THE PRESIDENTS

Editor

Fred L. Israel

VOLUME 8

Elections and Returns

Grolier Educational

SHERMAN TURNPIKE, DANBURY, CONNECTICUT

The publisher gratefully acknowledges permission from the sources to reproduce photos that appear on the cover.

Volume 1
J. Adams – New York Historical Society
J. Monroe – Library of Congress

Volume 2
J. K. Polk; A. Jackson; J. Tyler – Library of Congress
J. Q. Adams – National Archives

Volume 3
U. S. Grant – National Archives
A. Johnson; Z. Taylor – Library of Congress

Volume 4
B. Harrison; W. McKinley; J. A. Garfield – Library of Congress

Volume 5
H. Hoover; W. G. Harding – Library of Congress
T. Roosevelt – National Archives

Volume 6
D. D. Eisenhower – Library of Congress
L. B. Johnson – White House

Volume 7
B. Clinton – The White House
R. Reagan – Bush/Reagan Committee
G. Bush – Cynthia Johnson, The White House

Volume 8
T. Roosevelt – National Archives
B. Clinton – The White House

JH

Published 1997 exclusively for the school and library market by Grolier Educational

Sherman Turnpike, Danbury, Connecticut

© 1997 by Charles E. Smith Books, Inc.

Set: ISBN 0-7172-7642-2
Volume 8: ISBN 0-7172-7650-3

Library of Congress number:

The presidents.

    p. cm.

    Contents: v. 1. 1789–1825 (Washington–Monroe) — v. 2. 1825–1849 (Adams–Polk)

    v. 3. 1849–1877 (Taylor–Grant) — v. 4. 1877–1901 (Hayes–McKinley) — v. 5.1901–1933 (T. Roosevelt–Hoover)

    v. 6. 1933–1969 (F. D. Roosevelt–L. B. Johnson) — v. 7. 1969–1997 (Nixon–Clinton)

    v. 8. Documents, suggested reading, charts, tables, appendixes

1. Presidents – United States – Juvenile literature.
[1. Presidents.]
E176.1.P9175   1997
973.099 — dc20

96-31491
CIP
AC

For information, address the publisher
Grolier Educational, Sherman Turnpike, Danbury, Connecticut 06816

Printed in the United States of America

Cover design by Smart Graphics

TABLE OF CONTENTS

VOLUME EIGHT

INTRODUCTION

No branch of the federal government caused the authors of the Constitution as many problems as did the Executive. They feared a strong chief of state. After all, the American Revolution was, in part, a struggle against the King of England and the powerful royal governors. Surprisingly though, much power was granted to the president of the United States who is responsible only to the people. This was the boldest feature of the new Constitution. The president has varied duties. Above all, he must take care that the laws be faithfully executed. And also according to the Constitution, the president:

- is the commander in chief of the armed forces;
- has the power to make treaties with other nations (with the Senate's consent);
- appoints Supreme Court Justices and other members of the federal courts, ambassadors to other countries, department heads, and other high officials (all with the Senate's consent);
- signs into law or vetoes bills passed by Congress;
- calls special sessions of Congress in times of emergency.

In some countries, the power to lead is inherited. In others, men seize power through force. But in the United States, the people choose the nation's leader. The power of all the people to elect the president was not stated in the original Constitution. This came later. The United States is the first nation to have an elected president—and a president with a stated term of office. Every four years since the adoption of the Constitution in 1789, the nation has held a presidential election. Elections have been held even during major economic disruptions and wars. Indeed, these elections every four years are a vivid reminder of our democratic roots.

Who can vote for president of the United States? The original Constitution left voting qualifications to the states. At first, the states limited voting to white and very few black men who owned a certain amount of property. It was argued that only those with an economic or commercial interest in the nation should have a say in who could run the government. After the Civil War (1861–1865), the Fourteenth (1868) and Fifteenth (1870) Amendments to the Constitution guaranteed the vote to all men over the age of 21. The guarantee was only in theory. The Nineteenth Amendment (1920) extended the right to vote to women. The Nineteenth Amendment was a victory of the woman's suffrage movement which had worked for many years to achieve this goal. In 1964, the Twenty-fourth Amendment abolished poll taxes—a fee paid before a citizen was allowed to vote. This tax had kept many poor people, both black and white, from voting in several Southern states. And, the Twenty-sixth Amendment (1971) lowered the voting age to 18. (See Volume 8 for the complete text of the Constitution.)

In 1965, Congress passed the Voting Rights Act; it was renewed in 1985. This law, which carried out the requirements of the Fifteenth Amendment, made it illegal to interfere with anyone's right to vote. It forbade the use of literacy tests and, most important, the law mandated that federal voter registrars be sent into counties where less than 50 percent of the voting age population (black and white) was registered. This assumed that there must be serious barriers based on prejudice if so few had registered to vote. Those who had prevented African Americans from voting through fear and threat of violence now had to face the force of the federal government. Immediately, the number of African American voters in Southern states jumped dramatically from about 35 percent to 65 percent. In 1970, 1975, and 1982, Congress added amendments to the Voting Rights Act which helped other minorities such as Hispanics, Asians, Native Americans, and

Eskimos. For example, states must provide bilingual ballots in counties in which 5 percent or more of the population does not speak or read English. Today any citizen over the age of 18 has the right to vote in a presidential election. Many would argue that this is not only a right but also an obligation. However, all states deny the right to vote to anyone who is in prison.

Who can be president of the United States? There are formal constitutional requirements: one must be a "natural born citizen," at least 35 years old, and a resident of the United States for 14 years. The Constitution refers to the president as "he." It was probably beyond the thought process of the Founding Fathers that a woman, or a man who was not white, would ever be considered. The Twenty-second Amendment (1951), which deals with term limitations, uses "person" in referring to the president, recognizing that a woman could serve in that office.

How is the president elected? Most Americans assume that the president is elected by popular vote and the candidate with the highest number wins the election. This is not correct and may surprise those who thought they voted for Bill Clinton, Robert Dole, or Ross Perot in 1996. In fact, they voted for Clinton's or Dole's or Perot's electors who then elected the president. In the United States, the voters do not directly select the president. The Constitution provides a fairly complex—and some argue, an outdated—procedure for electing the president. Indeed, the electoral system devised by the Framers and modified by the Twelfth Amendment (1804) is unique. The records of the Constitutional Convention (1787) are silent in explaining the origins of the electoral system, usually referred to as the Electoral College. The several Federalist papers (Nos. 68–71) written by Alexander Hamilton in defense of the electoral system omit any source for the idea.

Under the electoral system of the United States, each state has the number of electoral voters equal to the size of its congressional delegation (House of Representatives plus Senate). Every 10 years, the census, as required by the Constitution, adjusts the number of representatives each state has in the House of Representatives because of population growth or loss. Every state always must have two senators. In the presidential election of 1996, for example, New York State had 33 electoral votes, because New York has 31 representatives and two senators. Alaska had three electoral votes, because Alaska has one representative and two senators. Since every congressional district must be approximately equal in population, we can say that the entire population of Alaska—the largest state in geographic size—is approximately equal in population to the 19th congressional district of New York City which covers the upper part of Manhattan Island.

There are 435 members of the House of Representatives. This number was fixed in 1910. There are 100 members of the Senate (50 states x 2 senators). This equals 535 electors. The Twenty-third Amendment (1961) gives the District of Columbia, the seat of our nation's capital, the electoral vote of the least populous state, three. So, the total electoral vote is 535 plus three or 538. To be elected president, a candidate must receive a majority, that is more than 50 percent, of the electoral votes: 270 electoral votes. If no candidate obtains a majority, the House of Representatives must choose the president from the top three candidates with each state delegation casting one vote. This happened in the 1824 presidential election. (See the article on John Quincy Adams.)

How does a political party choose its presidential nominee? Political parties play a crucial role—they select the candidates and provide the voters with a choice of alternatives.

In the early days of the Republic, the party's membership in Congress—the congressional caucus—chose presidential nominees. Sometimes state and local officials also put forward candidates. National party conventions where delegates were selected by state and local groups began by the 1830s. Each state had different delegate election procedures—some more democratic than others. Custom dictated that the convention sought the candidate. Potential nominees invariably seemed withdrawn and disinterested. They would rarely attend a nominating convention. Any attempt to pursue delegates was considered to be in bad taste. In fact, custom dictated that an official delegation went to the nominee's home to notify him of the party's decision and ask if he would accept. In the early years, convention officials sent a letter. By 1852, the candidate was informed in person. In the 1890s, these notification ceremonies dramatically increased in size. Madison Square Garden in New York City was the site for Grover Cleveland's 1892 notification.

By the first decade of the twentieth century, political reformers considered the convention system most undemocratic. They felt that it was a system dominated by patronage seeking party bosses who ignored the average voter. The primary system began as a way to increase participation in the nominating process. Candidates for the nation's highest office now actually sought the support of convention delegates. Theoretically, the primary allows all party members to choose their party's nominee. Most twentieth century conventions though, have seen a combination of delegates chosen by a political machine and elected in a primary. Today success in the primaries virtually assures the nomination. With few exceptions, the national conventions have become a rubber stamp for the candidate who did the best in the primaries.

The Campaign and Election. The presidential campaign is the great democratic exercise in politics. In recent elections, televised debates between the candidates have become a ritual, attracting record numbers of viewers. Public opinion polls continually monitor the nation's pulse. Commentators and writers analyze campaign strategies. Perhaps the winning strategy is to mobilize the party faithful and to persuade the independent voter that their candidate is the best. This is a costly process and since 1976, the general treasury provides major financial assistance to presidential campaigns. Public funding helps serious presidential candidates to present their qualifications without selling out to wealthy contributors and special interest groups.

Finally, on that first Tuesday after the first Monday in November, the voters make their choice. With the tragic exception of 1860, the American people have accepted the results. (See the article on Abraham Lincoln.) The election process works. Democracy has survived. Forty-one men have held the office of president of the United States. Each has been a powerful personality with varied leadership traits. Each had the opportunity to make major decisions both in foreign and domestic matters which affected the direction of the nation.

Join us as we proceed to study the men who helped to shape our history. We will also learn about their vice presidents, their cabinets, their families, and their homes and monuments.

Fred L. Israel
The City College of the City University of New York

ACKNOWLEDGMENTS

Sir Isaac Newton, the seventeenth-century English scientist who created calculus, discovered that white light is composed of many colors, discovered the law of gravity, and developed the standard laws of motion, once said, "If I have seen farther, it is because I have stood on the shoulders of giants." He meant that he used the work of those who came before him as a starting point for the development of his own ideas. This concept is as true in reference books as it is in science.

The White House Historical Association (740 Jackson Place N.W., Washington, D.C. 20503) supplied all the full page color paintings of the presidents, except seven. They are used with the permission of the White House

Historical Association, and we are grateful to them for their cooperation. The painting of James Monroe is Courtesy of the James Monroe Museum and Memorial Library, Fredericksburg, Virginia; the William Henry Harrison portrait is Courtesy of Grouseland; the John Tyler painting is Courtesy of Sherwood Forest Plantation; the Benjamin Harrison painting is from the President Benjamin Harrison Home; Harry Truman's photograph is from the U.S. Navy, Courtesy Harry S. Truman Library; George Bush's photograph is Courtesy of the Bush Presidential Materials Project; Bill Clinton's photograph is Courtesy of The White House. All the busts of the vice presidents are Courtesy of the Architect of the Capitol.

Over three dozen illustrations are credited to the Collection of David J. and Janice L. Frent. The Frents are friends and neighbors. Fred Israel and I both want to thank them very much for allowing us to show some of the treasures of their unequaled collection of political memorabilia.

The authors of the biographical pieces on the presidents are listed in each volume. They have provided the core of this work, and I am very grateful to them for their cooperation. Dr. Donald A. Ritchie, Associate Historian, United States Senate, wrote all the biographies of the vice presidents. Few people know more about this subject than Dr. Ritchie, and we appreciate his assistance.

Maribeth A. Corona (Editor, Charles E. Smith Books, Inc.) and I have written the sections on Family, Cabinet, and Places. Dr. Israel's editing of our work corrected and improved it greatly although we take full responsibility for any errors that remain. In preparing the material on places, three books served as a starting point: *Presidential Libraries and Museums, An Illustrated Guide,* Pat Hyland (Congressional Quarterly Inc., 1995); *Historic Homes of the American Presidents,* second edition, Irvin Haas (Dover Publications, 1991); and *Cabins, Cottages & Mansions, Homes of the Presidents of the United States,* Nancy D. Myers Benbow and Christopher H. Benbow (Thomas Publications, 1993). We wrote to every place noted in this work and our copy is based on the wealth of information returned to us. It is the most comprehensive and up-to-date collection of information available on this subject.

There is no single book on the families of the presidents. We relied on the abundance of biographies and autobiographies of members of the first families. Also helpful was *Children in the White House,* Christine Sadler (G.P. Putnam's Sons, 1967); *The Presidents' Mothers,* Doris Faber (St. Martin's Press, 1978); and *The First Ladies,* Margaret Brown Klapthor (White House Historical Association, 1989).

The Complete Book of U.S. Presidents, William A. DeGregorio (Wings Books, 1993) is an outstanding one-volume reference work, and we referred to it often. I also had the great pleasure of referring often to three encyclopedias which I had published earlier: *Encyclopedia of the American Presidency,* Leonard W. Levy and Louis Fisher (Simon & Schuster, 1994); *Encyclopedia of the American Constitution,* Leonard W. Levy, Kenneth L. Karst, and Dennis Mahoney (Macmillan & Free Press, 1986); and *Encyclopedia of the United States Congress,* Donald C. Bacon, Roger Davidson, and Morton H. Keller (Simon & Schuster, 1995). I also referred often to *Running for President, The Candidates and Their Images,* Arthur M. Schlesinger, Jr. (Simon & Schuster, 1994). Publishing this two-volume set also gave me the pleasure of working with Professor Schlesinger and the Associate Editors, Fred L. Israel and David J. Frent.

Most of the copyediting was done by Jerilyn Famighetti who was, as usual, prompt, accurate, and pleasant. Our partner in this endeavor was M.E. Aslett Corporation, 95 Campus Plaza, Edison, New Jersey. Although everyone at Aslett lent a hand, special thanks go to Elizabeth Geary, who designed the books; Brian Hewitt and Bob Bovasso, who scanned the images; and Joanne Morbit, who composed the pages. They designed every page and prepared the film for printing. The index was prepared by Jacqueline Flamm.

Charles E. Smith
Freehold, New Jersey

Presidential election results can be visually summarized in a map. The maps that follow are especially useful in revealing political patterns and trends. When studying each of these maps and the accompanying tables and text, ask yourself these questions: What states were won by each candidate? Does there appear to be a strong preference in some sections of the nation for a certain candidate? Why? What were the issues? Why do the states of the former Confederacy vote for the Democratic candidate in every presidential election between 1880 and 1944 with the exception of 1928? Why do so many of these states shift to the Republican nominee in recent decades? Which midwestern states are pivotal for the winning candidate in almost every election since the Civil War? Why?

Most Americans do not know how the president of the United States is elected. Many assume that the person with a popular vote majority wins the election, but this is not correct. The Founding Fathers devised a complex system for choosing the chief executive—a system which has worked since 1789.

At the Constitutional Convention (1787), some delegates favored having the president elected by the legislature, the practice most common in the states. Others thought this method would violate the principal of separation of powers among the three branches of the new government—executive, legislative, and judicial. Many delegates, including James Madison and Gouverneur Morris, strongly supported a popular election—that is, free adult men would vote for the president.

Two groups, however, objected to removing the choice from the national legislature. The first group was made up of the smaller states, such as New Jersey and Connecticut, which had gained equality with the larger states in the U.S. Senate. Each state, regardless of size, has two senators. The second group was made up of the slave states, which had gained greater voting power in the U.S. House of Representatives because of the so-called three-fifths compromise. This compromise resulted in a constitutional provision that counted five slaves, who could not vote, as equivalent to three free adult white persons for determining the number of representatives each state would have in the U.S. House of Representatives. Those favoring popular election of the president and those favoring election by Congress remained deadlocked until near the end of the Constitutional Convention. A Committee on Unfinished Parts chaired by David Brearly, a delegate from New Jersey, proposed the Electoral College. The Convention adopted this elaborate and complicated system.

Under this system, each state has as many presidential electors as it has representatives and senators (see Introduction). The method of choosing these electors is left to each state legislature. Most delegates assumed the presidential electors would vote for men from their own states, and they expected that no candidate would obtain the majority required for election. In that case, or if two candidates were tied, the election would be decided in the U.S. House of Representatives, where each state, regardless of population, would cast one vote and choose the president from the five candidates receiving the highest total in the Electoral College. In 1804, the Twelfth Amendment changed this to three candidates. (For the complete text of the Constitution see page 100.) This happened twice—in the elections of 1800 and 1824 when the U.S. House of Representatives chose Thomas Jefferson and John Quincy Adams, respectively, as president. This arrangement appeared to give the small states equal standing with the large states in the final choice of the president. The members of the Constitutional Convention assumed, in effect, that the president would be nominated by the large states in the Electoral College but actually elected by all the states in the U.S. House of Representatives.

The Founders gave each elector two votes but required that they cast at least one for a citizen of a state other than their own. They expected that the electors' combined second choice would identify a national candidate acceptable to most states whom, they anticipated, the U.S. House of Representatives would choose as president. The person with the second highest vote would be the vice president. The Twelfth Amendment (1804) changed this method of voting. It required electors to cast one ballot for president and vice president. This method of electing the president of the United States is a complicated compromise, but as Alexander Hamilton wrote in *Federalist 68,* if "the mode of appointment of the Chief Magistrate is . . . not perfect, it is at least excellent."

This method of electing the president assumed that each state would be the equivalent of a political party. Remember that the idea of a strong national government as opposed to a loose union of states had yet to emerge. State legislatures, in fact, chose electors through the 1830s, and popular voting for presidential electors began in some states by 1824. Four contenders for the presidency emerged in 1824. All claimed to be "Republicans." Two were "favorite sons" —Henry Clay of Kentucky and Andrew Jackson of Tennessee. (A "favorite son" is a candidate favored for the presidential nomination by the political leaders of a state or a region.) Another candidate was John Quincy Adams of Massachusetts. Adams served as secretary of state, 1817–1825, and many assumed he would succeed to the presidency. William Crawford of Georgia was the fourth candidate. No candidate had won a majority when the electoral votes were counted. Following the provisions of the Twelfth Amendment, the president was chosen by the U.S. House of Representatives from the three candidates with the highest number of electoral votes. Members of the House from each state vote as a unit, with each state having one vote. Adams was elected president. He won the vote of 13 states against Jackson's 7 and Crawford's 4. By 1840 every state, with the exception of South Carolina, had adopted popular voting for the electors. (The South Carolina state legislature chose its electors until the 1868 election.) Note, for example, that the vote cast for president in 1824 was about 365,000. This figure increased to nearly 2,500,000 in 1840, 16 years later, as additional state legislatures approved popular election of the electors.

The Electoral College worked smoothly in the first two presidential elections, 1789 and 1792, as George Washington was the unanimous choice of electors each time. (New York, North Carolina, and Rhode Island had not yet ratified the Constitution and did not participate in the first election.) The emergence of national political parties a few years later, however, made this elaborate procedure take on an entirely different meaning. The election of 1796 shows, for example, that John Adams was supported by the Federalist Party and Thomas Jefferson was backed by the Democratic-Republican Party, the predecessor of the present Democratic Party. Since a majority—not a plurality—of electors is needed to elect the president, two major national parties would come to dominate the U.S. political scene. Each political party, therefore, must be inclusive—rather than based on a single issue—in order to attract national rather than regional support.

The election of 1860 was a major exception to this idea of inclusiveness. Abraham Lincoln received only 39.9 percent of the popular vote—his three opponents combined received 60.1 percent. Six in 10 cast their vote for candidates who sharply differed with Lincoln on the most important issue of slavery and yet Lincoln was elected president. Lincoln's votes were concentrated in populous states and gave the Republicans 180 electoral votes—a clear majority. John Breckinridge received 72, John Bell received 39, and Stephen A. Douglas received 12, even though Douglas came in second in popular vote (29.5 percent). Lincoln won every free state except New Jersey, which divided its electoral vote between him and Douglas. Although Stephen A. Douglas won a majority of the popular vote in New Jersey, 4 of the state's 7 electors cast their vote for Lincoln. Lincoln did not receive a single popular vote in any future Confederate state except Virginia, where he received under 2,000 votes. Breckinridge carried the Deep South, while Bell and Douglas divided the border states. With this display of political unity among the Southern states, the slave states of the lower South began to secede in December 1860. Lincoln's election and the way in which we elect the president may have been causes of the Civil War.

Another unusual situation occurred in 1960. Mississippians who supported segregation and opposed civil rights for African Americans ran a slate of electors that were "unpledged" to any candidate for president. Mississippi Democratic electors promised to vote for John F. Kennedy if he carried the state and Republican electors promised that they would vote for Richard M. Nixon if he won. The "unpledged" electors made no commitment to a candidate. Instead, they stated that racial segregation in the South was their main concern. If the 1960 electoral vote between Kennedy and Nixon should be close, the "unpledged" electors in Mississippi planned to use their electoral votes to obtain from both Kennedy and Nixon a statement on what "integration" meant to each. The candidate who came closest to their segregationist views would receive the state's votes and win the election. However, this plan failed. Kennedy won a decisive electoral majority in the Electoral College. These "unpledged" electors cast the state's 8 electoral votes for Senator Harry F. Byrd, Sr. of Virginia, an openly declared segregationist. They convinced 7 other electors to do the same. That is, while 56.8 percent of Alabama voters cast their vote for Kennedy, technically giving him that state's 11 electoral votes, 6 of the 11 Alabama electors, although elected as Kennedy supporters, voted for Byrd. One Oklahoma elector who was chosen as a Nixon elector also voted for Byrd. By the 1970s, state laws had corrected this and electors are now bound to vote as they were directed by the voters. The Supreme Court, however, has yet to rule on the constitutionality of these state laws.

Several of these maps show occasions when the electoral votes of a state have been divided between candidates. The split electoral vote occurred for several reasons. Remember that voters are technically voting for electors who then vote for a presidential candidate. It is possible to split an electoral ticket. For example, in the 1996 presidential election, Pennsylvania had 23 electoral votes. In the voting booth, the names of Bill Clinton and Al Gore appeared above one lever and those of Robert Dole and Jack Kemp above another. Almost every voter in the state pulled down the lever for either of the major party candidates or for a minor party's nominees. In effect they cast one vote for 23 electors. Nevertheless, a voter could have requested a paper ballot listing the names of all the electors and may have chosen to vote for up to 23 electors of any party. This practice was more common before the use of voting machines. A paper ballot had the name of the party at the top, for example, Republican and the party's symbol. A list of each elector followed. An X in a designated box meant a vote for the complete electoral slate chosen by a party. But some chose to "split a ticket"—to vote for some and not others. This is why four Republican electors and three Democratic electors won in New Jersey in 1860. This also is the reason why eight Democratic electors and one Republican in California won in the 1892 election. And in 1892, one North Dakota elector voted for Grover Cleveland, who was not even on the ballot of this newly formed state. Split electoral votes were more common, when state legislatures chose the electors prior to the 1830s.

The results of a presidential election can be summarized in a map. Notice that each state is colored to show which candidate won that state's electoral vote. Check the map key to see how colors are used to identify the different candidates. Remember that a map which shows who won a state's electoral vote exaggerates the extent of a winning candidate's victory. Not all voters in Illinois, New York, and Massachusetts, for example, supported Lincoln in 1860. His opponents received many votes. But because Lincoln received more popular votes, he automatically won all of the electoral votes of these states. On the 1860 map, these three states are shown as states that Lincoln carried. The 1860 electoral map also shows how the nation's voters divided along sectional lines—North and South. It also shows that the border states (Missouri, Kentucky, Tennessee, and Virginia) favored the compromise candidates, Douglas and Bell.

On the 1896 electoral map, you will see that William McKinley, the Republican candidate, carried the heavily populated states in the Northeast and the Middle West. This election was a victory for industry over agriculture, the city over rural life, the interests of the North and East over the interests of the West and South. Oregon and California narrowly went for McKinley because of the excellent Republican Party organization in those states.

Continuing our look at what we can learn from a presidential electoral map, note that in the 1928 election, the voters overwhelmingly chose the Republican candidate, Herbert Hoover. He won 444 electoral votes to 87 for Alfred E. Smith, the Democratic candidate. The Republican Party broke the solid Democratic South for the first time since 1876 by carrying five states of the former Confederacy. Smith's loss, though, was not as hopeless as this map portrays it. He received twice as many popular votes than did the 1924 Democratic candidate, John W. Davis, and he won a majority in the nation's 12 largest cities.

Four years later, in 1932, Franklin D. Roosevelt, the Democratic candidate, reversed the 1928 Republican victory. Roosevelt carried 42 of the then 48 states. This electoral landslide does not reflect the 39.8 percent of the popular vote which President Herbert Hoover, the Republican candidate, received. Four in 10 voters did not vote for Roosevelt. This is not shown in the 1932 electoral map. The map does clearly show, however, that voters in every region blamed the Republicans for the Great Depression. Likewise, the 1972 electoral map shows a landslide for Richard M. Nixon—520 votes to 17 for George McGovern even though McGovern won 37.5 percent of the popular vote. And in 1984, Ronald Reagan received 525 votes to 13 for Walter Mondale although Mondale received 40.6 percent of the popular vote.

By studying the numerical charts, we can see that in 17 elections (1824, 1844, 1848, 1856, 1860, 1876, 1880, 1884, 1888, 1892, 1912, 1916, 1948, 1960, 1968, 1992, and 1996), the winning presidential candidate obtained less than 50 percent of the popular vote but, as the Constitution mandates, a majority of the electoral votes. In a very narrow popular victory, such as that of John F. Kennedy over Richard M. Nixon in 1960, 49.7 percent to 49.5 percent, Kennedy won a clear electoral majority—303 to 219. In this election the state winner-take-all system converted a very moderate popular triumph into a decisive electoral mandate.

In 1992, in a three-way race which included Ross Perot, Bill Clinton defeated President George Bush. Clinton received 43 percent of the popular vote and won 370 electoral votes—a clear majority. Although Perot polled 18.9 percent of the vote, he did not obtain a single electoral vote. In almost every presidential election, there has been at least one third party candidate who was deeply disenchanted with either the political or economic system. In 1912, Theodore Roosevelt ran as a third party candidate, as did Henry A. Wallace and J. Strom Thurmond in 1948 and George C. Wallace in 1968. However, it is almost impossible for a minor candidate to win a national election because of the way in which the president of the United States is elected through the Electoral College.

ELECTION MAPS
&
RESULTS

PRESIDENTIAL ELECTION OF
1789

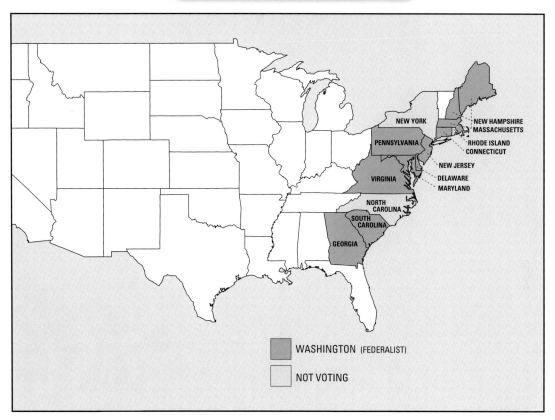

WASHINGTON (FEDERALIST)

NOT VOTING

States	Electoral Votes	Washington	Adams	Jay	Harrison	Rutledge	Hancock	Clinton	Huntington	Milton	Armstrong	Lincoln	Telfair
Connecticut	(14)	7	5	-	-	-	-	-	2	-	-	-	-
Delaware	(6)	3	-	3	-	-	-	-	-	-	-	-	-
Georgia	(10)	5	-	-	-	-	-	-	-	2	1	1	1
Maryland	(16)	6	-	-	6	-	-	-	-	-	-	-	-
Massachusetts	(20)	10	10	-	-	-	-	-	-	-	-	-	-
New Hampshire	(10)	5	5	-	-	-	-	-	-	-	-	-	-
New Jersey	(12)	6	1	5	-	-	-	-	-	-	-	-	-
New York	(16)	-	-	-	-	-	-	-	-	-	-	-	-
North Carolina	(14)	-	-	-	-	-	-	-	-	-	-	-	-
Pennsylvania	(20)	10	8	-	-	-	2	-	-	-	-	-	-
Rhode Island	(6)	-	-	-	-	-	-	-	-	-	-	-	-
South Carolina	(14)	7	-	-	-	6	1	-	-	-	-	-	-
Virginia	(24)	10	5	1	-	-	1	3	-	-	-	-	-
Totals	**(182)**	**69**	**34**	**9**	**6**	**6**	**4**	**3**	**2**	**2**	**1**	**1**	**1**

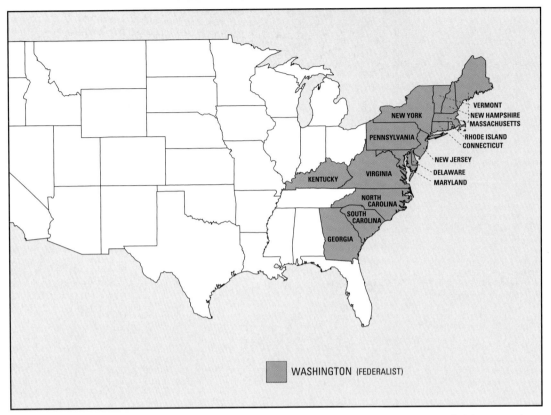

WASHINGTON (FEDERALIST)

States	Electoral Votes	Washington	Adams	Clinton	Jefferson	Burr
Connecticut	(18)	9	9	-	-	-
Delaware	(6)	3	3	-	-	-
Georgia	(8)	4	-	4	-	-
Kentucky	(8)	4	-	-	4	-
Maryland	(20)	8	8	-	-	-
Massachusetts	(32)	16	16	-	-	-
New Hampshire	(12)	6	6	-	-	-
New Jersey	(14)	7	7	-	-	-
New York	(24)	12	-	12	-	-
North Carolina	(24)	12	-	12	-	-
Pennsylvania	(30)	15	14	1	-	-
Rhode Island	(8)	4	4	-	-	-
South Carolina	(16)	8	7	-	-	1
Vermont	(8)	3	3	-	-	-
Virginia	(42)	21	-	21	-	-
Totals	**(270)**	**132**	**77**	**50**	**4**	**1**

PRESIDENTIAL ELECTION OF
1796

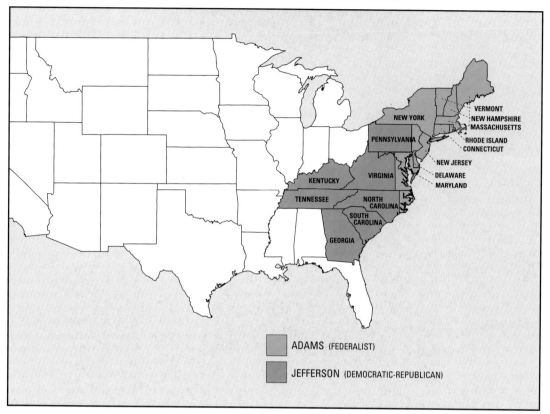

ADAMS (FEDERALIST)

JEFFERSON (DEMOCRATIC-REPUBLICAN)

States	Electoral Votes	J. Adams	Jefferson	T. Pinckney	Burr	S. Adams	Ellsworth	Clinton	Jay	Iredell	Henry	Johnston	Washington	C. Pinckney
Connecticut	(18)	9	–	4	–	–	–	–	5	–	–	–	–	–
Delaware	(6)	3	–	3	–	–	–	–	–	–	–	–	–	–
Georgia	(8)	–	4	–	–	–	–	4	–	–	–	–	–	–
Kentucky	(8)	–	4	–	4	–	–	–	–	–	–	–	–	–
Maryland	(20)	7	4	4	3	–	–	–	–	–	2	–	–	–
Massachusetts	(32)	16	–	13	–	–	1	–	–	–	–	2	–	–
New Hampshire	(12)	6	–	–	–	–	6	–	–	–	–	–	–	–
New Jersey	(14)	7	–	7	–	–	–	–	–	–	–	–	–	–
New York	(24)	12	–	12	–	–	–	–	–	–	–	–	–	–
North Carolina	(24)	1	11	1	6	–	–	–	–	3	–	–	1	1
Pennsylvania	(30)	1	14	2	13	–	–	–	–	–	–	–	–	–
Rhode Island	(8)	4	–	–	–	–	4	–	–	–	–	–	–	–
South Carolina	(16)	–	8	8	–	–	–	–	–	–	–	–	–	–
Tennessee	(6)	–	3	–	3	–	–	–	–	–	–	–	–	–
Vermont	(8)	4	–	4	–	–	–	–	–	–	–	–	–	–
Virginia	(42)	1	20	1	1	15	–	3	–	–	–	–	1	–
Totals	**(276)**	**71**	**68**	**59**	**30**	**15**	**11**	**7**	**5**	**3**	**2**	**2**	**2**	**1**

1800

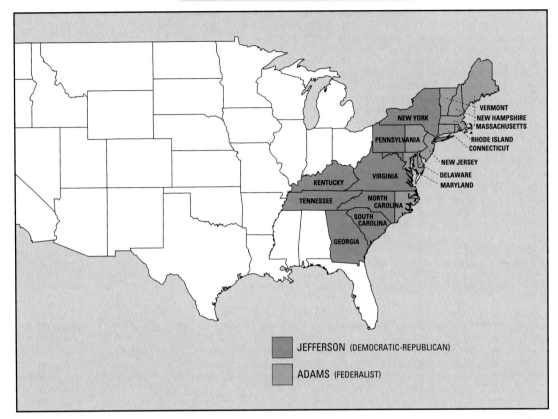

States	Electoral Votes	Jefferson	Burr	Adams	Pinckney	Jay
Connecticut	(18)	-	-	9	9	-
Delaware	(6)	-	-	3	3	-
Georgia	(8)	4	4	-	-	-
Kentucky	(8)	4	4	-	-	-
Maryland	(20)	5	5	5	5	-
Massachusetts	(32)	-	-	16	16	-
New Hampshire	(12)	-	-	6	6	-
New Jersey	(14)	-	-	7	7	-
New York	(24)	12	12	-	-	-
North Carolina	(24)	8	8	4	4	-
Pennsylvania	(30)	8	8	7	7	-
Rhode Island	(8)	-	-	4	3	1
South Carolina	(16)	8	8	-	-	-
Tennessee	(6)	3	3	-	-	-
Vermont	(8)	-	-	4	4	-
Virginia	(42)	21	21	-	-	-
Totals	**(276)**	**73**	**73**	**65**	**64**	**1**

PRESIDENTIAL ELECTION OF
1804

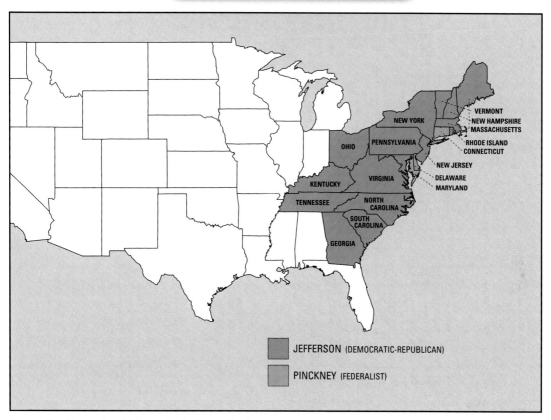

JEFFERSON (DEMOCRATIC-REPUBLICAN)

PINCKNEY (FEDERALIST)

Congressional Quarterly's Guide to U.S. Elections, 3rd. edition, copyright ©1994. Used with permission. All rights reserved.

States	Electoral Votes	Jefferson	Pinckney
Connecticut	(9)	-	9
Delaware	(3)	-	3
Georgia	(6)	6	-
Kentucky	(8)	8	-
Maryland	(11)	9	2
Massachusetts	(19)	19	-
New Hampshire	(7)	7	-
New Jersey	(8)	8	-
New York	(19)	19	-
North Carolina	(14)	14	-
Ohio	(3)	3	-
Pennsylvania	(20)	20	-
Rhode Island	(4)	4	-
South Carolina	(10)	10	-
Tennessee	(5)	5	-
Vermont	(6)	6	-
Virginia	(24)	24	-
Totals	**(176)**	**162**	**14**

PRESIDENTIAL ELECTION OF
1808

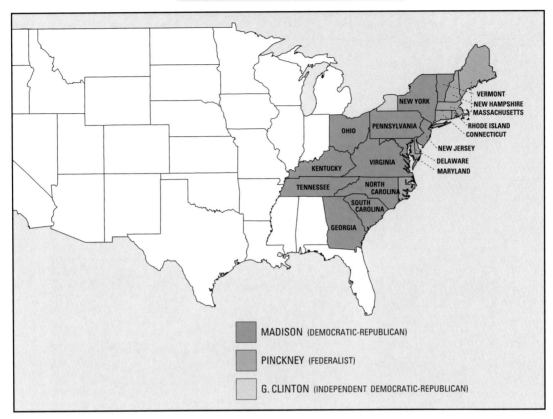

MADISON (DEMOCRATIC-REPUBLICAN)

PINCKNEY (FEDERALIST)

G. CLINTON (INDEPENDENT DEMOCRATIC-REPUBLICAN)

Congressional Quarterly's Guide to U.S. Elections, 3rd. edition, copyright ©1994. Used with permission. All rights reserved.

States	Electoral Votes	Madison	Pinckney	Clinton
Connecticut	(9)	-	9	-
Delaware	(3)	-	3	-
Georgia	(6)	6	-	-
Kentucky	(8)	7	-	-
Maryland	(11)	9	2	-
Massachusetts	(19)	-	19	-
New Hampshire	(7)	-	7	-
New Jersey	(8)	8	-	-
New York	(19)	13	-	6
North Carolina	(14)	11	3	-
Ohio	(3)	3	-	-
Pennsylvania	(20)	20	-	-
Rhode Island	(4)	-	4	-
South Carolina	(10)	10	-	-
Tennessee	(5)	5	-	-
Vermont	(6)	6	-	-
Virginia	(24)	24	-	-
Totals	**(176)**	**122**	**47**	**6**

PRESIDENTIAL ELECTION OF
1812

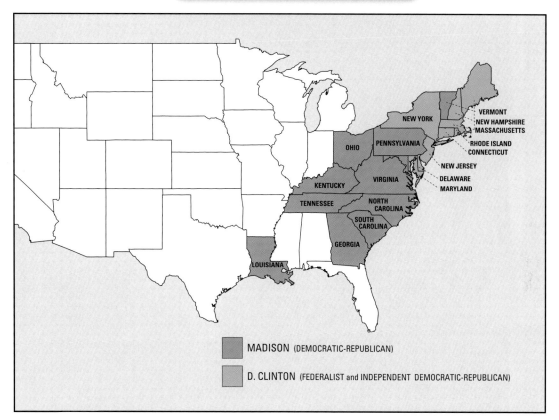

MADISON (DEMOCRATIC-REPUBLICAN)

D. CLINTON (FEDERALIST and INDEPENDENT DEMOCRATIC-REPUBLICAN)

States	Electoral Votes	Madison	Clinton
Connecticut	(9)	-	9
Delaware	(4)	-	4
Georgia	(8)	8	-
Kentucky	(12)	12	-
Louisiana	(3)	3	-
Maryland	(11)	6	5
Massachusetts	(22)	-	22
New Hampshire	(8)	-	8
New Jersey	(8)	-	8
New York	(29)	-	29
North Carolina	(15)	15	-
Ohio	(8)	7	-
Pennsylvania	(25)	25	-
Rhode Island	(4)	-	4
South Carolina	(11)	11	-
Tennessee	(8)	8	-
Vermont	(8)	8	-
Virginia	(25)	25	-
Totals	**(218)**	**128**	**89**

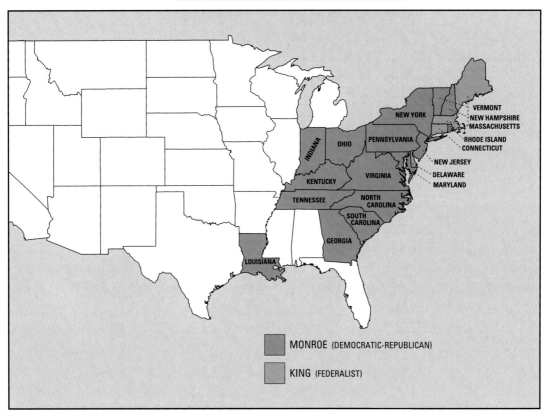

PRESIDENTIAL ELECTION OF

1816

MONROE (DEMOCRATIC-REPUBLICAN)

KING (FEDERALIST)

States	Electoral Votes	Monroe	King
Connecticut	(9)	-	9
Delaware	(4)	-	3
Georgia	(8)	8	-
Indiana	(3)	3	-
Kentucky	(12)	12	-
Louisiana	(3)	3	-
Maryland	(11)	8	-
Massachusetts	(22)	-	22
New Hampshire	(8)	8	-
New Jersey	(8)	8	-
New York	(29)	29	-
North Carolina	(15)	15	-
Ohio	(8)	8	-
Pennsylvania	(25)	25	-
Rhode Island	(4)	4	-
South Carolina	(11)	11	-
Tennessee	(8)	8	-
Vermont	(8)	8	-
Virginia	(25)	25	-
Totals	**(221)**	**183**	**34**

PRESIDENTIAL ELECTION OF
1820

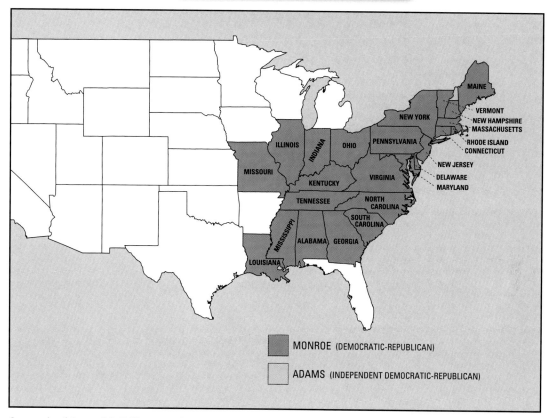

States	Electoral Votes	Monroe	Adams
Alabama	(3)	3	-
Connecticut	(9)	9	-
Delaware	(4)	4	-
Georgia	(8)	8	-
Illinois	(3)	3	-
Indiana	(3)	3	-
Kentucky	(12)	12	-
Louisiana	(3)	3	-
Maine	(9)	9	-
Maryland	(11)	11	-
Massachusetts	(15)	15	-
Mississippi	(3)	2	-
Missouri	(3)	3	-
New Hampshire	(8)	7	1
New Jersey	(8)	8	-
New York	(29)	29	-
North Carolina	(15)	15	-
Ohio	(8)	8	-
Pennsylvania	(25)	24	-
Rhode Island	(4)	4	-
South Carolina	(11)	11	-
Tennessee	(8)	7	-
Vermont	(8)	8	-
Virginia	(25)	25	-
Totals	**(235)**	**231**	**1**

PRESIDENTIAL ELECTION OF
1824

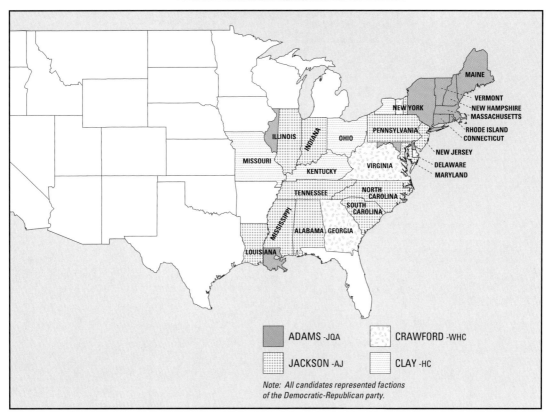

	ADAMS -JQA		CRAWFORD -WHC
	JACKSON -AJ		CLAY -HC

Note: All candidates represented factions
of the Democratic-Republican party.

Congressional Quarterly's Guide to U.S. Elections, 3rd. edition, copyright ©1994. Used with permission. All rights reserved.

States	Electoral Votes	Jackson	Adams	Crawford	Clay
Alabama	(5)	5	-	-	-
Connecticut	(8)	-	8	-	-
Delaware	(3)	-	1	2	-
Georgia	(9)	-	-	9	-
Illinois	(3)	2	1	-	-
Indiana	(5)	5	-	-	-
Kentucky	(14)	-	-	-	14
Louisiana	(5)	3	2	-	-
Maine	(9)	-	9	-	-
Maryland	(11)	7	3	1	-
Massachusetts	(15)	-	15	-	-
Mississippi	(3)	3	-	-	-
Missouri	(3)	-	-	-	3
New Hampshire	(8)	-	8	-	-
New Jersey	(8)	8	-	-	-
New York	(36)	1	26	5	4
North Carolina	(15)	15	-	-	-
Ohio	(16)	-	-	-	16
Pennsylvania	(28)	28	-	-	-
Rhode Island	(4)	-	4	-	-
South Carolina	(11)	11	-	-	-
Tennessee	(11)	11	-	-	-
Vermont	(7)	-	7	-	-
Virginia	(24)	-	-	24	-
Totals	(261)	99	84	41	37

1824

PRESIDENTIAL ELECTION RETURNS

STATE	TOTAL VOTE	JOHN Q. ADAMS (Democratic-Republican)		ANDREW JACKSON (Democratic-Republican)		HENRY CLAY (Democratic-Republican)		WILLIAM H. CRAWFORD (Democratic-Republican)		OTHER		PLURALITY	
		Votes	%	Votes	%	Votes	%	Votes	%	Votes	%		
Alabama	13,603	2,422	17.8	9,429	69.3	96	0.7	1,656	12.2	—		7,007	AJ
Connecticut	10,647	7,494	70.4	—		—		1,965	18.5	1,188	11.2	5,529	JQA
Illinois	4,671	1,516	32.5	1,272	27.2	1,036	22.2	847	18.1	—		244	JQA
Indiana	15,838	3,071	19.4	7,444	47.0	5,316	33.6	—		7		2,128	AJ
Kentucky	23,338	—		6,356	27.2	16,982	72.8	—		—		10,626	HC
Maine	12,625	10,289	81.5	—		—		2,336	18.5	—		7,953	JQA
Maryland	33,214	14,632	44.1	14,523	43.7	695	2.1	3,364	10.1	—		109	JQA
Massachusetts	42,056	30,687	73.0	—		—		—		11,369	27.0	24,071	JQA
Mississippi	4,894	1,654	33.8	3,121	63.8	—		119	2.4	—		1,467	AJ
Missouri	3,432	159	4.6	1,166	34.0	2,042	59.5	32	0.9	33	1.0	876	HC
New Hampshire	10,032	9,389	93.6	—		—		643	6.4	—		8,746	JQA
New Jersey	19,837	8,309	41.9	10,332	52.1	—		1,196	6.0	—		2,023	AJ
North Carolina	36,109	—		20,231	56.0	—		15,622	43.3	256	0.7	4,609	AJ
Ohio	50,024	12,280	24.5	18,489	37.0	19,255	38.5	—		—		766	HC
Pennsylvania	47,073	5,441	11.6	35,736	75.9	1,690	3.6	4,206	8.9	—		30,295	AJ
Rhode Island	2,344	2,144	91.5	—		—		—		200	8.5	1,944	JQA
Tennessee	20,725	216	1.0	20,197	97.5	—		312	1.5	—		19,885	AJ
Virginia	15,371	3,419	22.2	2,975	19.4	419	2.7	8,558	55.7	—		5,139	WHC
Totals	365,833	113,122	30.9	151,271	41.3	47,531	13.0	40,856	11.2	13,053	3.6	38,149	AJ

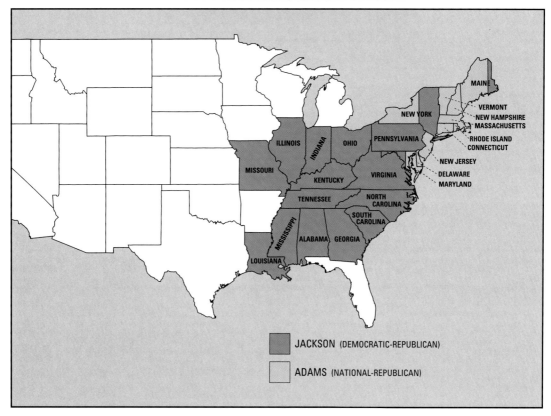

PRESIDENTIAL ELECTION OF
1828

JACKSON (DEMOCRATIC-REPUBLICAN)

ADAMS (NATIONAL-REPUBLICAN)

Congressional Quarterly's Guide to U.S. Elections, 3rd. edition, copyright ©1994. Used with permission. All rights reserved.

States	Electoral Votes	Jackson	Adams
Alabama	(5)	5	-
Connecticut	(8)	-	8
Delaware	(3)	-	3
Georgia	(9)	9	-
Illinois	(3)	3	-
Indiana	(5)	5	-
Kentucky	(14)	14	-
Louisiana	(5)	5	-
Maine	(9)	1	8
Maryland	(11)	5	6
Massachusetts	(15)	-	15
Mississippi	(3)	3	-
Missouri	(3)	3	-
New Hampshire	(8)	-	8
New Jersey	(8)	-	8
New York	(36)	20	16
North Carolina	(15)	15	-
Ohio	(16)	16	-
Pennsylvania	(28)	28	-
Rhode Island	(4)	-	4
South Carolina	(11)	11	-
Tennessee	(11)	11	-
Vermont	(7)	-	7
Virginia	(24)	24	-
Totals	**(261)**	**178**	**83**

1828

PRESIDENTIAL ELECTION RETURNS

STATE	TOTAL VOTE	ANDREW JACKSON (Democratic-Republican)		JOHN Q. ADAMS (National-Republican)		OTHER		PLURALITY	
		Votes	%	Votes	%	Votes	%		
Alabama	18,618	16,736	89.9	1,878	10.1	4		14,858	DR
Connecticut	19,378	4,448	23.0	13,829	71.4	1,101	5.7	9,381	NR
Georgia	20,004	19,362	96.8	642	3.2	—		18,720	DR
Illinois	14,222	9,560	67.2	4,662	32.8	—		4,898	DR
Indiana	39,210	22,201	56.6	17,009	43.4	—		5,192	DR
Kentucky	70,776	39,308	55.5	31,468	44.5	—		7,840	DR
Louisiana	8,687	4,605	53.0	4,082	47.0	—		523	DR
Maine	34,789	13,927	40.0	20,773	59.7	89	0.3	6,846	NR
Maryland	45,796	22,782	49.7	23,014	50.3	—		232	NR
Massachusetts	39,074	6,012	15.4	29,836	76.4	3,226	8.3	23,824	NR
Mississippi	8,344	6,763	81.1	1,581	18.9	—		5,182	DR
Missouri	11,654	8,232	70.6	3,422	29.4	—		4,810	DR
New Hampshire	44,035	20,212	45.9	23,823	54.1	—		3,611	NR
New Jersey	45,570	21,809	47.9	23,753	52.1	8		1,944	NR
New York	270,975	139,412	51.4	131,563	48.6	—		7,849	DR
North Carolina	51,747	37,814	73.1	13,918	26.9	15		23,896	DR
Ohio	131,049	67,596	51.6	63,453	48.4	—		4,143	DR
Pennsylvania	152,220	101,457	66.7	50,763	33.3	—		50,694	DR
Rhode Island	3,580	820	22.9	2,755	77.0	5	0.1	1,935	NR
Tennessee	46,533	44,293	95.2	2,240	4.8	—		42,053	DR
Vermont	32,833	8,350	25.4	24,363	74.2	120	0.4	16,013	NR
Virginia	38,924	26,854	69.0	12,070	31.0	—		14,784	DR
Totals	**1,148,018**	**642,553**	**56.0**	**500,897**	**43.6**	**4,568**	**0.4**	**141,656**	**DR**

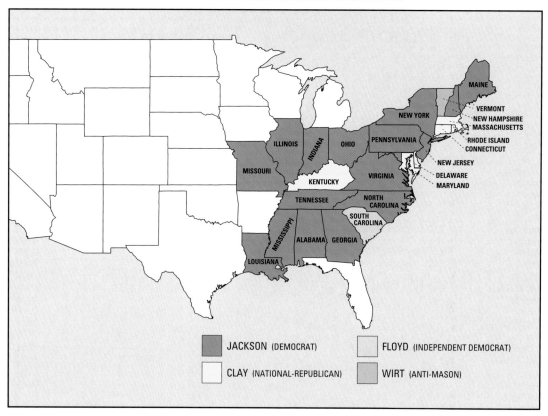

PRESIDENTIAL ELECTION OF

1832

JACKSON (DEMOCRAT)　　FLOYD (INDEPENDENT DEMOCRAT)

CLAY (NATIONAL-REPUBLICAN)　　WIRT (ANTI-MASON)

Congressional Quarterly's Guide to U.S. Elections, 3rd. edition, copyright ©1994. Used with permission. All rights reserved.

States	Electoral Votes	Jackson	Clay	Floyd	Wirt
Alabama	(7)	7	-	-	-
Connecticut	(8)	-	8	-	-
Delaware	(3)	-	3	-	-
Georgia	(11)	11	-	-	-
Illinois	(5)	5	-	-	-
Indiana	(9)	9	-	-	-
Kentucky	(15)	-	15	-	-
Louisiana	(5)	5	-	-	-
Maine	(10)	10	-	-	-
Maryland	(10)	3	5	-	-
Massachusetts	(14)	-	14	-	-
Mississippi	(4)	4	-	-	-
Missouri	(4)	4	-	-	-
New Hampshire	(7)	7	-	-	-
New Jersey	(8)	8	-	-	-
New York	(42)	42	-	-	-
North Carolina	(15)	15	-	-	-
Ohio	(21)	21	-	-	-
Pennsylvania	(30)	30	-	-	-
Rhode Island	(4)	-	4	-	-
South Carolina	(11)	-	-	11	-
Tennessee	(15)	15	-	-	-
Vermont	(7)	-	-	-	7
Virginia	(23)	23	-	-	-
Totals	**(288)**	**219**	**49**	**11**	**7**

16

1832

PRESIDENTIAL ELECTION RETURNS

STATE	TOTAL VOTE	ANDREW JACKSON (Democrat)		HENRY CLAY (National-Republican)		WILLIAM WIRT (Anti-Mason)		OTHER		PLURALITY	
		Votes	%	Votes	%	Votes	%	Votes	%		
Alabama	14,291	14,286	100.0	5		—		—		14,281	D
Connecticut	32,833	11,269	34.3	18,155	55.3	3,409	10.4	—		6,886	NR
Delaware	8,386	4,110	49.0	4,276	51.0	—		—		166	NR
Georgia	20,750	20,750	100.0	—		—		—		20,750	D
Illinois	21,481	14,609	68.0	6,745	31.4	97	0.5	30	0.1	7,864	D
Indiana	57,152	31,652	55.4	25,473	44.6	27		—		6,179	D
Kentucky	79,741	36,292	45.5	43,449	54.5	—		—		7,157	NR
Louisiana	6,337	3,908	61.7	2,429	38.3	—		—		1,479	D
Maine	62,153	33,978	54.7	27,331	44.0	844	1.4	—		6,647	D
Maryland	38,316	19,156	50.0	19,160	50.0	—		—		4	NR
Massachusetts	67,619	13,933	20.6	31,963	47.3	14,692	21.7	7,031	10.4	17,271	NR
Mississippi	5,750	5,750	100.0	—		—		—		5,750	D
Missouri	5,192	5,192	100.0	—		—		—		5,192	D
New Hampshire	43,793	24,855	56.8	18,938	43.2	—		—		5,917	D
New Jersey	47,760	23,826	49.9	23,466	49.1	468	1.0	—		360	D
New York	323,393	168,497	52.1	154,896	47.9	—		—		13,601	D
North Carolina	29,799	25,261	84.8	4,538	15.2	—		—		20,723	D
Ohio	158,350	81,246	51.3	76,566	48.4	538	0.3	—		4,680	D
Pennsylvania	157,679	90,973	57.7	—		66,706	42.3	—		24,267	D
Rhode Island	5,747	2,051	35.7	2,871	50.0	819	14.3	6	0.1	820	NR
Tennessee	29,425	28,078	95.4	1,347	4.6	—		—		26,731	D
Vermont	32,344	7,865	24.3	11,161	34.5	13,112	40.5	206	0.6	1,951	AM
Virginia	45,682	34,243	75.0	11,436	25.0	3		—		22,807	D
Totals	**1,293,973**	**701,780**	**54.2**	**484,205**	**37.4**	**100,715**	**7.8**	**7,273**	**0.6**	**217,575**	**D**

PRESIDENTIAL ELECTION OF
1836

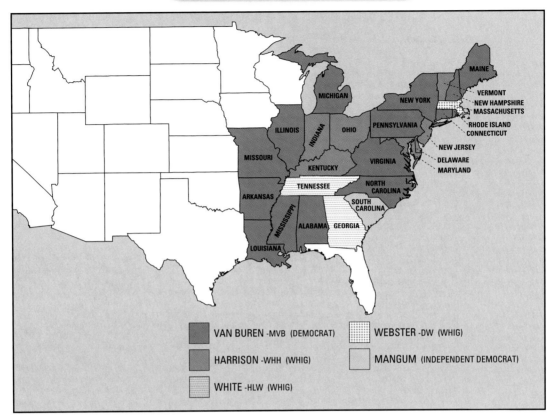

	VAN BUREN -MVB (DEMOCRAT)		WEBSTER -DW (WHIG)
	HARRISON -WHH (WHIG)		MANGUM (INDEPENDENT DEMOCRAT)
	WHITE -HLW (WHIG)		

Congressional Quarterly's Guide to U.S. Elections, 3rd. edition, copyright ©1994. Used with permission. All rights reserved.

States	Electoral Votes	Van Buren	Harrison	White	Webster	Mangum
Alabama	(7)	7	-	-	-	-
Arkansas	(3)	3	-	-	-	-
Connecticut	(8)	8	-	-	-	-
Delaware	(3)	-	3	-	-	-
Georgia	(11)	-	-	11	-	-
Illinois	(5)	5	-	-	-	-
Indiana	(9)	-	9	-	-	-
Kentucky	(15)	-	15	-	-	-
Louisiana	(5)	5	-	-	-	-
Maine	(10)	10	-	-	-	-
Maryland	(10)	-	10	-	-	-
Massachusetts	(14)	-	-	-	14	-
Michigan	(3)	3	-	-	-	-
Mississippi	(4)	4	-	-	-	-
Missouri	(4)	4	-	-	-	-
New Hampshire	(7)	7	-	-	-	-
New Jersey	(8)	-	8	-	-	-
New York	(42)	42	-	-	-	-
North Carolina	(15)	15	-	-	-	-
Ohio	(21)	-	21	-	-	-
Pennsylvania	(30)	30	-	-	-	-
Rhode Island	(4)	4	-	-	-	-
South Carolina	(11)	-	-	-	-	11
Tennessee	(15)	-	-	15	-	-
Vermont	(7)	-	7	-	-	-
Virginia	(23)	23	-	-	-	-
Totals	**(294)**	**170**	**73**	**26**	**14**	**11**

1836

PRESIDENTIAL ELECTION RETURNS

STATE	TOTAL VOTE	MARTIN VAN BUREN (Democrat)		WILLIAM H. HARRISON (Whig)		HUGH L. WHITE (Whig)		DANIEL WEBSTER (Whig)		OTHER		PLURALITY	
		Votes	%	Votes	%	Votes	%	Votes	%	Votes	%		
Alabama	37,296	20,638	55.3	—		16,658	44.7	—		—		3,980	MVB
Arkansas	3,714	2,380	64.1			1,334	35.9	—		—		1,046	MVB
Connecticut	38,093	19,294	50.6	18,799	49.4	—		—		—		495	MVB
Delaware	8,895	4,154	46.7	4,736	53.2	—		—		5	0.1	582	WHH
Georgia	47,259	22,778	48.2	—		24,481	51.8	—		—		1,703	HLW
Illinois	33,589	18,369	54.7	15,220	45.3	—		—		—		3,149	MVB
Indiana	74,423	33,084	44.5	41,339	55.5	—		—		—		8,255	WHH
Kentucky	70,090	33,229	47.4	36,861	52.6	—		—		—		3,632	WHH
Louisiana	7,425	3,842	51.7	—		3,583	48.3	—		—		259	MVB
Maine	38,740	22,825	58.9	14,803	38.2	—		—		1,112	2.9	8,022	MVB
Maryland	48,119	22,267	46.3	25,852	53.7	—		—		—		3,585	WHH
Massachusetts	74,732	33,486	44.8	—		—		41,201	55.1	45	0.1	33,486	DW
Michigan	12,052	6,507	54.0	5,545	46.0	—		—		—		962	MVB
Mississippi	20,079	10,297	51.3	—		9,782	48.7	—		—		515	MVB
Missouri	18,332	10,995	60.0	—		7,337	40.0	—		—		3,658	MVB
New Hampshire	24,925	18,697	75.0	6,228	25.0	—		—		—		12,469	MVB
New Jersey	51,729	25,592	49.5	26,137	50.5	—		—		—		545	WHH
New York	305,343	166,795	54.6	138,548	45.4	—		—		—		28,247	MVB
North Carolina	50,153	26,631	53.1	—		23,521	46.9	—		1		3,110	MVB
Ohio	202,931	97,122	47.9	105,809	52.1	—		—		—		8,687	WHH
Pennsylvania	178,701	91,466	51.2	87,235	48.8	—		—		—		4,231	MVB
Rhode Island	5,673	2,962	52.2	2,710	47.8	—		—		1		252	MVB
Tennessee	62,197	26,170	42.1	—		36,027	57.9	—		—		9,857	HLW
Vermont	35,099	14,040	4	20,994	59.8	—		—		65	0.2	6,954	WHH
Virginia	53,945	30,556	56.6	—		23,384	43.3	—		5		7,172	MVB
Totals	**1,503,534**	**764,176**	**50.8**	**550,816**	**36.6**	**146,107**	**9.7**	**41,201**	**2.7**	**1,234**	**0.1**	**213,360**	**MVB**

1840

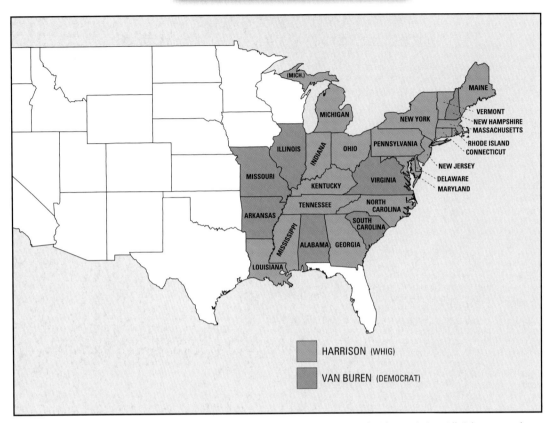

Congressional Quarterly's Guide to U.S. Elections, 3rd. edition, copyright ©1994. Used with permission. All rights reserved.

States	Electoral Votes	Harrison	Van Buren
Alabama	(7)	-	7
Arkansas	(3)	-	3
Connecticut	(8)	8	-
Delaware	(3)	3	-
Georgia	(11)	11	-
Illinois	(5)	-	5
Indiana	(9)	9	-
Kentucky	(15)	15	-
Louisiana	(5)	5	-
Maine	(10)	10	-
Maryland	(10)	10	-
Massachusetts	(14)	14	-
Michigan	(3)	3	-
Mississippi	(4)	4	-
Missouri	(4)	-	4
New Hampshire	(7)	-	7
New Jersey	(8)	8	-
New York	(42)	42	-
North Carolina	(15)	15	-
Ohio	(21)	21	-
Pennsylvania	(30)	30	-
Rhode Island	(4)	4	-
South Carolina	(11)	-	11
Tennessee	(15)	15	-
Vermont	(7)	7	-
Virginia	(23)	-	23
Totals	**(294)**	**234**	**60**

1840

PRESIDENTIAL ELECTION RETURNS

STATE	TOTAL VOTE	WILLIAM H. HARRISON (Whig)		MARTIN VAN BUREN (Democrat)		JAMES G. BIRNEY (Liberty)		OTHER		PLURALITY	
		Votes	%	Votes	%	Votes	%	Votes	%		
Alabama	62,511	28,515	45.6	33,996	54.4	—		—		5,481	D
Arkansas	11,839	5,160	43.6	6,679	56.4	—		—		1,519	D
Connecticut	56,879	31,598	55.6	25,281	44.4	—		—		6,317	W
Delaware	10,852	5,967	55.0	4,872	44.9	—		13	0.1	1,095	W
Georgia	72,322	40,339	55.8	31,983	44.2	—		—		8,356	W
Illinois	93,175	45,574	48.9	47,441	50.9	160	0.2	—		1,867	D
Indiana	117,605	65,280	55.5	51,696	44.0	30		599	0.5	13,584	W
Kentucky	91,104	58,488	64.2	32,616	35.8	—		—		25,872	W
Louisiana	18,912	11,296	59.7	7,616	40.3	—		—		3,680	W
Maine	92,802	46,612	50.2	46,190	49.8	—		—		422	W
Maryland	62,280	33,528	53.8	28,752	46.2	—		—		4,776	W
Massachusetts	126,825	72,852	57.4	52,355	41.3	1,618	1.3	—		20,497	W
Michigan	44,029	22,933	52.1	21,096	47.9	—		—		1,837	W
Mississippi	36,525	19,515	53.4	17,010	46.6	—		—		2,505	W
Missouri	52,923	22,954	43.4	29,969	56.6	—		—		7,015	D
New Hampshire	59,956	26,310	43.9	32,774	54.7	872	1.5	—		6,464	D
New Jersey	64,454	33,351	51.7	31,034	48.1	69	0.1	—		2,317	W
New York	441,543	226,001	51.2	212,733	48.2	2,809	0.6	—		13,268	W
North Carolina	80,735	46,567	57.7	34,168	42.3	—		—		12,399	W
Ohio	272,890	148,043	54.3	123,944	45.4	903	0.3	—		24,099	W
Pennsylvania	287,695	144,023	50.1	143,672	49.9	—		—		351	W
Rhode Island	8,631	5,213	60.4	3,263	37.8	19	0.2	136	1.6	1,950	W
Tennessee	108,145	60,194	55.7	47,951	44.3	—		—		12,243	W
Vermont	50,782	32,440	63.9	18,006	35.5	317	0.6	19		14,434	W
Virginia	86,394	42,637	49.4	43,757	50.6	—		—		1,120	D
Totals	**2,411,808**	**1,275,390**	**52.9**	**1,128,854**	**46.8**	**6,797**	**0.3**	**767**		**146,536**	**W**

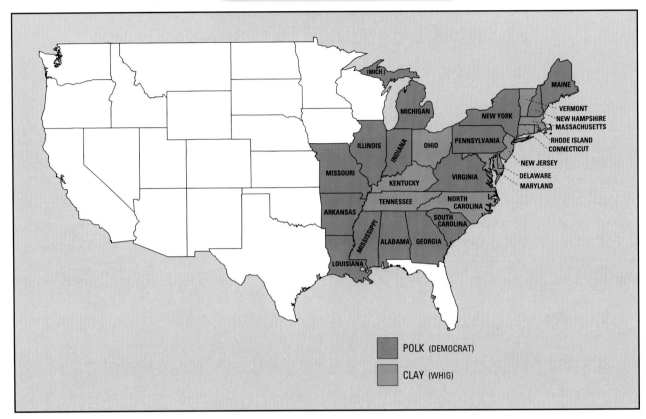

PRESIDENTIAL ELECTION OF
1844

POLK (DEMOCRAT)

CLAY (WHIG)

States	Electoral Votes	Polk	Clay
Alabama	(9)	9	-
Arkansas	(3)	3	-
Connecticut	(6)	-	6
Delaware	(3)	-	3
Georgia	(10)	10	-
Illinois	(9)	9	-
Indiana	(12)	12	-
Kentucky	(12)	-	12
Louisiana	(6)	6	-
Maine	(9)	9	-
Maryland	(8)	-	8
Massachusetts	(12)	-	12
Michigan	(5)	5	-
Mississippi	(6)	6	-
Missouri	(7)	7	-
New Hampshire	(6)	6	-
New Jersey	(7)	-	7
New York	(36)	36	-
North Carolina	(11)	-	11
Ohio	(23)	-	23
Pennsylvania	(26)	26	-
Rhode Island	(4)	-	4
South Carolina	(9)	9	-
Tennessee	(13)	-	13
Vermont	(6)	-	6
Virginia	(17)	17	-
Totals	**(275)**	**170**	**105**

1844

PRESIDENTIAL ELECTION RETURNS

STATE	TOTAL VOTE	JAMES K. POLK (Democrat)		HENRY CLAY (Whig)		JAMES G. BIRNEY (Liberty)		OTHER		PLURALITY	
		Votes	%	Votes	%	Votes	%	Votes	%		
Alabama	63,403	37,401	59.0	26,002	41.0	—		—		11,399	D
Arkansas	15,150	9,546	63.0	5,604	37.0	—		—		3,942	D
Connecticut	64,616	29,841	46.2	32,832	50.8	1,943	3.0	—		2,991	W
Delaware	12,247	5,970	48.7	6,271	51.2	—		6		301	W
Georgia	86,247	44,147	51.2	42,100	48.8	—		—		2,047	D
Illinois	109,057	58,795	53.9	45,854	42.0	3,469	3.2	939	0.9	12,941	D
Indiana	140,157	70,183	50.1	67,866	48.4	2,108	1.5	—		2,317	D
Kentucky	113,237	51,988	45.9	61,249	54.1	—		—		9,261	W
Louisiana	26,865	13,782	51.3	13,083	48.7	—		—		699	D
Maine	84,933	45,719	53.8	34,378	40.5	4,836	5.7	—		11,341	D
Maryland	68,690	32,706	47.6	35,984	52.4	—		—		3,278	W
Massachusetts	132,037	53,039	40.2	67,062	50.8	10,830	8.2	1,106	0.8	14,023	W
Michigan	55,560	27,737	49.9	24,185	43.5	3,638	6.5	—		3,552	D
Mississippi	45,004	25,846	57.4	19,158	42.6	—		—		6,688	D
Missouri	72,522	41,322	57.0	31,200	43.0	—		—		10,122	D
New Hampshire	49,187	27,160	55.2	17,866	36.3	4,161	8.5	—		9,294	D
New Jersey	75,944	37,495	49.4	38,318	50.5	131	0.2	—		823	W
New York	485,882	237,588	48.9	232,482	47.9	15,812	3.3	—		5,106	D
North Carolina	82,521	39,287	47.6	43,232	52.4	—		2		3,945	W
Ohio	312,300	149,127	47.8	155,091	49.7	8,082	2.6	—		5,964	W
Pennsylvania	331,645	167,311	50.4	161,195	48.6	3,139	0.9	—		6,116	D
Rhode Island	12,194	4,867	39.9	7,322	60.0	—		5		2,455	W
Tennessee	119,957	59,917	49.9	60,040	50.1	—		—		123	W
Vermont	48,765	18,041	37.0	26,770	54.9	3,954	8.1	—		8,729	W
Virginia	95,539	50,679	53.0	44,860	47.0	—		—		5,819	D
Totals	2,703,659	1,339,494	49.5	1,300,004	48.1	62,103	2.3	2,058	0.1	39,490	D

PRESIDENTIAL ELECTION OF
1848

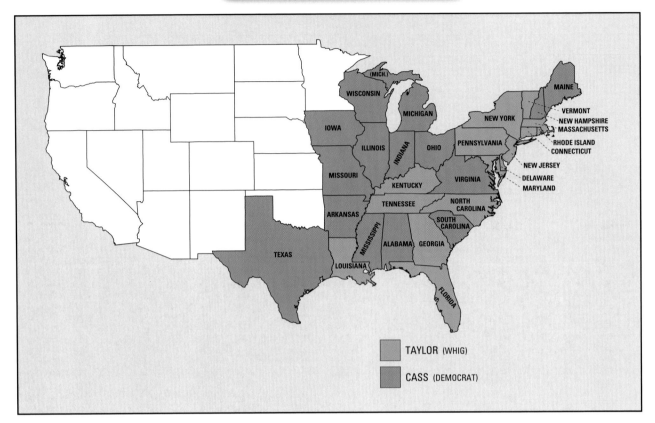

States	Electoral Votes	Taylor	Cass	States	Electoral Votes	Taylor	Cass
Alabama	(9)	–	9	Mississippi	(6)	–	6
Arkansas	(3)	–	3	Missouri	(7)	–	7
Connecticut	(6)	6	–	New Hampshire	(6)	–	6
Delaware	(3)	3	–	New Jersey	(7)	7	–
Florida	(3)	3	–	New York	(36)	36	–
Georgia	(10)	10	–	North Carolina	(11)	11	–
Illinois	(9)	–	9	Ohio	(23)	–	23
Indiana	(12)	–	12	Pennsylvania	(26)	26	–
Iowa	(4)	–	4	Rhode Island	(4)	4	–
Kentucky	(12)	12	–	South Carolina	(9)	–	9
Louisiana	(6)	6	–	Tennessee	(13)	13	–
Maine	(9)	–	9	Texas	(4)	–	4
Maryland	(8)	8	–	Vermont	(6)	6	–
Massachusetts	(12)	12	–	Virginia	(17)	–	17
Michigan	(5)	–	5	Wisconsin	(4)	–	4
				Totals	**(290)**	**163**	**127**

1848

PRESIDENTIAL ELECTION RETURNS

STATE	TOTAL VOTE	ZACHARY TAYLOR (Whig)		LEWIS CASS (Democrat)		MARTIN VAN BUREN (Free Soil)		OTHER		PLURALITY	
		Votes	%	Votes	%	Votes	%	Votes	%		
Alabama	61,659	30,482	49.4	31,173	50.6	—		4		691	D
Arkansas	16,888	7,587	44.9	9,301	55.1	—		—		1,714	D
Connecticut	62,398	30,318	48.6	27,051	43.4	5,005	8.0	24		3,267	W
Delaware	12,432	6,440	51.8	5,910	47.5	82	0.7	—		530	W
Florida	7,203	4,120	57.2	3,083	42.8	—		—		1,037	W
Georgia	92,317	47,532	51.5	44,785	48.5	—		—		2,747	W
Illinois	124,596	52,853	42.4	55,952	44.9	15,702	12.6	89	0.1	3,099	D
Indiana	152,394	69,668	45.7	74,695	49.0	8,031	5.3	—		5,027	D
Iowa	22,271	9,930	44.6	11,238	50.5	1,103	5.0	—		1,308	D
Kentucky	116,865	67,145	57.5	49,720	42.5	—		—		17,425	W
Louisiana	33,866	18,487	54.6	15,379	45.4	—		—		3,108	W
Maine	87,625	35,273	40.3	40,195	45.9	12,157	13.9	—		4,922	D
Maryland	72,359	37,702	52.1	34,528	47.7	129	0.2	—		3,174	W
Massachusetts	134,748	61,072	45.3	35,281	26.2	38,333	28.4	62		22,739	W
Michigan	65,082	23,947	36.8	30,742	47.2	10,393	16.0	—		6,795	D
Mississippi	52,456	25,911	49.4	26,545	50.6	—		—		634	D
Missouri	72,748	32,671	44.9	40,077	55.1	—		—		7,406	D
New Hampshire	50,104	14,781	29.5	27,763	55.4	7,560	15.1	—		12,982	D
New Jersey	77,745	40,015	51.5	36,901	47.5	829	1.1	—		3,114	W
New York	455,944	218,583	47.9	114,319	25.1	120,497	26.4	2,545	0.6	98,086	W
North Carolina	79,826	44,054	55.2	35,772	44.8	—		—		8,282	W
Ohio	328,987	138,656	42.1	154,782	47.0	35,523	10.8	26		16,126	D
Pennsylvania	369,092	185,730	50.3	172,186	46.7	11,176	3.0	—		13,544	W
Rhode Island	11,049	6,705	60.7	3,613	32.7	726	6.6	5		3,092	W
Tennessee	122,463	64,321	52.5	58,142	47.5	—		—		6,179	W
Texas	17,000	5,281	31.1	11,644	68.5	—		75	0.4	6,363	D
Vermont	47,897	23,117	48.3	10,943	22.8	13,837	28.9	—		9,280	W
Virginia	92,004	45,265	49.2	46,739	50.8	—		—		1,474	D
Wisconsin	39,166	13,747	35.1	15,001	38.3	10,418	26.6	—		1,254	D
Totals	2,879,184	1,361,393	47.3	1,223,460	42.5	291,501	10.1	2,830	0.1	137,933	W

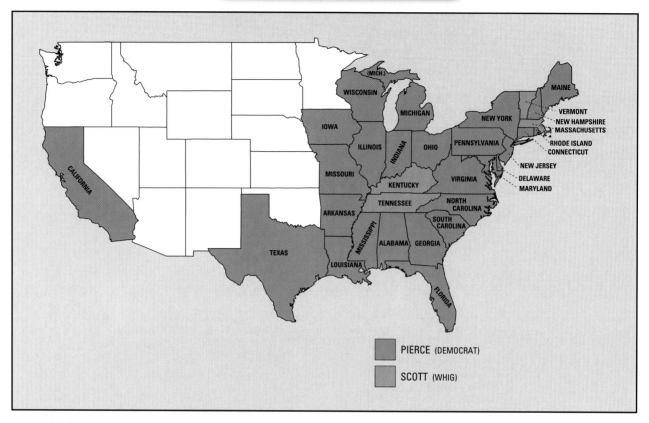

PRESIDENTIAL ELECTION OF
1852

PIERCE (DEMOCRAT)

SCOTT (WHIG)

States	Electoral Votes	Pierce	Scott	States	Electoral Votes	Pierce	Scott
Alabama	(9)	9	-	Mississippi	(7)	7	-
Arkansas	(4)	4	-	Missouri	(9)	9	-
California	(4)	4	-	New Hampshire	(5)	5	-
Connecticut	(6)	6	-	New Jersey	(7)	7	-
Delaware	(3)	3	-	New York	(35)	35	-
Florida	(3)	3	-	North Carolina	(10)	10	-
Georgia	(10)	10	-	Ohio	(23)	23	-
Illinois	(11)	11	-	Pennsylvania	(27)	27	-
Indiana	(13)	13	-	Rhode Island	(4)	4	-
Iowa	(4)	4	-	South Carolina	(8)	8	-
Kentucky	(12)	-	12	Tennessee	(12)	-	12
Louisiana	(6)	6	-	Texas	(4)	4	-
Maine	(8)	8	-	Vermont	(5)	-	5
Maryland	(8)	8	-	Virginia	(15)	15	-
Massachusetts	(13)	-	13	Wisconsin	(5)	5	-
Michigan	(6)	6	-	**Totals**	**(296)**	**254**	**42**

1852

PRESIDENTIAL ELECTION RETURNS

STATE	TOTAL VOTE	FRANKLIN PIERCE (Democrat)		WINFIELD SCOTT (Whig)		JOHN P. HALE (Free Soil)		OTHER		PLURALITY	
		Votes	%	Votes	%	Votes	%	Votes	%		
Alabama	44,147	26,881	60.9	15,061	34.1	—		2,205	5.0	11,820	D
Arkansas	19,577	12,173	62.2	7,404	37.8	—		—		4,769	D
California	76,810	40,721	53.0	35,972	46.8	61	0.1	56	0.1	4,749	D
Connecticut	66,781	33,249	49.8	30,359	45.5	3,161	4.7	12		2,890	D
Delaware	12,673	6,318	49.9	6,293	49.7	62	0.5	—		25	D
Florida	7,193	4,318	60.0	2,875	40.0	—		—		1,443	D
Georgia	62,626	40,516	64.7	16,660	26.6	—		5,450	8.7	23,856	D
Illinois	154,974	80,378	51.9	64,733	41.8	9,863	6.4	—		15,645	D
Indiana	183,176	95,340	52.0	80,907	44.2	6,929	3.8	—		14,433	D
Iowa	35,364	17,763	50.2	15,856	44.8	1,606	4.5	139	0.4	1,907	D
Kentucky	111,643	53,949	48.3	57,428	51.4	266	0.2	—		3,479	W
Louisiana	35,902	18,647	51.9	17,255	48.1	—		—		1,392	D
Maine	82,182	41,609	50.6	32,543	39.6	8,030	9.8	—		9,066	D
Maryland	75,120	40,022	53.3	35,077	46.7	21		—		4,945	D
Massachusetts	127,103	44,569	35.1	52,683	41.4	28,023	22.0	1,828	1.4	8,114	W
Michigan	82,939	41,842	50.4	33,860	40.8	7,237	8.7	—		7,982	D
Mississippi	44,454	26,896	60.5	17,558	39.5	—		—		9,338	D
Missouri	68,801	38,817	56.4	29,984	43.6	—		—		8,833	D
New Hampshire	50,535	28,503	56.4	15,486	30.6	6,546	13.0	—		13,017	D
New Jersey	83,926	44,301	52.8	38,551	45.9	336	0.4	738	0.9	5,750	D
New York	522,294	262,083	50.2	234,882	45.0	25,329	4.8	—		27,201	D
North Carolina	78,891	39,788	50.4	39,043	49.5	—		60	0.1	745	D
Ohio	352,903	169,193	47.9	152,577	43.2	31,133	8.8	—		16,616	D
Pennsylvania	387,920	198,568	51.2	179,182	46.2	8,500	2.2	1,670	0.4	19,386	D
Rhode Island	17,005	8,735	51.4	7,626	44.8	644	3.8	—		1,109	D
Tennessee	115,486	56,900	49.3	58,586	50.7	—		—		1,686	W
Texas	20,223	14,857	73.5	5,356	26.5	—		10		9,501	D
Vermont	43,838	13,044	29.8	22,173	50.6	8,621	19.7	—		9,129	W
Virginia	132,604	73,872	55.7	58,732	44.3	—		—		15,140	D
Wisconsin	64,740	33,658	52.0	22,240	34.4	8,842	13.7	—		11,418	D
Totals	3,161,830	1,607,510	50.8	1,386,942	43.9	155,210	4.9	12,168	0.4	220,568	D

PRESIDENTIAL ELECTION OF
1856

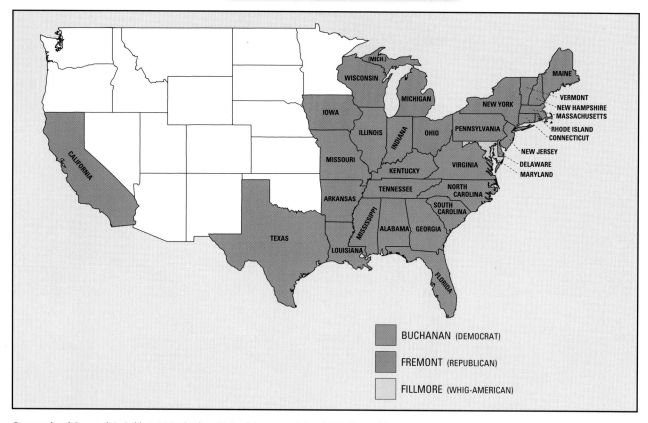

BUCHANAN (DEMOCRAT)

FREMONT (REPUBLICAN)

FILLMORE (WHIG-AMERICAN)

Congressional Quarterly's Guide to U.S. Elections, 3rd. edition, copyright ©1994. Used with permission. All rights reserved.

States	Electoral Votes	Buchanan	Fremont	Fillmore	States	Electoral Votes	Buchanan	Fremont	Fillmore
Alabama	(9)	9	-	-	Mississippi	(7)	7	-	-
Arkansas	(4)	4	-	-	Missouri	(9)	9	-	-
California	(4)	4	-	-	New Hampshire	(5)	-	5	-
Connecticut	(6)	-	6	-	New Jersey	(7)	7	-	-
Delaware	(3)	3	-	-	New York	(35)	-	35	-
Florida	(3)	3	-	-	North Carolina	(10)	10	-	-
Georgia	(10)	10	-	-	Ohio	(23)	-	23	-
Illinois	(11)	11	-	-	Pennsylvania	(27)	27	-	-
Indiana	(13)	13	-	-	Rhode Island	(4)	-	4	-
Iowa	(4)	-	4	-	South Carolina	(8)	8	-	-
Kentucky	(12)	12	-	-	Tennessee	(12)	12	-	-
Louisiana	(6)	6	-	-	Texas	(4)	4	-	-
Maine	(8)	-	8	-	Vermont	(5)	-	5	-
Maryland	(8)	-	-	8	Virginia	(15)	15	-	-
Massachusetts	(13)	-	13	-	Wisconsin	(5)	-	5	-
Michigan	(6)	-	6	-	Totals	(296)	174	114	8

1856

PRESIDENTIAL ELECTION RETURNS

STATE	TOTAL VOTE	JAMES BUCHANAN (Democrat)		JOHN C. FREMONT (Republican)		MILLARD FILLMORE (Whig-American)		OTHER		PLURALITY	
		Votes	%	Votes	%	Votes	%	Votes	%		
Alabama	75,291	46,739	62.1	—		28,552	37.9	—		18,187	D
Arkansas	32,642	21,910	67.1	—		10,732	32.9	—		11,178	D
California	110,255	53,342	48.4	20,704	18.8	36,195	32.8	14		17,147	D
Connecticut	80,360	35,028	43.6	42,717	53.2	2,615	3.3	—		7,689	R
Delaware	14,598	8,004	54.8	310	2.1	6,275	43.0	9	0.1	1,729	D
Florida	11,191	6,358	56.8	—		4,833	43.2	—		1,525	D
Georgia	99,020	56,581	57.1	—		42,439	42.9	—		14,142	D
Illinois	239,334	105,528	44.1	96,275	40.2	37,531	15.7	—		9,253	D
Indiana	235,401	118,670	50.4	94,375	40.1	22,356	9.5	—		24,295	D
Iowa	92,310	37,568	40.7	45,073	48.8	9,669	10.5	—		7,505	R
Kentucky	142,058	74,642	52.5	—		67,416	47.5	—		7,226	D
Louisiana	42,873	22,164	51.7	—		20,709	48.3	—		1,455	D
Maine	109,689	39,140	35.7	67,279	61.3	3,270	3.0	—		28,139	R
Maryland	86,860	39,123	45.0	285	0.3	47,452	54.6	—		8,329	WA
Massachusetts	170,048	39,244	23.1	108,172	63.6	19,626	11.5	3,006	1.8	68,928	R
Michigan	125,558	52,136	41.5	71,762	57.2	1,660	1.3	—		19,626	R
Mississippi	59,647	35,456	59.4	—		24,191	40.6	—		11,265	D
Missouri	106,486	57,964	54.4	—		48,522	45.6	—		9,442	D
New Hampshire	69,774	31,891	45.7	37,473	53.7	410	0.6	—		5,582	R
New Jersey	99,396	46,943	47.2	28,338	28.5	24,115	24.3	—		18,605	D
New York	596,486	195,878	32.8	276,004	46.3	124,604	20.9	—		80,126	R
North Carolina	84,963	48,243	56.8	—		36,720	43.2	—		11,523	D
Ohio	386,640	170,874	44.2	187,497	48.5	28,121	7.3	148		16,623	R
Pennsylvania	460,937	230,772	50.1	147,963	32.1	82,202	17.8	—		82,809	D
Rhode Island	19,822	6,680	33.7	11,467	57.8	1,675	8.5	—		4,787	R
Tennessee	133,582	69,704	52.2	—		63,878	47.8	—		5,826	D
Texas	48,005	31,995	66.6	—		16,010	33.4	—		15,985	D
Vermont	50,675	10,569	20.9	39,561	78.1	545	1.1	—		28,992	R
Virginia	150,233	90,083	60.0	—		60,150	40.0	—		29,933	D
Wisconsin	120,513	52,843	43.8	67,090	55.7	580	0.5	—		14,247	R
Totals	**4,054,647**	**1,836,072**	**45.3**	**1,342,345**	**33.1**	**873,053**	**21.5**	**3,177**	**0.1**	**493,727**	**D**

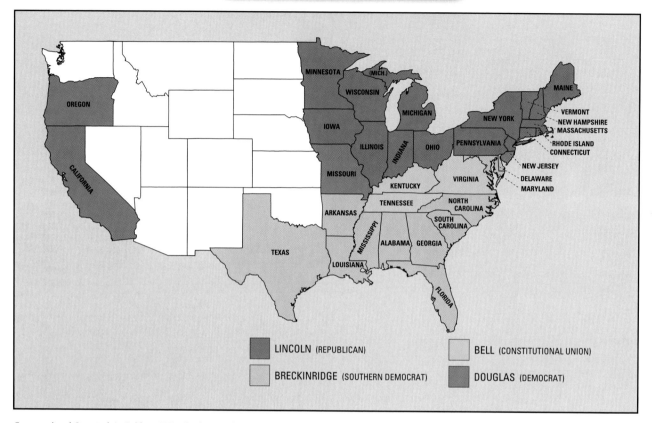

PRESIDENTIAL ELECTION OF 1860

States	Electoral Votes	Lincoln	Breckinridge	Bell	Douglas	States	Electoral Votes	Lincoln	Breckinridge	Bell	Douglas
Alabama	(9)	–	9	–	–	Mississippi	(7)	–	7	–	–
Arkansas	(4)	–	4	–	–	Missouri	(9)	–	–	–	9
California	(4)	4	–	–	–	New Hampshire	(5)	5	–	–	–
Connecticut	(6)	6	–	–	–	New Jersey	(7)	4	–	–	3
Delaware	(3)	–	3	–	–	New York	(35)	35	–	–	–
Florida	(3)	–	3	–	–	North Carolina	(10)	–	10	–	–
Georgia	(10)	–	10	–	–	Ohio	(23)	23	–	–	–
Illinois	(11)	11	–	–	–	Oregon	(3)	3	–	–	–
Indiana	(13)	13	–	–	–	Pennsylvania	(27)	27	–	–	–
Iowa	(4)	4	–	–	–	Rhode Island	(4)	4	–	–	–
Kentucky	(12)	–	–	12	–	South Carolina	(8)	–	8	–	–
Louisiana	(6)	–	6	–	–	Tennessee	(12)	–	–	12	–
Maine	(8)	8	–	–	–	Texas	(4)	–	4	–	–
Maryland	(8)	–	8	–	–	Vermont	(5)	5	–	–	–
Massachusetts	(13)	13	–	–	–	Virginia	(15)	–	–	15	–
Michigan	(6)	6	–	–	–	Wisconsin	(5)	5	–	–	–
Minnesota	(4)	4	–	–	–	**Totals**	**(303)**	**180**	**72**	**39**	**12**

1860

PRESIDENTIAL ELECTION RETURNS

STATE	TOTAL VOTE	ABRAHAM LINCOLN (Republican)		STEPHEN A. DOUGLAS (Democrat)		JOHN C. BRECKINRIDGE (Southern Democrat)		JOHN BELL (Constitutional Union)		OTHER		PLURALITY	
		Votes	%	Votes	%	Votes	%	Votes	%	Votes	%		
Alabama	90,122	—		13,618	15.1	48,669	54.0	27,835	30.9	—		20,834	SD
Arkansas	54,152	—		5,357	9.9	28,732	53.1	20,063	37.0	—		8,669	SD
California	119,827	38,733	32.3	37,999	31.7	33,969	28.3	9,111	7.6	15		734	R
Connecticut	74,819	43,488	58.1	15,431	20.6	14,372	19.2	1,528	2.0	—		28,057	R
Delaware	16,115	3,822	23.7	1,066	6.6	7,339	45.5	3,888	24.1	—		3,451	SD
Florida	13,301	—		223	1.7	8,277	62.2	4,801	36.1	—		3,476	SD
Georgia	106,717	—		11,581	10.9	52,176	48.9	42,960	40.3	—		9,216	SD
Illinois	339,666	172,171	50.7	160,215	47.2	2,331	0.7	4,914	1.4	35		11,956	R
Indiana	272,143	139,033	51.1	115,509	42.4	12,295	4.5	5,306	1.9	—		23,524	R
Iowa	128,739	70,302	54.6	55,639	43.2	1,035	0.8	1,763	1.4	—		14,663	R
Kentucky	146,216	1,364	0.9	25,651	17.5	53,143	36.3	66,058	45.2	—		12,915	CU
Louisiana	50,510	—		7,625	15.1	22,681	44.9	20,204	40.0	—		2,477	SD
Maine	100,918	62,811	62.2	29,693	29.4	6,368	6.3	2,046	2.0	—		33,118	R
Maryland	92,502	2,294	2.5	5,966	6.4	42,482	45.9	41,760	45.1	—		722	SD
Massachusetts	169,876	106,684	62.8	34,370	20.2	6,163	3.6	22,331	13.1	328	0.2	72,314	R
Michigan	154,758	88,481	57.2	65,057	42.0	805	0.5	415	0.3	—		23,424	R
Minnesota	34,804	22,069	63.4	11,920	34.2	748	2.1	50	0.1	17		10,149	R
Mississippi	69,095	—		3,282	4.7	40,768	59.0	25,045	36.2	—		15,723	SD
Missouri	165,563	17,028	10.3	58,801	35.5	31,362	18.9	58,372	35.3	—		429	D
New Hampshire	65,943	37,519	56.9	25,887	39.3	2,125	3.2	412	0.6	—		11,632	R
New Jersey	121,215	58,346	48.1	62,869	51.9	—		—		—		4,523	D
New York	675,156	362,646	53.7	312,510	46.3	—		—		—		50,136	R
North Carolina	96,712	—		2,737	2.8	48,846	50.5	45,129	46.7	—		3,717	SD
Ohio	442,866	231,709	52.3	187,421	42.3	11,406	2.6	12,194	2.8	136		44,288	R
Oregon	14,758	5,329	36.1	4,136	28.0	5,075	34.4	218	1.5	—		254	R
Pennsylvania	476,442	268,030	56.3	16,765	3.5	178,871	37.5	12,776	2.7	—		89,159	R
Rhode Island	19,951	12,244	61.4	7,707	38.6	—		—		—		4,537	R
Tennessee	146,106	—		11,281	7.7	65,097	44.6	69,728	47.7	—		4,631	CU
Texas	62,855	—		18		47,454	75.5	15,383	24.5	—		32,071	SD
Vermont	44,644	33,808	75.7	8,649	19.4	218	0.5	1,969	4.4	—		25,159	R
Virginia	166,891	1,887	1.1	16,198	9.7	74,325	44.5	74,481	44.6	—		156	CU
Wisconsin	152,179	86,110	56.6	65,021	42.7	887	0.6	161	0.1	—		21,089	R
Totals	4,685,561	1,865,908	39.9	1,380,202	29.5	848,019	18.1	590,901	12.6	531		485,706	R

PRESIDENTIAL ELECTION OF

1864

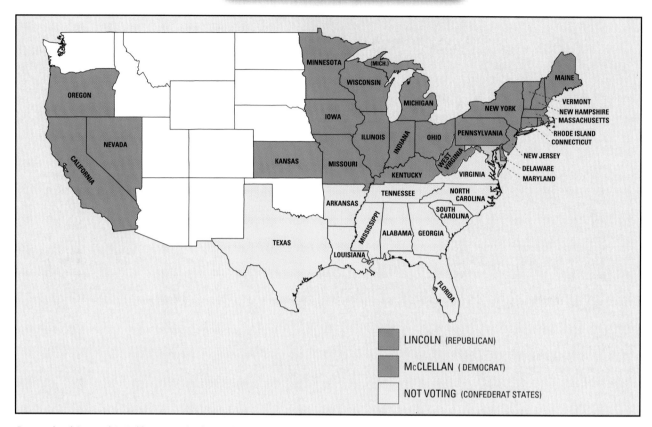

LINCOLN (REPUBLICAN)

McCLELLAN (DEMOCRAT)

NOT VOTING (CONFEDERAT STATES)

States	Electoral Votes	Lincoln	McClellan	States	Electoral Votes	Lincoln	McClellan
California	(5)	5	-	Missouri	(11)	11	-
Connecticut	(6)	6	-	Nevada	(3)	2	-
Delaware	(3)	-	3	New Hampshire	(5)	5	-
Illinois	(16)	16	-	New Jersey	(7)	-	7
Indiana	(13)	13	-	New York	(33)	33	-
Iowa	(8)	8	-	Ohio	(21)	21	-
Kansas	(3)	3	-	Oregon	(3)	3	-
Kentucky	(11)	-	11	Pennsylvania	(26)	26	-
Maine	(7)	7	-	Rhode Island	(4)	4	-
Maryland	(7)	7	-	Vermont	(5)	5	-
Massachusetts	(12)	12	-	West Virginia	(5)	5	-
Michigan	(8)	8	-	Wisconsin	(8)	8	-
Minnesota	(4)	4	-	**Totals**	**(234)**	**212**	**21**

1864

PRESIDENTIAL ELECTION RETURNS

STATE	TOTAL VOTE	ABRAHAM LINCOLN (Republican)		GEORGE B. McCLELLAN (Democrat)		OTHER		PLURALITY	
		Votes	%	Votes	%	Votes	%		
California	105,890	62,053	58.6	43,837	41.4	—		18,216	R
Connecticut	86,958	44,673	51.4	42,285	48.6	—		2,388	R
Delaware	16,922	8,155	48.2	8,767	51.8	—		612	D
Illinois	348,236	189,512	54.4	158,724	45.6	—		30,788	R
Indiana	280,117	149,887	53.5	130,230	46.5	—		19,657	R
Iowa	132,947	83,858	63.1	49,089	36.9	—		34,769	R
Kansas	21,580	17,089	79.2	3,836	17.8	655	3.0	13,253	R
Kentucky	92,088	27,787	30.2	64,301	69.8	—		36,514	D
Maine	114,797	67,805	59.1	46,992	40.9	—		20,813	R
Maryland	72,892	40,153	55.1	32,739	44.9	—		7,414	R
Massachusetts	175,493	126,742	72.2	48,745	27.8	6		77,997	R
Michigan	165,279	91,133	55.1	74,146	44.9	—		16,987	R
Minnesota	42,433	25,031	59.0	17,376	40.9	26	0.1	7,655	R
Missouri	104,346	72,750	69.7	31,596	30.3	—		41,154	R
Nevada	16,420	9,826	59.8	6,594	40.2	—		3,232	R
New Hampshire	69,630	36,596	52.6	33,034	47.4	—		3,562	R
New Jersey	128,744	60,724	47.2	68,020	52.8	—		7,296	D
New York	730,721	368,735	50.5	361,986	49.5	—		6,749	R
Ohio	471,283	265,674	56.4	205,609	43.6	—		60,065	R
Oregon	18,350	9,888	53.9	8,457	46.1	5		1,431	R
Pennsylvania	573,735	296,292	51.6	277,443	48.4	—		18,849	R
Rhode Island	23,067	14,349	62.2	8,718	37.8	—		5,631	R
Vermont	55,740	42,419	76.1	13,321	23.9	—		29,098	R
West Virginia	34,877	23,799	68.2	11,078	31.8	—		12,721	R
Wisconsin	149,342	83,458	55.9	65,884	44.1	—		17,574	R
Totals	4,031,887	2,218,388	55.0	1,812,807	45.0	692		405,581	R

PRESIDENTIAL ELECTION OF
1868

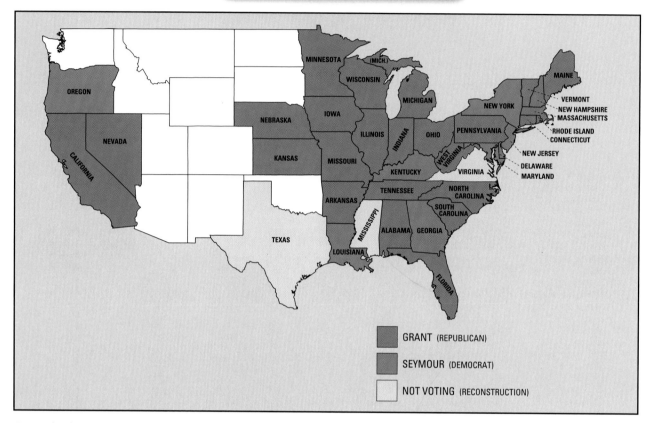

GRANT (REPUBLICAN)

SEYMOUR (DEMOCRAT)

NOT VOTING (RECONSTRUCTION)

States	Electoral Votes	Grant	Seymour	States	Electoral Votes	Grant	Seymour
Alabama	(8)	8	-	Missouri	(11)	11	-
Arkansas	(5)	5	-	Nebraska	(3)	3	-
California	(5)	5	-	Nevada	(3)	3	-
Connecticut	(6)	6	-	New Hampshire	(5)	5	-
Delaware	(3)	-	3	New Jersey	(7)	-	7
Florida	(3)	3	-	New York	(33)	-	33
Georgia	(9)	-	9	North Carolina	(9)	9	-
Illinois	(16)	16	-	Ohio	(21)	21	-
Indiana	(13)	13	-	Oregon	(3)	-	3
Iowa	(8)	8	-	Pennsylvania	(26)	26	-
Kansas	(3)	3	-	Rhode Island	(4)	4	-
Kentucky	(11)	-	11	South Carolina	(6)	6	-
Louisiana	(7)	-	7	Tennessee	(10)	10	-
Maine	(7)	7	-	Vermont	(5)	5	-
Maryland	(7)	-	7	West Virginia	(5)	5	-
Massachusetts	(12)	12	-	Wisconsin	(8)	8	-
Michigan	(8)	8	-				
Minnesota	(4)	4	-	**Totals**	**(294)**	**214**	**80**

1868

PRESIDENTIAL ELECTION RETURNS

STATE	TOTAL VOTE	ULYSSES S. GRANT (Republican)		HORATIO SEYMOUR (Democrat)		OTHER		PLURALITY	
		Votes	%	Votes	%	Votes	%		
Alabama	149,594	76,667	51.3	72,921	48.7	6		3,746	R
Arkansas	41,190	22,112	53.7	19,078	46.3	—		3,034	R
California	108,656	54,588	50.2	54,068	49.8	—		520	R
Connecticut	98,570	50,789	51.5	47,781	48.5	—		3,008	R
Delaware	18,571	7,614	41.0	10,957	59.0	—		3,343	D
Georgia	159,816	57,109	35.7	102,707	64.3	—		45,598	D
Illinois	449,420	250,304	55.7	199,116	44.3	—		51,188	R
Indiana	343,528	176,548	51.4	166,980	48.6	—		9,568	R
Iowa	194,439	120,399	61.9	74,040	38.1	—		46,359	R
Kansas	43,630	30,027	68.8	13,600	31.2	3		16,427	R
Kentucky	155,455	39,566	25.5	115,889	74.5	—		76,323	D
Louisiana	113,488	33,263	29.3	80,225	70.7	—		46,962	D
Maine	112,962	70,502	62.4	42,460	37.6	—		28,042	R
Maryland	92,795	30,438	32.8	62,357	67.2	—		31,919	D
Massachusetts	195,508	136,379	69.8	59,103	30.2	26		77,276	R
Michigan	225,632	128,563	57.0	97,069	43.0	—		31,494	R
Minnesota	71,620	43,545	60.8	28,075	39.2	—		15,470	R
Missouri	152,488	86,860	57.0	65,628	43.0	—		21,232	R
Nebraska	15,291	9,772	63.9	5,519	36.1	—		4,253	R
Nevada	11,689	6,474	55.4	5,215	44.6	—		1,259	R
New Hampshire	68,304	37,718	55.2	30,575	44.8	11		7,143	R
New Jersey	163,133	80,132	49.1	83,001	50.9	—		2,869	D
New York	849,771	419,888	49.4	429,883	50.6	—		9,995	D
North Carolina	181,498	96,939	53.4	84,559	46.6	—		12,380	R
Ohio	518,665	280,159	54.0	238,506	46.0	—		41,653	R
Oregon	22,086	10,961	49.6	11,125	50.4	—		164	D
Pennsylvania	655,662	342,280	52.2	313,382	47.8	—		28,898	R
Rhode Island	19,511	13,017	66.7	6,494	33.3	—		6,523	R
South Carolina	107,538	62,301	57.9	45,237	42.1	—		17,064	R
Tennessee	82,757	56,628	68.4	26,129	31.6	—		30,499	R
Vermont	56,224	44,173	78.6	12,051	21.4	—		32,122	R
West Virginia	49,321	29,015	58.8	20,306	41.2	—		8,709	R
Wisconsin	193,628	108,920	56.3	84,708	43.7	—		24,212	R
Totals	5,722,440	3,013,650	52.7	2,708,744	47.3	46		304,906	R

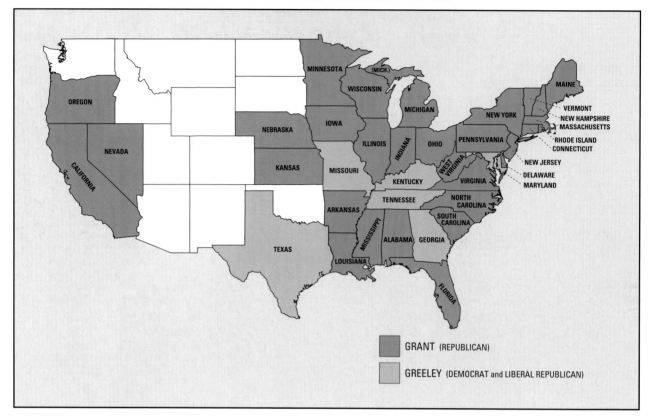

PRESIDENTIAL ELECTION OF
1872

States	Electoral Votes	Grant	Hendricks	Brown	Jenkins	Davis
Alabama	(10)	10	-	-	-	-
Arkansas	(6)	-	-	-	-	-
California	(6)	6	-	-	-	-
Connecticut	(6)	6	-	-	-	-
Delaware	(3)	3	-	-	-	-
Florida	(4)	4	-	-	-	-
Georgia	(11)	-	-	6	2	-
Illinois	(21)	21	-	-	-	-
Indiana	(15)	15	-	-	-	-
Iowa	(11)	11	-	-	-	-
Kansas	(5)	5	-	-	-	-
Kentucky	(12)	-	8	4	-	-
Louisiana	(8)	-	-	-	-	-
Maine	(7)	7	-	-	-	-
Maryland	(8)	-	8	-	-	-
Massachusetts	(13)	13	-	-	-	-
Michigan	(11)	11	-	-	-	-
Minnesota	(5)	5	-	-	-	-
Mississippi	(8)	8	-	-	-	-
Missouri	(15)	-	6	8	-	1
Nebraska	(3)	3	-	-	-	-
Nevada	(3)	3	-	-	-	-
New Hampshire	(5)	5	-	-	-	-
New Jersey	(9)	9	-	-	-	-
New York	(35)	35	-	-	-	-
North Carolina	(10)	10	-	-	-	-
Ohio	(22)	22	-	-	-	-
Oregon	(3)	3	-	-	-	-
Pennsylvania	(29)	29	-	-	-	-
Rhode Island	(4)	4	-	-	-	-
South Carolina	(7)	7	-	-	-	-
Tennessee	(12)	-	12	-	-	-
Texas	(8)	-	8	-	-	-
Vermont	(5)	5	-	-	-	-
Virginia	(11)	11	-	-	-	-
West Virginia	(5)	5	-	-	-	-
Wisconsin	(10)	10	-	-	-	-
Totals	**(366)**	**286**	**42**	**18**	**2**	**1**

1872

PRESIDENTIAL ELECTION RETURNS

STATE	TOTAL VOTE	ULYSSES S. GRANT (Republican)		HORACE GREELEY (Democrat, Liberal Republican)		CHARLES O'CONOR (Straight Out Democrat)		OTHER		PLURALITY	
		Votes	%	Votes	%	Votes	%	Votes	%		
Alabama	169,716	90,272	53.2	79,444	46.8	—		—		10,828	R
Arkansas	79,300	41,373	52.2	37,927	47.8	—		—		3,446	R
California	95,785	54,007	56.4	40,717	42.5	1,061	1.1	—		13,290	R
Connecticut	95,992	50,307	52.4	45,685	47.6	—		—		4,622	R
Delaware	21,822	11,129	51.0	10,205	46.8	488	2.2	—		924	R
Florida	33,190	17,763	53.5	15,427	46.5	—		—		2,336	R
Georgia	138,906	62,550	45.0	76,356	55.0	—		—		13,806	D
Illinois	429,971	241,936	56.3	184,884	43.0	3,151	0.7	—		57,052	R
Indiana	349,779	186,147	53.2	163,632	46.8	—		—		22,515	R
Iowa	216,365	131,566	60.8	71,189	32.9	2,221	1.0	11,389	5.3	60,377	R
Kansas	100,512	66,805	66.5	32,970	32.8	156	0.2	581	0.6	33,835	R
Kentucky	191,135	88,766	46.4	99,995	52.3	2,374	1.2	—		11,229	D
Louisiana	128,692	71,663	55.7	57,029	44.3	—		—		14,634	R
Maine	90,523	61,426	67.9	29,097	32.1	—		—		32,329	R
Maryland	134,447	66,760	49.7	67,687	50.3	—		—		927	D
Massachusetts	192,650	133,455	69.3	59,195	30.7	—		—		74,260	R
Michigan	221,569	138,768	62.6	78,651	35.5	2,879	1.3	1,271	0.6	60,117	R
Minnesota	91,339	56,040	61.4	35,131	38.5	—		168	0.2	20,909	R
Mississippi	129,457	82,175	63.5	47,282	36.5	—		—		34,893	R
Missouri	273,059	119,196	43.7	151,434	55.5	2,429	0.9	—		32,238	D
Nebraska	25,932	18,329	70.7	7,603	29.3	—		—		10,726	R
Nevada	14,649	8,413	57.4	6,236	42.6	—		—		2,177	R
New Hampshire	68,906	37,168	53.9	31,425	45.6	—		313	0.5	5,743	R
New Jersey	168,112	91,656	54.5	76,456	45.5	—		—		15,200	R
New York	828,020	440,738	53.2	387,282	46.8	—		—		53,456	R
North Carolina	165,163	94,772	57.4	70,130	42.5	261	0.2	—		24,642	R
Ohio	529,435	281,852	53.2	244,320	46.1	1,163	0.2	2,100	0.4	37,532	R
Oregon	20,107	11,818	58.8	7,742	38.5	547	2.7	—		4,076	R
Pennsylvania	561,629	349,589	62.2	212,040	37.8	—		—		137,549	R
Rhode Island	18,994	13,665	71.9	5,329	28.1	—		—		8,336	R
South Carolina	95,452	72,290	75.7	22,699	23.8	204	0.2	259	0.3	49,591	R
Tennessee	179,046	85,655	47.8	93,391	52.2	—		—		7,736	D
Texas	115,700	47,910	41.4	67,675	58.5	115	0.1	—		19,765	D
Vermont	52,408	41,481	79.2	10,927	20.8	—		—		30,554	R
Virginia	185,195	93,463	50.5	91,647	49.5	85		—		1,816	R
West Virginia	62,467	32,320	51.7	29,532	47.3	615	1.0	—		2,788	R
Wisconsin	192,255	105,012	54.6	86,390	44.9	853	0.4	—		18,622	R
Totals	6,467,679	3,598,235	55.6	2,834,761	43.8	18,602	0.3	16,081	0.3	763,474	R

PRESIDENTIAL ELECTION OF
1876

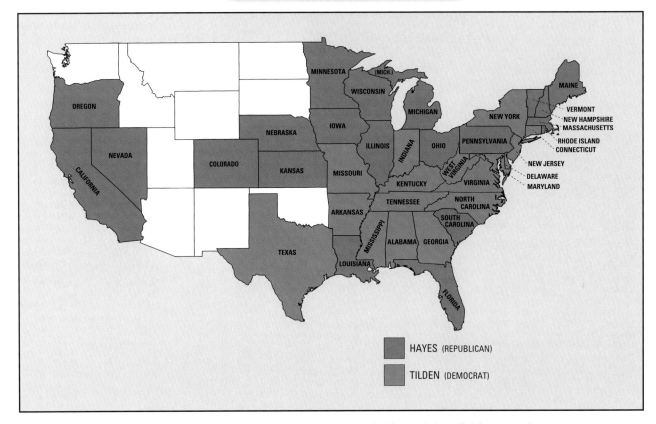

HAYES (REPUBLICAN)

TILDEN (DEMOCRAT)

Congressional Quarterly's Guide to U.S. Elections, 3rd. edition, copyright ©1994. Used with permission. All rights reserved.

States	Electoral Votes	Hayes	Tilden	States	Electoral Votes	Hayes	Tilden
Alabama	(10)	-	10	Missouri	(15)	-	15
Arkansas	(6)	-	6	Nebraska	(3)	3	-
California	(6)	6	-	Nevada	(3)	3	-
Colorado	(3)	3	-	New Hampshire	(5)	5	-
Connecticut	(6)	-	6	New Jersey	(9)	-	9
Delaware	(3)	-	3	New York	(35)	-	35
Florida	(4)	4	-	North Carolina	(10)	-	10
Georgia	(11)	-	11	Ohio	(22)	22	-
Illinois	(21)	21	-	Oregon	(3)	3	-
Indiana	(15)	-	15	Pennsylvania	(29)	29	-
Iowa	(11)	11	-	Rhode Island	(4)	4	-
Kansas	(5)	5	-	South Carolina	(7)	7	-
Kentucky	(12)	-	12	Tennessee	(12)	-	12
Louisiana	(8)	8	-	Texas	(8)	-	8
Maine	(7)	7	-	Vermont	(5)	5	-
Maryland	(8)	-	8	Virginia	(11)	-	11
Massachusetts	(13)	13	-	West Virginia	(5)	-	5
Michigan	(11)	11	-	Wisconsin	(10)	10	-
Minnesota	(5)	5	-				
Mississippi	(8)	-	8	**Totals**	**(369)**	**185**	**184**

1876

PRESIDENTIAL ELECTION RETURNS

STATE	TOTAL VOTE	RUTHERFORD B. HAYES (Republican)		SAMUEL J. TILDEN (Democrat)		PETER COOPER (Greenback)		OTHER		PLURALITY	
		Votes	%	Votes	%	Votes	%	Votes	%		
Alabama	171,699	68,708	40.0	102,989	60.0	—		2		34,281	D
Arkansas	96,946	38,649	39.9	58,086	59.9	211	0.2	—		19,437	D
California	155,784	79,258	50.9	76,460	49.1	47		19		2,798	R
Connecticut	122,134	59,033	48.3	61,927	50.7	774	0.6	400	0.3	2,894	D
Delaware	24,133	10,752	44.6	13,381	55.4	—		—		2,629	D
Florida	46,776	23,849	51.0	22,927	49.0	—		—		922	R
Georgia	180,690	50,533	28.0	130,157	72.0	—		—		79,624	D
Illinois	554,368	278,232	50.2	258,611	46.6	17,207	3.1	318	0.1	19,621	R
Indiana	431,073	208,011	48.3	213,529	49.5	9,533	2.2	—		5,518	D
Iowa	293,398	171,326	58.4	112,121	38.2	9,431	3.2	520	0.2	59,205	R
Kansas	124,134	78,324	63.1	37,902	30.5	7,770	6.3	138	0.1	40,422	R
Kentucky	260,626	97,568	37.4	160,060	61.4	—		2,998	1.2	62,492	D
Louisiana	145,823	75,315	51.6	70,508	48.4	—		—		4,807	R
Maine	117,045	66,300	56.6	49,917	42.6	—		828	0.7	16,383	R
Maryland	163,759	71,980	44.0	91,779	56.0	—		—		19,799	D
Massachusetts	259,619	150,063	57.8	108,777	41.9	—		779	0.3	41,286	R
Michigan	318,426	166,901	52.4	141,665	44.5	9,023	2.8	837	0.3	25,236	R
Minnesota	124,160	72,962	58.8	48,799	39.3	2,399	1.9	—		24,163	R
Mississippi	164,776	52,603	31.9	112,173	68.1	—		—		59,570	D
Missouri	350,610	145,027	41.4	202,086	57.6	3,497	1.0	—		57,059	D
Nebraska	49,258	31,915	64.8	17,343	35.2	—		—		14,572	R
Nevada	19,691	10,383	52.7	9,308	47.3	—		—		1,075	R
New Hampshire	80,143	41,540	51.8	38,510	48.1	—		93	0.1	3,030	R
New Jersey	220,193	103,517	47.0	115,962	52.7	714	0.3	—		12,445	D
New York	1,015,503	489,207	48.2	521,949	51.4	1,978	0.2	2,369	0.2	32,742	D
North Carolina	233,911	108,484	46.4	125,427	53.6	—		—		16,943	D
Ohio	658,650	330,698	50.2	323,182	49.1	3,058	0.5	1,712	0.3	7,516	R
Oregon	29,873	15,207	50.9	14,157	47.4	509	1.7	—		1,050	R
Pennsylvania	758,973	384,157	50.6	366,204	48.2	7,209	0.9	1,403	0.2	17,953	R
Rhode Island	26,499	15,787	59.6	10,712	40.4	—		—		5,075	R
South Carolina	182,683	91,786	50.2	90,897	49.8	—		—		889	R
Tennessee	222,743	89,566	40.2	133,177	59.8	—		—		43,611	D
Texas	151,431	45,013	29.7	106,372	70.2	—		46		61,359	D
Vermont	64,460	44,092	68.4	20,254	31.4	—		114	0.2	23,838	R
Virginia	236,288	95,518	40.4	140,770	59.6	—		—		45,252	D
West Virginia	99,647	41,997	42.1	56,546	56.7	1,104	1.1	—		14,549	D
Wisconsin	257,176	130,050	50.6	123,922	48.2	1,509	0.6	1,695	0.7	6,128	R
Totals	8,413,101	4,034,311	48.0	4,288,546	51.0	75,973	0.9	14,271	0.2	254,235	D

PRESIDENTIAL ELECTION OF

1880

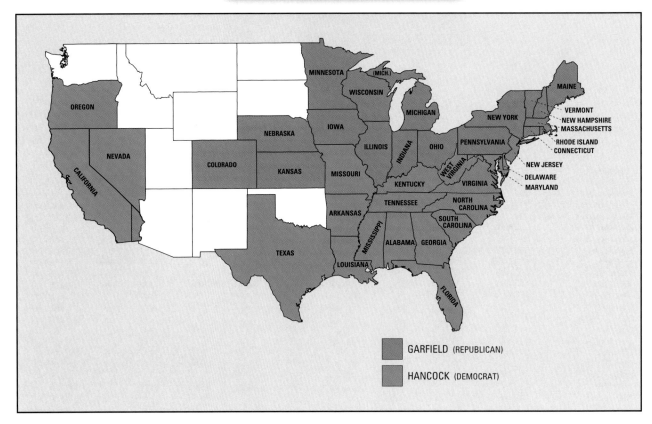

GARFIELD (REPUBLICAN)

HANCOCK (DEMOCRAT)

States	Electoral Votes	Garfield	Hancock	States	Electoral Votes	Garfield	Hancock
Alabama	(10)	-	10	Mississippi	(8)	-	8
Arkansas	(6)	-	6	Missouri	(15)	-	15
California	(6)	1	5	Nebraska	(3)	3	-
Colorado	(3)	3	-	Nevada	(3)	-	3
Connecticut	(6)	6	-	New Hampshire	(5)	5	-
Delaware	(3)	-	3	New Jersey	(9)	-	9
Florida	(4)	-	4	New York	(35)	35	-
Georgia	(11)	-	11	North Carolina	(10)	-	10
Illinois	(21)	21	-	Ohio	(22)	22	-
Indiana	(15)	15	-	Oregon	(3)	3	-
Iowa	(11)	11	-	Pennsylvania	(29)	29	-
Kansas	(5)	5	-	Rhode Island	(4)	4	-
Kentucky	(12)	-	12	South Carolina	(7)	-	7
Louisiana	(8)	-	8	Tennessee	(12)	-	12
Maine	(7)	7	-	Texas	(8)	-	8
Maryland	(8)	-	8	Vermont	(5)	5	-
Massachusetts	(13)	13	-	Virginia	(11)	-	11
Michigan	(11)	11	-	West Virginia	(5)	-	5
Minnesota	(5)	5	-	Wisconsin	(10)	10	-
				Totals	**(369)**	**214**	**155**

1880

Presidential Election Returns

STATE	TOTAL VOTE	JAMES A. GARFIELD (Republican)		WINFIELD S. HANCOCK (Democrat)		JAMES B. WEAVER (Greenback)		OTHER		PLURALITY	
		Votes	%	Votes	%	Votes	%	Votes	%		
Alabama	151,902	56,350	37.1	91,130	60.0	4,422	2.9	—		34,780	D
Arkansas	107,772	41,661	38.7	60,489	56.1	4,079	3.8	1,543	1.4	18,828	D
California	164,218	80,282	48.9	80,426	49.0	3,381	2.1	129	0.1	144	D
Colorado	53,546	27,450	51.3	24,647	46.0	1,435	2.7	14		2,803	R
Connecticut	132,798	67,071	50.5	64,411	48.5	868	0.7	448	0.3	2,660	R
Delaware	29,458	14,148	48.0	15,181	51.5	129	0.4	—		1,033	D
Florida	51,618	23,654	45.8	27,964	54.2	—		—		4,310	D
Georgia	157,451	54,470	34.6	102,981	65.4	—		—		48,511	D
Illinois	622,305	318,036	51.1	277,321	44.6	26,358	4.2	590	0.1	40,715	R
Indiana	470,758	232,169	49.3	225,523	47.9	13,066	2.8	—		6,646	R
Iowa	323,140	183,904	56.9	105,845	32.8	32,327	10.0	1,064	0.3	78,059	R
Kansas	201,054	121,520	60.4	59,789	29.7	19,710	9.8	35		61,731	R
Kentucky	267,104	106,490	39.9	148,875	55.7	11,506	4.3	233	0.1	42,385	D
Louisiana	104,462	38,978	37.3	65,047	62.3	437	0.4	—		26,069	D
Maine	143,903	74,052	51.5	65,211	45.3	4,409	3.1	231	0.2	8,841	R
Maryland	172,221	78,515	45.6	93,706	54.4	—		—		15,191	D
Massachusetts	282,505	165,198	58.5	111,960	39.6	4,548	1.6	799	0.3	53,238	R
Michigan	353,076	185,335	52.5	131,596	37.3	34,895	9.9	1,250	0.4	53,739	R
Minnesota	150,806	93,939	62.3	53,314	35.4	3,267	2.2	286	0.2	40,625	R
Mississippi	117,068	34,844	29.8	75,750	64.7	5,797	5.0	677	0.6	40,906	D
Missouri	397,289	153,647	38.7	208,600	52.5	35,042	8.8	—		54,953	D
Nebraska	87,355	54,979	62.9	28,523	32.7	3,853	4.4	—		26,456	R
Nevada	18,343	8,732	47.6	9,611	52.4	—		—		879	D
New Hampshire	86,361	44,856	51.9	40,797	47.2	528	0.6	180	0.2	4,059	R
New Jersey	245,928	120,555	49.0	122,565	49.8	2,617	1.1	191	0.1	2,010	D
New York	1,103,945	555,544	50.3	534,511	48.4	12,373	1.1	1,517	0.1	21,033	R
North Carolina	240,946	115,616	48.0	124,204	51.5	1,126	0.5	—		8,588	D
Ohio	724,984	375,048	51.7	340,867	47.0	6,456	0.9	2,613	0.4	34,181	R
Oregon	40,841	20,619	50.5	19,955	48.9	267	0.7	—		664	R
Pennsylvania	874,783	444,704	50.8	407,428	46.6	20,667	2.4	1,984	0.2	37,276	R
Rhode Island	29,235	18,195	62.2	10,779	36.9	236	0.8	25	0.1	7,416	R
South Carolina	169,793	57,954	34.1	111,236	65.5	567	0.3	36		53,282	D
Tennessee	243,263	107,677	44.3	129,569	53.3	6,017	2.5	—		21,892	D
Texas	233,632	50,217	21.5	156,010	66.8	27,405	11.7	—		105,793	D
Vermont	65,098	45,567	70.0	18,316	28.1	1,215	1.9	—		27,251	R
Virginia	211,616	83,533	39.5	128,083	60.5	—		—		44,550	D
West Virginia	112,641	46,243	41.1	57,390	50.9	9,008	8.0	—		11,147	D
Wisconsin	267,202	144,406	54.0	114,650	42.9	7,986	3.0	160	0.1	29,756	R
Totals	9,210,420	4,446,158	48.3	4,444,260	48.3	305,997	3.3	14,005	0.2	1,898	R

PRESIDENTIAL ELECTION OF

1884

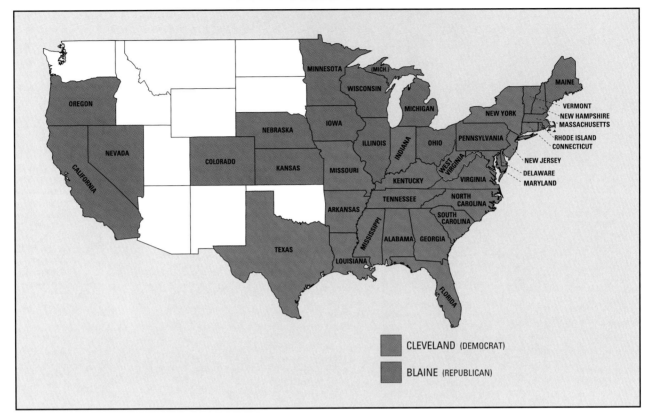

CLEVELAND (DEMOCRAT)

BLAINE (REPUBLICAN)

Congressional Quarterly's Guide to U.S. Elections, 3rd. edition, copyright ©1994. Used with permission. All rights reserved.

States	Electoral Votes	Cleveland	Blaine	States	Electoral Votes	Cleveland	Blaine
Alabama	(10)	10	-	Mississippi	(9)	9	-
Arkansas	(7)	7	-	Missouri	(16)	16	-
California	(8)	-	8	Nebraska	(5)	-	5
Colorado	(3)	-	3	Nevada	(3)	-	3
Connecticut	(6)	6	-	New Hampshire	(4)	-	4
Delaware	(3)	3	-	New Jersey	(9)	9	-
Florida	(4)	4	-	New York	(36)	36	-
Georgia	(12)	12	-	North Carolina	(11)	11	-
Illinois	(22)	-	22	Ohio	(23)	-	23
Indiana	(15)	15	-	Oregon	(3)	-	3
Iowa	(13)	-	13	Pennsylvania	(30)	-	30
Kansas	(9)	-	9	Rhode Island	(4)	-	4
Kentucky	(13)	13	-	South Carolina	(9)	9	-
Louisiana	(8)	8	-	Tennessee	(12)	12	-
Maine	(6)	-	6	Texas	(13)	13	-
Maryland	(8)	8	-	Vermont	(4)	-	4
Massachusetts	(14)	-	14	Virginia	(12)	12	-
Michigan	(13)	-	13	West Virginia	(6)	6	-
Minnesota	(7)	-	7	Wisconsin	(11)	-	11
				Totals	**(401)**	**219**	**182**

1884

PRESIDENTIAL ELECTION RETURNS

STATE	TOTAL VOTE	GROVER CLEVELAND (Democrat)		JAMES G. BLAINE (Republican)		BENJAMIN F. BUTLER (Greenback)		JOHN P. ST. JOHN (Prohibition)		OTHER		PLURALITY	
		Votes	%	Votes	%	Votes	%	Votes	%	Votes	%		
Alabama	153,624	92,736	60.4	59,444	38.7	762	0.5	610	0.4	72		33,292	D
Arkansas	125,779	72,734	57.8	51,198	40.7	1,847	1.5	—		—		21,536	D
California	196,988	89,288	45.3	102,369	52.0	2,037	1.0	2,965	1.5	329	0.2	13,081	R
Colorado	66,519	27,723	41.7	36,084	54.2	1,956	2.9	756	1.1	—		8,361	R
Connecticut	137,221	67,167	48.9	65,879	48.0	1,682	1.2	2,493	1.8	—		1,288	D
Delaware	29,984	16,957	56.6	12,953	43.2	10		64	0.2	—		4,004	D
Florida	59,990	31,769	53.0	28,031	46.7	—		72	0.1	118	0.2	3,738	D
Georgia	143,610	94,667	65.9	48,603	33.8	145	0.1	195	0.1	—		46,064	D
Illinois	672,670	312,351	46.4	337,469	50.2	10,776	1.6	12,074	1.8	—		25,118	R
Indiana	491,649	244,989	49.8	238,466	48.5	8,194	1.7	—		—		6,523	D
Iowa	393,542	177,316	45.1	197,089	50.1	16,341	4.2	1,499	0.4	1,297	0.3	19,773	R
Kansas	250,991	90,111	35.9	154,410	61.5	1,691	0.7	4,311	1.7	468	0.2	64,299	R
Kentucky	274,910	152,961	55.6	118,690	43.2	120		3,139	1.1	—		34,271	D
Louisiana	113,234	62,594	55.3	46,347	40.9	3,955	3.5	338	0.3	—		16,247	D
Maine	127,114	52,153	41.0	72,217	56.8	578	0.5	2,160	1.7	6		20,064	R
Maryland	209,823	96,866	46.2	85,748	40.9	24,382	11.6	2,827	1.3	—		11,118	D
Massachusetts	321,253	122,352	38.1	146,724	45.7	42,252	13.2	9,923	3.1	2		24,372	R
Michigan	364,490	149,835	41.1	192,669	52.9	3,583	1.0	18,403	5.0	—		42,834	R
Minnesota	186,434	70,065	37.6	111,685	59.9	—		4,684	2.5	—		41,620	R
Mississippi	120,688	77,653	64.3	43,035	35.7	—		—		—		34,618	D
Missouri	441,268	236,023	53.5	203,081	46.0	—		2,164	0.5	—		32,942	D
Nebraska	134,202	54,391	40.5	76,912	57.3	—		2,899	2.2	—		22,521	R
Nevada	12,779	5,577	43.6	7,176	56.2	26	0.2	—		—		1,599	R
New Hampshire	84,586	39,198	46.3	43,254	51.1	554	0.7	1,580	1.9	—		4,056	R
New Jersey	260,853	127,747	49.0	123,436	47.3	3,486	1.3	6,156	2.4	28		4,311	D
New York	1,167,003	563,048	48.2	562,001	48.2	16,955	1.5	24,999	2.1	—		1,047	D
North Carolina	268,356	142,905	53.3	125,021	46.6	—		430	0.2	—		17,884	D
Ohio	784,620	368,280	46.9	400,092	51.0	5,179	0.7	11,069	1.4	—		31,812	R
Oregon	52,683	24,598	46.7	26,845	51.0	726	1.4	479	0.9	35	0.1	2,247	R
Pennsylvania	899,710	394,772	43.9	472,792	52.5	16,992	1.9	15,154	1.7	—		78,020	R
Rhode Island	32,771	12,391	37.8	19,030	58.1	422	1.3	928	2.8	—		6,639	R
South Carolina	92,812	69,845	75.3	21,730	23.4	—		—		1,237	1.3	48,115	D
Tennessee	259,978	133,770	51.5	124,101	47.7	957	0.4	1,150	0.4	—		9,669	D
Texas	321,242	223,209	69.5	91,234	28.4	3,310	1.0	3,489	1.1	—		131,975	D
Vermont	59,409	17,331	29.2	39,514	66.5	785	1.3	1,752	2.9	27		22,183	R
Virginia	284,977	145,491	51.1	139,356	48.9	—		130		—		6,135	D
West Virginia	132,145	67,311	50.9	63,096	47.7	799	0.6	939	0.7	—		4,215	D
Wisconsin	319,847	146,447	45.8	161,155	50.4	4,594	1.4	7,651	2.4	—		14,708	R
Totals	10,049,754	4,874,621	48.5	4,848,936	48.2	175,096	1.7	147,482	1.5	3,619		25,685	D

1888

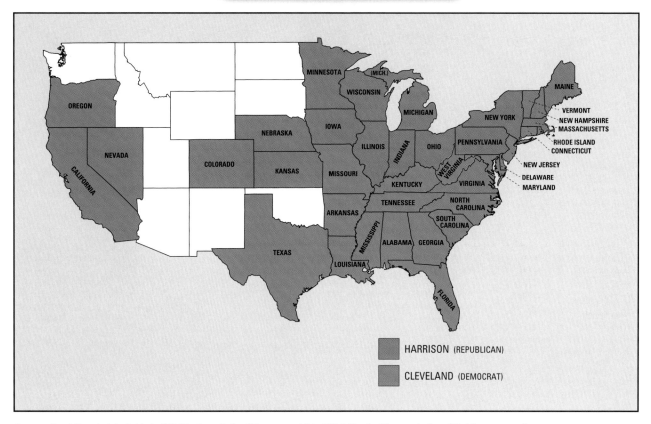

HARRISON (REPUBLICAN)

CLEVELAND (DEMOCRAT)

States	Electoral Votes	Harrison	Cleveland	States	Electoral Votes	Harrison	Cleveland
Alabama	(10)	-	10	Mississippi	(9)	-	9
Arkansas	(7)	-	7	Missouri	(16)	-	16
California	(8)	8	-	Nebraska	(5)	5	-
Colorado	(3)	3	-	Nevada	(3)	3	-
Connecticut	(6)	-	6	New Hampshire	(4)	4	-
Delaware	(3)	-	3	New Jersey	(9)	-	9
Florida	(4)	-	4	New York	(36)	36	-
Georgia	(12)	-	12	North Carolina	(11)	-	11
Illinois	(22)	22	-	Ohio	(23)	23	-
Indiana	(15)	15	-	Oregon	(3)	3	-
Iowa	(13)	13	-	Pennsylvania	(30)	30	-
Kansas	(9)	9	-	Rhode Island	(4)	4	-
Kentucky	(13)	-	13	South Carolina	(9)	-	9
Louisiana	(8)	-	8	Tennessee	(12)	-	12
Maine	(6)	6	-	Texas	(13)	-	13
Maryland	(8)	-	8	Vermont	(4)	4	-
Massachusetts	(14)	14	-	Virginia	(12)	-	12
Michigan	(13)	13	-	West Virginia	(6)	-	6
Minnesota	(7)	7	-	Wisconsin	(11)	11	-
				Totals	**(401)**	**233**	**168**

1888

PRESIDENTIAL ELECTION RETURNS

STATE	TOTAL VOTE	BENJAMIN HARRISON (Republican)		GROVER CLEVELAND (Democrat)		CLINTON B. FISK (Prohibition)		ALSON J. STREETER (Union Labor)		OTHER		PLURALITY	
		Votes	%	Votes	%	Votes	%	Votes	%	Votes	%		
Alabama	175,085	57,177	32.7	117,314	67.0	594	0.3	—		—		60,137	D
Arkansas	157,058	59,752	38.0	86,062	54.8	614	0.4	10,630	6.8	—		26,310	D
California	251,339	124,816	49.7	117,729	46.8	5,761	2.3	—		3,033	1.2	7,087	R
Colorado	91,946	50,772	55.2	37,549	40.8	2,182	2.4	1,266	1.4	177	0.2	13,223	R
Connecticut	153,978	74,584	48.4	74,920	48.7	4,234	2.7	240	0.2	—		336	D
Delaware	29,764	12,950	43.5	16,414	55.1	399	1.3	—		1		3,464	D
Florida	66,500	26,529	39.9	39,557	59.5	414	0.6	—		—		13,028	D
Georgia	142,936	40,499	28.3	100,493	70.3	1,808	1.3	136	0.1	—		59,994	D
Illinois	747,813	370,475	49.5	348,351	46.6	21,703	2.9	7,134	1.0	150		22,124	R
Indiana	536,988	263,366	49.0	260,990	48.6	9,939	1.9	2,693	0.5	—		2,376	R
Iowa	404,694	211,607	52.3	179,876	44.4	3,550	0.9	9,105	2.2	556	0.1	31,731	R
Kansas	331,133	182,845	55.2	102,739	31.0	6,774	2.0	37,838	11.4	937	0.3	80,106	R
Kentucky	344,868	155,138	45.0	183,830	53.3	5,223	1.5	677	0.2	—		28,692	D
Louisiana	115,891	30,660	26.5	85,032	73.4	160	0.1	39		—		54,372	D
Maine	128,253	73,730	57.5	50,472	39.4	2,691	2.1	1,344	1.0	16		23,258	R
Maryland	210,941	99,986	47.4	106,188	50.3	4,767	2.3	—		—		6,202	D
Massachusetts	344,243	183,892	53.4	151,590	44.0	8,701	2.5	—		60		32,302	R
Michigan	475,356	236,387	49.7	213,469	44.9	20,945	4.4	4,555	1.0	—		22,918	R
Minnesota	263,162	142,492	54.1	104,372	39.7	15,201	5.8	1,097	0.4	—		38,120	R
Mississippi	115,786	30,095	26.0	85,451	73.8	240	0.2	—		—		55,356	D
Missouri	521,359	236,252	45.3	261,943	50.2	4,539	0.9	18,625	3.6	—		25,691	D
Nebraska	202,630	108,417	53.5	80,552	39.8	9,435	4.7	4,226	2.1	—		27,865	R
Nevada	12,573	7,229	57.5	5,303	42.2	41	0.3	—		—		1,926	R
New Hampshire	90,770	45,734	50.4	43,382	47.8	1,596	1.8	—		58	0.1	2,352	R
New Jersey	303,634	144,347	47.5	151,493	49.9	7,794	2.6	—		—		7,146	D
New York	1,319,748	650,338	49.3	635,965	48.2	30,231	2.3	627		2,587	0.2	14,373	R
North Carolina	285,563	134,784	47.2	147,902	51.8	2,840	1.0	—		37		13,118	D
Ohio	839,357	416,054	49.6	395,456	47.1	24,356	2.9	3,491	0.4	—		20,598	R
Oregon	61,889	33,291	53.8	26,518	42.8	1,676	2.7	—		404	0.7	6,773	R
Pennsylvania	997,568	526,091	52.7	446,633	44.8	20,947	2.1	3,873	0.4	24		79,458	R
Rhode Island	40,775	21,969	53.9	17,530	43.0	1,251	3.1	18		7		4,439	R
South Carolina	79,997	13,736	17.2	65,824	82.3	—		—		437	0.5	52,088	D
Tennessee	303,694	138,978	45.8	158,699	52.3	5,969	2.0	48		—		19,721	D
Texas	354,412	88,604	25.0	232,189	65.5	4,739	1.3	28,880	8.1	—		143,585	D
Vermont	63,476	45,193	71.2	16,788	26.4	1,460	2.3	—		35	0.1	28,405	R
Virginia	304,087	150,399	49.5	152,004	50.0	1,684	0.6	—		—		1,605	D
West Virginia	159,440	78,171	49.0	78,677	49.3	1,084	0.7	1,508	0.9	—		506	D
Wisconsin	354,614	176,553	49.8	155,232	43.8	14,277	4.0	8,552	2.4	—		21,321	R
Totals	11,383,320	5,443,892	47.8	5,534,488	48.6	249,819	2.2	146,602	1.3	8,519	0.1	90,596	D

PRESIDENTIAL ELECTION OF
1892

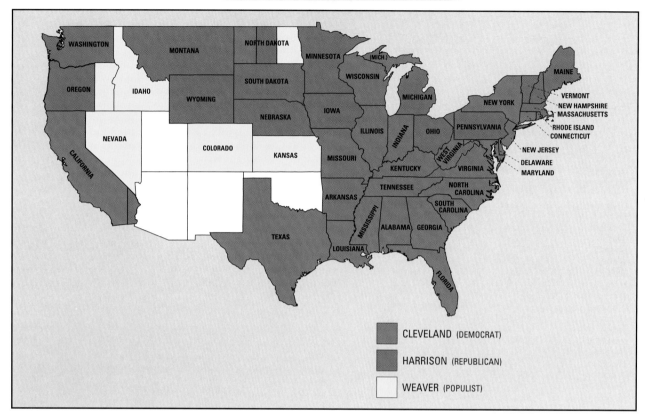

CLEVELAND (DEMOCRAT)

HARRISON (REPUBLICAN)

WEAVER (POPULIST)

Congressional Quarterly's Guide to U.S. Elections, 3rd. edition, copyright ©1994. Used with permission. All rights reserved.

States	Electoral Votes	Cleveland	Harrison	Weaver	States	Electoral Votes	Cleveland	Harrison	Weaver
Alabama	(11)	11	-	-	Montana	(3)	-	3	-
Arkansas	(8)	8	-	-	Nebraska	(8)	-	8	-
California	(9)	8	1	-	Nevada	(3)	-	-	3
Colorado	(4)	-	-	4	New Hampshire	(4)	-	4	-
Connecticut	(6)	6	-	-	New Jersey	(10)	10	-	-
Delaware	(3)	3	-	-	New York	(36)	36	-	-
Florida	(4)	4	-	-	North Carolina	(11)	11	-	-
Georgia	(13)	13	-	-	North Dakota	(3)	1	1	1
Idaho	(3)	-	-	3	Ohio	(23)	1	22	-
Illinois	(24)	24	-	-	Oregon	(4)	-	3	1
Indiana	(15)	15	-	-	Pennsylvania	(32)	-	32	-
Iowa	(13)	-	13	-	Rhode Island	(4)	-	4	-
Kansas	(10)	-	-	10	South Carolina	(9)	9	-	-
Kentucky	(13)	13	-	-	South Dakota	(4)	-	4	-
Louisiana	(8)	8	-	-	Tennessee	(12)	12	-	-
Maine	(6)	-	6	-	Texas	(15)	15	-	-
Maryland	(8)	8	-	-	Vermont	(4)	-	4	-
Massachusetts	(15)	-	15	-	Virginia	(12)	12	-	-
Michigan	(14)	5	9	-	Washington	(4)	-	4	-
Minnesota	(9)	-	9	-	West Virginia	(6)	6	-	-
Mississippi	(9)	9	-	-	Wisconsin	(12)	12	-	-
Missouri	(17)	17	-	-	Wyoming	(3)	-	3	-
					Totals	**(444)**	**277**	**145**	**22**

1892

PRESIDENTIAL ELECTION RETURNS

STATE	TOTAL VOTE	GROVER CLEVELAND (Democrat)		BENJAMIN HARRISON (Republican)		JAMES B. WEAVER (Populist)		JOHN BIDWELL (Prohibition)		OTHER		PLURALITY	
		Votes	%	Votes	%	Votes	%	Votes	%	Votes	%		
Alabama	232,543	138,135	59.4	9,184	3.9	84,984	36.5	240	0.1	—		53,151	D
Arkansas	148,117	87,834	59.3	47,072	31.8	11,831	8.0	113	0.1	1,267	0.9	40,762	D
California	269,585	118,151	43.8	118,027	43.8	25,311	9.4	8,096	3.0	—		124	D
Colorado	93,881	—		38,620	41.1	53,584	57.1	1,677	1.8	—		14,964	POP
Connecticut	164,593	82,395	50.1	77,030	46.8	809	0.5	4,026	2.4	333	0.2	5,365	D
Delaware	37,235	18,581	49.9	18,077	48.5			564	1.5	13		504	D
Florida	35,471	30,153	85.0	—		4,843	13.7	475	1.3	—		25,310	D
Georgia	223,126	129,446	58.0	48,408	21.7	41,939	18.8	988	0.4	2,345	1.1	81,038	D
Idaho	19,407	—		8,599	44.3	10,520	54.2	288	1.5	—		1,921	POP
Illinois	873,667	426,281	48.8	399,308	45.7	22,207	2.5	25,871	3.0	—		26,973	D
Indiana	553,613	262,740	47.5	255,615	46.2	22,208	4.0	13,050	2.4	—		7,125	D
Iowa	443,159	196,367	44.3	219,795	49.6	20,595	4.6	6,402	1.4	—		23,428	R
Kansas	323,591	—		156,134	48.3	162,888	50.3	4,569	1.4	—		6,754	POP
Kentucky	340,864	175,461	51.5	135,462	39.7	23,500	6.9	6,441	1.9	—		39,999	D
Louisiana	114,889	87,926	76.5	26,963	23.5	—		—		—		60,963	D
Maine	116,451	48,049	41.3	62,936	54.0	2,396	2.1	3,066	2.6	4		14,887	R
Maryland	213,275	113,866	53.4	92,736	43.5	796	0.4	5,877	2.8	—		21,130	D
Massachusetts	391,028	176,813	45.2	202,814	51.9	3,210	0.8	7,539	1.9	652	0.2	26,001	R
Michigan	466,917	202,396	43.3	222,708	47.7	20,031	4.3	20,857	4.5	925	0.2	20,312	R
Minnesota	267,841	100,589	37.6	122,736	45.8	30,399	11.3	14,117	5.3	—		22,147	R
Mississippi	52,519	40,030	76.2	1,398	2.7	10,118	19.3	973	1.9	—		29,912	D
Missouri	541,583	268,400	49.6	227,646	42.0	41,204	7.6	4,333	0.8	—		40,754	D
Montana	44,461	17,690	39.8	18,871	42.4	7,338	16.5	562	1.3	—		1,181	R
Nebraska	200,205	24,956	12.5	87,213	43.6	83,134	41.5	4,902	2.4	—		4,079	R
Nevada	10,826	703	6.5	2,811	26.0	7,226	66.7	86	0.8	—		4,415	POP
New Hampshire	89,328	42,081	47.1	45,658	51.1	292	0.3	1,297	1.5	—		3,577	R
New Jersey	337,485	170,987	50.7	156,059	46.2	969	0.3	8,133	2.4	1,337	0.4	14,928	D
New York	1,336,793	654,868	49.0	609,350	45.6	16,429	1.2	38,190	2.9	17,956	1.3	45,518	D
North Carolina	280,270	132,951	47.4	100,346	35.8	44,336	15.8	2,637	0.9	—		32,605	D
North Dakota	36,118	—		17,519	48.5	17,700	49.0	899	2.5	—		181	POP
Ohio	850,164	404,115	47.5	405,187	47.7	14,850	1.7	26,012	3.1	—		1,072	R
Oregon	78,378	14,243	18.2	35,002	44.7	26,875	34.3	2,258	2.9	—		8,127	R
Pennsylvania	1,003,000	452,264	45.1	516,011	51.4	8,714	0.9	25,123	2.5	888	0.1	63,747	R
Rhode Island	53,196	24,336	45.7	26,975	50.7	228	0.4	1,654	3.1	3		2,639	R
South Carolina	70,504	54,680	77.6	13,345	18.9	2,407	3.4	—		72	0.1	41,335	D
South Dakota	70,160	8,894	12.7	34,714	49.5	26,552	37.8	—		—		8,162	R
Tennessee	265,732	136,468	51.4	100,537	37.8	23,918	9.0	4,809	1.8	—		35,931	D
Texas	410,860	236,979	57.7	70,982	17.3	96,649	23.5	2,164	0.5	4,086	1.0	140,330	D
Vermont	55,793	16,325	29.3	37,992	68.1	42	0.1	1,424	2.6	10		21,667	R
Virginia	292,238	164,136	56.2	113,098	38.7	12,275	4.2	2,729	0.9	—		51,038	D
Washington	87,968	29,802	33.9	36,459	41.4	19,165	21.8	2,542	2.9	—		6,657	R
West Virginia	171,079	84,467	49.4	80,292	46.9	4,167	2.4	2,153	1.3	—		4,175	D
Wisconsin	371,481	177,325	47.7	171,101	46.1	9,919	2.7	13,136	3.5	—		6,224	D
Wyoming	16,703	—		8,454	50.6	7,722	46.2	498	3.0	29	0.2	732	R
Totals	12,056,097	5,551,883	46.1	5,179,244	43.0	1,024,280	8.5	270,770	2.2	29,920	0.2	372,639	D

PRESIDENTIAL ELECTION OF
1896

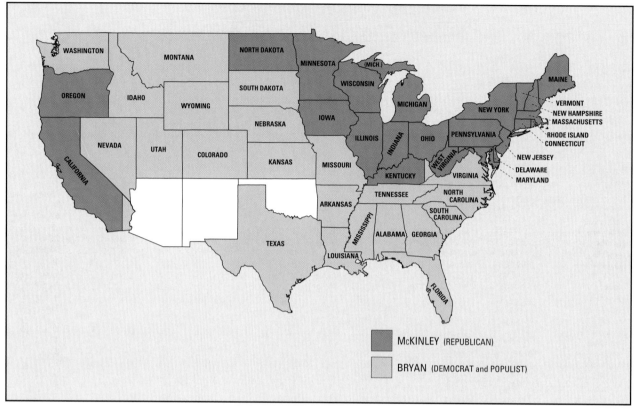

McKINLEY (REPUBLICAN)

BRYAN (DEMOCRAT and POPULIST)

States	Electoral Votes	McKinley	Bryan	States	Electoral Votes	McKinley	Bryan
Alabama	(11)	-	11	Nebraska	(8)	-	8
Arkansas	(8)	-	8	Nevada	(3)	-	3
California	(9)	8	1	New Hampshire	(4)	4	-
Colorado	(4)	-	4	New Jersey	(10)	10	-
Connecticut	(6)	6	-	New York	(36)	36	-
Delaware	(3)	3	-	North Carolina	(11)	-	11
Florida	(4)	-	4	North Dakota	(3)	3	-
Georgia	(13)	-	13	Ohio	(23)	23	-
Idaho	(3)	-	3	Oregon	(4)	4	-
Illinois	(24)	24	-	Pennsylvania	(32)	32	-
Indiana	(15)	15	-	Rhode Island	(4)	4	-
Iowa	(13)	13	-	South Carolina	(9)	-	9
Kansas	(10)	-	10	South Dakota	(4)	-	4
Kentucky	(13)	12	1	Tennessee	(12)	-	12
Louisiana	(8)	-	8	Texas	(15)	-	15
Maine	(6)	6	-	Utah	(3)	-	3
Maryland	(8)	8	-	Vermont	(4)	4	-
Massachusetts	(15)	15	-	Virginia	(12)	-	12
Michigan	(14)	14	-	Washington	(4)	-	4
Minnesota	(9)	9	-	West Virginia	(6)	6	-
Mississippi	(9)	-	9	Wisconsin	(12)	12	-
Missouri	(17)	-	17	Wyoming	(3)	-	3
Montana	(3)	-	3	**Totals**	**(447)**	**271**	**176**

1896

PRESIDENTIAL ELECTION RETURNS

STATE	TOTAL VOTE	WILLIAM McKINLEY (Republican)		WILLIAM J. BRYAN (Democrat, Populist)		JOHN M. PALMER (National Democrat)		JOSHUA LEVERING (Prohibition)		OTHER		PLURALITY	
		Votes	%	Votes	%	Votes	%	Votes	%	Votes	%		
Alabama	194,580	55,673	28.6	130,298	67.0	6,375	3.3	2,234	1.1	—		74,625	D
Arkansas	149,396	37,512	25.1	110,103	73.7	—		889	0.6	892	0.6	72,591	D
California	298,598	146,756	49.1	144,877	48.5	1,730	0.6	2,573	0.9	2,662	0.9	1,879	R
Colorado	189,539	26,271	13.9	161,005	84.9	1		1,717	0.9	545	0.3	134,734	D
Connecticut	174,394	110,285	63.2	56,740	32.5	4,336	2.5	1,806	1.0	1,227	0.7	53,545	R
Delaware	38,456	20,450	53.2	16,574	43.1	966	2.5	466	1.2	—		3,876	R
Florida	46,488	11,298	24.3	32,756	70.5	1,778	3.8	656	1.4	—		21,458	D
Georgia	162,480	59,395	36.6	93,885	57.8	3,670	2.3	5,483	3.4	47		34,490	D
Idaho	29,631	6,324	21.3	23,135	78.1	—		172	0.6	—		16,811	D
Illinois	1,090,766	607,130	55.7	465,593	42.7	6,307	0.6	9,796	0.9	1,940	0.2	141,537	R
Indiana	637,089	323,754	50.8	305,538	48.0	2,145	0.3	3,061	0.5	2,591	0.4	18,216	R
Iowa	521,550	289,293	55.5	223,744	42.9	4,516	0.9	3,192	0.6	805	0.2	65,549	R
Kansas	336,085	159,484	47.5	173,049	51.5	1,209	0.4	1,723	0.5	620	0.2	13,565	D
Kentucky	445,928	218,171	48.9	217,894	48.9	5,084	1.1	4,779	1.1	—		277	R
Louisiana	101,046	22,037	21.8	77,175	76.4	1,834	1.8	—		—		55,138	D
Maine	118,419	80,403	67.9	34,587	29.2	1,867	1.6	1,562	1.3	—		45,816	R
Maryland	250,249	136,959	54.7	104,150	41.6	2,499	1.0	5,918	2.4	723	0.3	32,809	R
Massachusetts	401,269	278,976	69.5	105,414	26.3	11,749	2.9	2,998	0.7	2,132	0.5	173,562	R
Michigan	545,583	293,336	53.8	237,164	43.5	6,923	1.3	4,978	0.9	3,182	0.6	56,172	R
Minnesota	341,762	193,503	56.6	139,735	40.9	3,222	0.9	4,348	1.3	954	0.3	53,768	R
Mississippi	69,591	4,819	6.9	63,355	91.0	1,021	1.5	396	0.6	—		58,536	D
Missouri	674,032	304,940	45.2	363,667	54.0	2,365	0.4	2,169	0.3	891	0.1	58,727	D
Montana	53,330	10,509	19.7	42,628	79.9	—		193	0.4	—		32,119	D
Nebraska	223,181	103,064	46.2	115,007	51.5	2,885	1.3	1,242	0.6	983	0.4	11,943	D
Nevada	10,286	1,938	18.8	8,348	81.2	—		—		—		6,410	D
New Hampshire	83,670	57,444	68.7	21,650	25.9	3,520	4.2	779	0.9	277	0.3	35,794	R
New Jersey	371,014	221,367	59.7	133,675	36.0	6,373	1.7	—		9,599	2.6	87,692	R
New York	1,423,876	819,838	57.6	551,369	38.7	18,950	1.3	16,052	1.1	17,667	1.2	268,469	R
North Carolina	331,337	155,122	46.8	174,408	52.6	578	0.2	635	0.2	594	0.2	19,286	D
North Dakota	47,391	26,335	55.6	20,686	43.6	—		358	0.8	12		5,649	R
Ohio	1,014,295	525,991	51.9	477,497	47.1	1,858	0.2	5,068	0.5	3,881	0.4	48,494	R
Oregon	97,335	48,700	50.0	46,739	48.0	977	1.0	919	0.9	—		1,961	R
Pennsylvania	1,194,355	728,300	61.0	433,228	36.3	11,000	0.9	19,274	1.6	2,553	0.2	295,072	R
Rhode Island	54,785	37,437	68.3	14,459	26.4	1,166	2.1	1,160	2.1	563	1.0	22,978	R
South Carolina	68,938	9,313	13.5	58,801	85.3	824	1.2	—		—		49,488	D
South Dakota	82,937	41,040	49.5	41,225	49.7	—		672	0.8	—		185	D
Tennessee	320,903	148,683	46.3	167,168	52.1	1,953	0.6	3,099	1.0	—		18,485	D
Texas	541,018	163,894	30.3	370,308	68.4	5,022	0.9	1,794	0.3	—		206,414	D
Utah	78,098	13,491	17.3	64,607	82.7	—		—		—		51,116	D
Vermont	63,568	51,127	80.4	10,367	16.3	1,341	2.1	733	1.2	—		40,760	R
Virginia	294,674	135,379	45.9	154,708	52.5	2,129	0.7	2,350	0.8	108		19,329	D
Washington	93,583	39,153	41.8	53,314	57.0	—		968	1.0	148	0.2	14,161	D
West Virginia	201,757	105,379	52.2	94,480	46.8	678	0.3	1,220	0.6	—		10,899	R
Wisconsin	447,409	268,135	59.9	165,523	37.0	4,584	1.0	7,507	1.7	1,660	0.4	102,612	R
Wyoming	21,067	10,072	47.8	10,862	51.6	—		133	0.6	—		790	D
Totals	**13,935,738**	**7,108,480**	**51.0**	**6,511,495**	**46.7**	**133,435**	**1.0**	**125,072**	**0.9**	**57,256**	**0.4**	**596,985**	**R**

PRESIDENTIAL ELECTION OF

1900

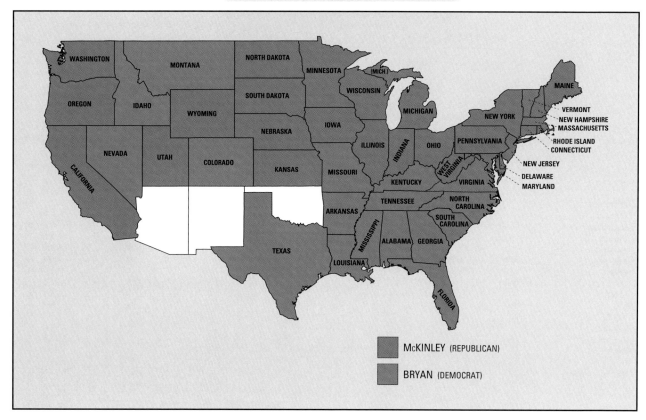

States	Electoral Votes	McKinley	Bryan	States	Electoral Votes	McKinley	Bryan
Alabama	(11)	-	11	Nebraska	(8)	8	-
Arkansas	(8)	-	8	Nevada	(3)	-	3
California	(9)	9	-	New Hampshire	(4)	4	-
Colorado	(4)	-	4	New Jersey	(10)	10	-
Connecticut	(6)	6	-	New York	(36)	36	-
Delaware	(3)	3	-	North Carolina	(11)	-	11
Florida	(4)	-	4	North Dakota	(3)	3	-
Georgia	(13)	-	13	Ohio	(23)	23	-
Idaho	(3)	-	3	Oregon	(4)	4	-
Illinois	(24)	24	-	Pennsylvania	(32)	32	-
Indiana	(15)	15	-	Rhode Island	(4)	4	-
Iowa	(13)	13	-	South Carolina	(9)	-	9
Kansas	(10)	10	-	South Dakota	(4)	4	-
Kentucky	(13)	-	13	Tennessee	(12)	-	12
Louisiana	(8)	-	8	Texas	(15)	-	15
Maine	(6)	6	-	Utah	(3)	3	-
Maryland	(8)	8	-	Vermont	(4)	4	-
Massachusetts	(15)	15	-	Virginia	(12)	-	12
Michigan	(14)	14	-	Washington	(4)	4	-
Minnesota	(9)	9	-	West Virginia	(6)	6	-
Mississippi	(9)	-	9	Wisconsin	(12)	12	-
Missouri	(17)	-	17	Wyoming	(3)	3	-
Montana	(3)	-	3	**Totals**	**(447)**	**292**	**155**

1900

PRESIDENTIAL ELECTION RETURNS

STATE	TOTAL VOTE	WILLIAM McKINLEY (Republican)		WILLIAM J. BRYAN (Democrat)		JOHN G. WOOLEY (Prohibition)		EUGENE V. DEBS (Socialist)		OTHER		PLURALITY	
		Votes	%	Votes	%	Votes	%	Votes	%	Votes	%		
Alabama	159,692	55,612	34.8	97,129	60.8	2,763	1.7	—		4,188	2.6	41,517	D
Arkansas	127,966	44,800	35.0	81,242	63.5	584	0.5	—		1,340	1.0	36,442	D
California	302,318	164,755	54.5	124,985	41.3	5,024	1.7	—		7,554	2.5	39,770	R
Colorado	220,895	92,701	42.0	122,705	55.5	3,790	1.7	686	0.3	1,013	0.5	30,004	D
Connecticut	180,195	102,572	56.9	74,014	41.1	1,617	0.9	1,029	0.6	963	0.5	28,558	R
Delaware	41,989	22,535	53.7	18,852	44.9	546	1.3	56	0.1	—		3,683	R
Florida	39,649	7,355	18.6	28,273	71.3	2,244	5.7	634	1.6	1,143	2.9	20,918	D
Georgia	121,410	34,260	28.2	81,180	66.9	1,402	1.2	—		4,568	3.8	46,920	D
Idaho	57,984	27,198	46.9	29,484	50.8	857	1.5	—		445	0.8	2,286	D
Illinois	1,131,898	597,985	52.8	503,061	44.4	17,626	1.6	9,687	0.9	3,539	0.3	94,924	R
Indiana	664,094	336,063	50.6	309,584	46.6	13,718	2.1	2,374	0.4	2,355	0.4	26,479	R
Iowa	530,345	307,799	58.0	209,261	39.5	9,502	1.8	2,743	0.5	1,040	0.2	98,538	R
Kansas	353,766	185,955	52.6	162,601	46.0	3,605	1.0	1,605	0.5	—		23,354	R
Kentucky	468,265	227,132	48.5	235,126	50.2	2,890	0.6	766	0.2	2,351	0.5	7,994	D
Louisiana	67,906	14,234	21.0	53,668	79.0	—		—		4		39,434	D
Maine	105,693	65,412	61.9	36,822	34.8	2,581	2.4	878	0.8	—		28,590	R
Maryland	264,386	136,151	51.5	122,237	46.2	4,574	1.7	900	0.3	524	0.2	13,914	R
Massachusetts	414,804	238,866	57.6	156,997	37.8	6,202	1.5	9,607	2.3	3,132	0.8	81,869	R
Michigan	543,789	316,014	58.1	211,432	38.9	11,804	2.2	2,820	0.5	1,719	0.3	104,582	R
Minnesota	316,311	190,461	60.2	112,901	35.7	8,555	2.7	3,065	1.0	1,329	0.4	77,560	R
Mississippi	59,055	5,707	9.7	51,706	87.6	—		—		1,642	2.8	45,999	D
Missouri	683,658	314,092	45.9	351,922	51.5	5,965	0.9	6,139	0.9	5,540	0.8	37,830	D
Montana	63,856	25,409	39.8	37,311	58.4	306	0.5	711	1.1	119	0.2	11,902	D
Nebraska	241,430	121,835	50.5	114,013	47.2	3,655	1.5	823	0.3	1,104	0.5	7,822	R
Nevada	10,196	3,849	37.8	6,347	62.2	—		—		—		2,498	D
New Hampshire	92,364	54,799	59.3	35,489	38.4	1,270	1.4	790	0.9	16		19,310	R
New Jersey	401,050	221,707	55.3	164,808	41.1	7,183	1.8	4,609	1.1	2,743	0.7	56,899	R
New York	1,548,043	822,013	53.1	678,462	43.8	22,077	1.4	12,869	0.8	12,622	0.8	143,551	R
North Carolina	292,518	132,997	45.5	157,733	53.9	990	0.3	—		798	0.3	24,736	D
North Dakota	57,783	35,898	62.1	20,524	35.5	735	1.3	517	0.9	109	0.2	15,374	R
Ohio	1,040,073	543,918	52.3	474,882	45.7	10,203	1.0	4,847	0.5	6,223	0.6	69,036	R
Oregon	83,251	46,172	55.5	32,810	39.4	2,536	3.0	1,464	1.8	269	0.3	13,362	R
Pennsylvania	1,173,210	712,665	60.7	424,232	36.2	27,908	2.4	4,831	0.4	3,574	0.3	288,433	R
Rhode Island	56,548	33,784	59.7	19,812	35.0	1,529	2.7	—		1,423	2.5	13,972	R
South Carolina	50,698	3,525	7.0	47,173	93.0	—		—		—		43,648	D
South Dakota	96,169	54,574	56.7	39,538	41.1	1,541	1.6	176	0.2	340	0.4	15,036	R
Tennessee	273,860	123,108	45.0	145,240	53.0	3,844	1.4	346	0.1	1,322	0.5	22,132	D
Texas	424,334	131,174	30.9	267,945	63.1	2,642	0.6	1,846	0.4	20,727	4.9	136,771	D
Utah	93,071	47,089	50.6	44,949	48.3	205	0.2	717	0.8	111	0.1	2,140	R
Vermont	56,212	42,569	75.7	12,849	22.9	383	0.7	39	0.1	372	0.7	29,720	R
Virginia	264,208	115,769	43.8	146,079	55.3	2,130	0.8	—		230	0.1	30,310	D
Washington	107,523	57,455	53.4	44,833	41.7	2,363	2.2	2,006	1.9	866	0.8	12,622	R
West Virginia	220,796	119,829	54.3	98,807	44.8	1,628	0.7	286	0.1	246	0.1	21,022	R
Wisconsin	442,501	265,760	60.1	159,163	36.0	10,027	2.3	7,048	1.6	503	0.1	106,597	R
Wyoming	24,708	14,482	58.6	10,164	41.1	—		21	0.1	41	0.2	4,318	R
Totals	13,970,470	7,218,039	51.7	6,358,345	45.5	209,004	1.5	86,935	0.6	98,147	0.7	859,694	R

PRESIDENTIAL ELECTION OF
1904

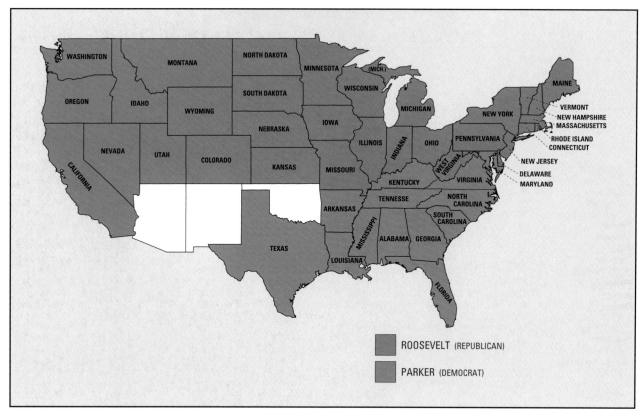

ROOSEVELT (REPUBLICAN)

PARKER (DEMOCRAT)

Congressional Quarterly's Guide to U.S. Elections, 3rd. edition, copyright ©1994. Used with permission. All rights reserved.

States	Electoral Votes	Roosevelt	Parker	States	Electoral Votes	Roosevelt	Parker
Alabama	(11)	-	11	Nebraska	(8)	8	-
Arkansas	(9)	-	9	Nevada	(3)	3	-
California	(10)	10	-	New Hampshire	(4)	4	-
Colorado	(5)	5	-	New Jersey	(12)	12	-
Connecticut	(7)	7	-	New York	(39)	39	-
Delaware	(3)	3	-	North Carolina	(12)	-	12
Florida	(5)	-	5	North Dakota	(4)	4	-
Georgia	(13)	-	13	Ohio	(23)	23	-
Idaho	(3)	3	-	Oregon	(4)	4	-
Illinois	(27)	27	-	Pennsylvania	(34)	34	-
Indiana	(15)	15	-	Rhode Island	(4)	4	-
Iowa	(13)	13	-	South Carolina	(9)	-	9
Kansas	(10)	10	-	South Dakota	(4)	4	-
Kentucky	(13)	-	13	Tennessee	(12)	-	12
Louisiana	(9)	-	9	Texas	(18)	-	18
Maine	(6)	6	-	Utah	(3)	3	-
Maryland	(8)	1	7	Vermont	(4)	4	-
Massachusetts	(16)	16	-	Virginia	(12)	-	12
Michigan	(14)	14	-	Washington	(5)	5	-
Minnesota	(11)	11	-	West Virginia	(7)	7	-
Mississippi	(10)	-	10	Wisconsin	(13)	13	-
Missouri	(18)	18	-	Wyoming	(3)	3	-
Montana	(3)	3	-	**Totals**	**(476)**	**336**	**140**

52

1904

PRESIDENTIAL ELECTION RETURNS

STATE	TOTAL VOTE	THEODORE ROOSEVELT (Republican)		ALTON B. PARKER (Democrat)		EUGENE V. DEBS (Socialist)		SILAS C. SWALLOW (Prohibition)		OTHER		PLURALITY	
		Votes	%	Votes	%	Votes	%	Votes	%	Votes	%		
Alabama	108,785	22,472	20.7	79,797	73.4	853	0.8	612	0.6	5,051	4.6	57,325	D
Arkansas	116,328	46,760	40.2	64,434	55.4	1,816	1.6	992	0.9	2,326	2.0	17,674	D
California	331,768	205,226	61.9	89,294	26.9	29,535	8.9	7,380	2.2	333	0.1	115,932	R
Colorado	243,667	134,661	55.3	100,105	41.1	4,304	1.8	3,438	1.4	1,159	0.5	34,556	R
Connecticut	191,136	111,089	58.1	72,909	38.1	4,543	2.4	1,506	0.8	1,089	0.6	38,180	R
Delaware	43,856	23,705	54.1	19,347	44.1	146	0.3	607	1.4	51	0.1	4,358	R
Florida	38,705	8,314	21.5	26,449	68.3	2,337	6.0	—		1,605	4.1	18,135	D
Georgia	130,986	24,004	18.3	83,466	63.7	196	0.1	685	0.5	22,635	17.3	59,462	D
Idaho	72,577	47,783	65.8	18,480	25.5	4,949	6.8	1,013	1.4	352	0.5	29,303	R
Illinois	1,076,495	632,645	58.8	327,606	30.4	69,225	6.4	34,770	3.2	12,249	1.1	305,039	R
Indiana	682,206	368,289	54.0	274,356	40.2	12,023	1.8	23,496	3.4	4,042	0.6	93,933	R
Iowa	485,703	307,907	63.4	149,141	30.7	14,847	3.1	11,601	2.4	2,207	0.5	158,766	R
Kansas	329,047	213,455	64.9	86,164	26.2	15,869	4.8	7,306	2.2	6,253	1.9	127,291	R
Kentucky	435,946	205,457	47.1	217,170	49.8	3,599	0.8	6,603	1.5	3,117	0.7	11,713	D
Louisiana	53,908	5,205	9.7	47,708	88.5	995	1.8	—		—		42,503	D
Maine	97,023	65,432	67.4	27,642	28.5	2,102	2.2	1,510	1.6	337	0.3	37,790	R
Maryland	224,229	109,497	48.8	109,446	48.8	2,247	1.0	3,034	1.4	5		51	R
Massachusetts	445,100	257,813	57.9	165,746	37.2	13,604	3.1	4,279	1.0	3,658	0.8	92,067	R
Michigan	520,443	361,863	69.5	134,163	25.8	8,942	1.7	13,312	2.6	2,163	0.4	227,700	R
Minnesota	292,860	216,651	74.0	55,187	18.8	11,692	4.0	6,253	2.1	3,077	1.1	161,464	R
Mississippi	58,721	3,280	5.6	53,480	91.1	462	0.8	—		1,499	2.6	50,200	D
Missouri	643,861	321,449	49.9	296,312	46.0	13,009	2.0	7,191	1.1	5,900	0.9	25,137	R
Montana	63,568	33,994	53.5	21,816	34.3	5,675	8.9	339	0.5	1,744	2.7	12,178	R
Nebraska	225,732	138,558	61.4	52,921	23.4	7,412	3.3	6,323	2.8	20,518	9.1	85,637	R
Nevada	12,115	6,864	56.7	3,982	32.9	925	7.6	—		344	2.8	2,882	R
New Hampshire	90,151	54,157	60.1	34,071	37.8	1,090	1.2	750	0.8	83	0.1	20,086	R
New Jersey	432,247	245,164	56.7	164,566	38.1	9,587	2.2	6,845	1.6	6,085	1.4	80,598	R
New York	1,617,765	859,533	53.1	683,981	42.3	36,883	2.3	20,787	1.3	16,581	1.0	175,552	R
North Carolina	207,818	82,442	39.7	124,091	59.7	124	0.1	342	0.2	819	0.4	41,649	D
North Dakota	70,014	52,595	75.1	14,273	20.4	2,009	2.9	1,137	1.6	—		38,322	R
Ohio	1,004,395	600,095	59.7	344,674	34.3	36,260	3.6	19,339	1.9	4,027	0.4	255,421	R
Oregon	89,656	60,309	67.3	17,327	19.3	7,479	8.3	3,795	4.2	746	0.8	42,982	R
Pennsylvania	1,236,738	840,949	68.0	337,998	27.3	21,863	1.8	33,717	2.7	2,211	0.2	502,951	R
Rhode Island	68,656	41,605	60.6	24,839	36.2	956	1.4	768	1.1	488	0.7	16,766	R
South Carolina	55,890	2,570	4.6	53,320	95.4	—		—		—		50,750	D
South Dakota	101,395	72,083	71.1	21,969	21.7	3,138	3.1	2,965	2.9	1,240	1.2	50,114	R
Tennessee	242,750	105,363	43.4	131,653	54.2	1,354	0.6	1,889	0.8	2,491	1.0	26,290	D
Texas	233,609	51,307	22.0	167,088	71.5	2,788	1.2	3,933	1.7	8,493	3.6	115,781	D
Utah	101,626	62,446	61.4	33,413	32.9	5,767	5.7	—		—		29,033	R
Vermont	51,888	40,459	78.0	9,777	18.8	859	1.7	792	1.5	1		30,682	R
Virginia	130,410	48,180	36.9	80,649	61.8	202	0.2	1,379	1.1	—		32,469	D
Washington	145,151	101,540	70.0	28,098	19.4	10,023	6.9	3,229	2.2	2,261	1.6	73,442	R
West Virginia	239,986	132,620	55.3	100,855	42.0	1,573	0.7	4,599	1.9	339	0.1	31,765	R
Wisconsin	443,440	280,314	63.2	124,205	28.0	28,240	6.4	9,872	2.2	809	0.2	156,109	R
Wyoming	30,614	20,489	66.9	8,930	29.2	987	3.2	208	0.7	—		11,559	R
Totals	13,518,964	7,626,593	56.4	5,082,898	37.6	402,489	3.0	258,596	1.9	148,388	1.1	2,543,695	R

PRESIDENTIAL ELECTION OF

1908

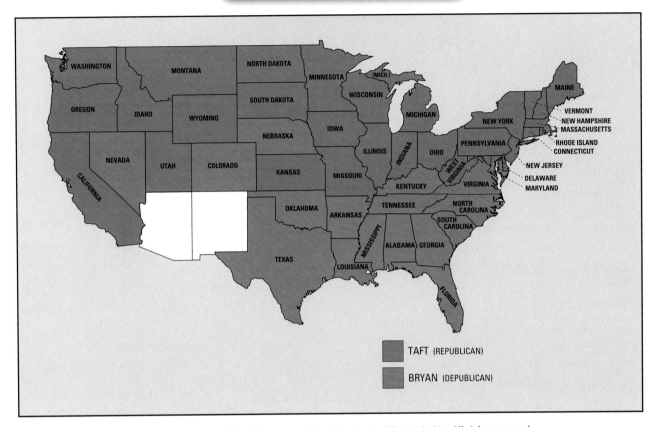

TAFT (REPUBLICAN)

BRYAN (DEPUBLICAN)

Congressional Quarterly's Guide to U.S. Elections, 3rd. edition, copyright ©1994. Used with permission. All rights reserved.

States	Electoral Votes	Taft	Bryan	States	Electoral Votes	Taft	Bryan
Alabama	(11)	-	11	Nebraska	(8)	-	8
Arkansas	(9)	-	9	Nevada	(3)	-	3
California	(10)	10	-	New Hampshire	(4)	4	-
Colorado	(5)	-	5	New Jersey	(12)	12	-
Connecticut	(7)	7	-	New York	(39)	39	-
Delaware	(3)	3	-	North Carolina	(12)	-	12
Florida	(5)	-	5	North Dakota	(4)	4	-
Georgia	(13)	-	13	Ohio	(23)	23	-
Idaho	(3)	3	-	Oklahoma	(7)	-	7
Illinois	(27)	27	-	Oregon	(4)	4	-
Indiana	(15)	15	-	Pennsylvania	(34)	34	-
Iowa	(13)	13	-	Rhode Island	(4)	4	-
Kansas	(10)	10	-	South Carolina	(9)	-	9
Kentucky	(13)	-	13	South Dakota	(4)	4	-
Louisiana	(9)	-	9	Tennessee	(12)	-	12
Maine	(6)	6	-	Texas	(18)	-	18
Maryland	(8)	2	6	Utah	(3)	3	-
Massachusetts	(16)	16	-	Vermont	(4)	4	-
Michigan	(14)	14	-	Virginia	(12)	-	12
Minnesota	(11)	11	-	Washington	(5)	5	-
Mississippi	(10)	-	10	West Virginia	(7)	7	-
Missouri	(18)	18	-	Wisconsin	(13)	13	-
Montana	(3)	3	-	Wyoming	(3)	3	-
				Totals	**(483)**	**321**	**162**

1908

PRESIDENTIAL ELECTION RETURNS

STATE	TOTAL VOTE	WILLIAM H. TAFT (Republican)		WILLIAM J. BRYAN (Democrat)		EUGENE V. DEBS (Socialist)		EUGENE W. CHAFIN (Prohibition)		OTHER		PLURALITY	
		Votes	%	Votes	%	Votes	%	Votes	%	Votes	%		
Alabama	105,152	25,561	24.3	74,391	70.7	1,450	1.4	690	0.7	3,060	2.9	48,830	D
Arkansas	151,845	56,684	37.3	87,020	57.3	5,842	3.8	1,026	0.7	1,273	0.8	30,336	D
California	386,625	214,398	55.5	127,492	33.0	28,659	7.4	11,770	3.0	4,306	1.1	86,906	R
Colorado	263,858	123,693	46.9	126,644	48.0	7,960	3.0	5,559	2.1	2		2,951	D
Connecticut	189,903	112,815	59.4	68,255	35.9	5,113	2.7	2,380	1.3	1,340	0.7	44,560	R
Delaware	48,007	25,014	52.1	22,055	45.9	239	0.5	670	1.4	29	0.1	2,959	R
Florida	49,360	10,654	21.6	31,104	63.0	3,747	7.6	1,356	2.7	2,499	5.1	20,450	D
Georgia	132,504	41,355	31.2	72,350	54.6	584	0.4	1,452	1.1	16,763	12.7	30,995	D
Idaho	97,293	52,621	54.1	36,162	37.2	6,400	6.6	1,986	2.0	124	0.1	16,459	R
Illinois	1,155,254	629,932	54.5	450,810	39.0	34,711	3.0	29,364	2.5	10,437	0.9	179,122	R
Indiana	721,117	348,993	48.4	338,262	46.9	13,476	1.9	18,036	2.5	2,350	0.3	10,731	R
Iowa	494,770	275,210	55.6	200,771	40.6	8,287	1.7	9,837	2.0	665	0.1	74,439	R
Kansas	376,043	197,316	52.5	161,209	42.9	12,420	3.3	5,030	1.3	68		36,107	R
Kentucky	490,719	235,711	48.0	244,092	49.7	4,093	0.8	5,885	1.2	938	0.2	8,381	D
Louisiana	75,117	8,958	11.9	63,568	84.6	2,514	3.3	—		77	0.1	54,610	D
Maine	106,335	66,987	63.0	35,403	33.3	1,758	1.7	1,487	1.4	700	0.7	31,584	R
Maryland	238,531	116,513	48.8	115,908	48.6	2,323	1.0	3,302	1.4	485	0.2	605	R
Massachusetts	456,905	265,966	58.2	155,533	34.0	10,778	2.4	4,373	1.0	20,255	4.4	110,433	R
Michigan	538,124	333,313	61.9	174,619	32.4	11,527	2.1	16,785	3.1	1,880	0.3	158,694	R
Minnesota	330,254	195,843	59.3	109,401	33.1	14,472	4.4	10,114	3.1	424	0.1	86,442	R
Mississippi	66,904	4,363	6.5	60,287	90.1	978	1.5	—		1,276	1.9	55,924	D
Missouri	715,841	347,203	48.5	346,574	48.4	15,431	2.2	4,209	0.6	2,424	0.3	629	R
Montana	69,233	32,471	46.9	29,511	42.6	5,920	8.6	838	1.2	493	0.7	2,960	R
Nebraska	266,799	126,997	47.6	131,099	49.1	3,524	1.3	5,179	1.9	—		4,102	D
Nevada	24,526	10,775	43.9	11,212	45.7	2,103	8.6	—		436	1.8	437	D
New Hampshire	89,595	53,144	59.3	33,655	37.6	1,299	1.4	905	1.0	592	0.7	19,489	R
New Jersey	467,111	265,298	56.8	182,522	39.1	10,249	2.2	4,930	1.1	4,112	0.9	82,776	R
New York	1,638,350	870,070	53.1	667,468	40.7	38,451	2.3	22,667	1.4	39,694	2.4	202,602	R
North Carolina	252,554	114,887	45.5	136,928	54.2	372	0.1	354	0.1	13		22,041	D
North Dakota	94,524	57,680	61.0	32,884	34.8	2,421	2.6	1,496	1.6	43		24,796	R
Ohio	1,121,552	572,312	51.0	502,721	44.8	33,795	3.0	11,402	1.0	1,322	0.1	69,591	R
Oklahoma	254,260	110,473	43.4	122,362	48.1	21,425	8.4	—		—		11,889	D
Oregon	110,539	62,454	56.5	37,792	34.2	7,322	6.6	2,682	2.4	289	0.3	24,662	R
Pennyvlania	1,267,450	745,779	58.8	448,782	35.4	33,914	2.7	36,694	2.9	2,281	0.2	296,997	R
Rhode Island	72,317	43,942	60.8	24,706	34.2	1,365	1.9	1,016	1.4	1,288	1.8	19,236	R
South Carolina	66,379	3,945	5.9	62,288	93.8	100	0.2	—		46	0.1	58,343	D
South Dakota	114,775	67,536	58.8	40,266	35.1	2,846	2.5	4,039	3.5	88	0.1	27,270	R
Tennessee	257,180	117,977	45.9	135,608	52.7	1,870	0.7	301	0.1	1,424	0.6	17,631	D
Texas	292,913	65,605	22.4	216,662	74.0	7,779	2.7	1,626	0.6	1,241	0.4	151,057	D
Utah	108,757	61,165	56.2	42,610	39.2	4,890	4.5	—		92	0.1	18,555	R
Vermont	52,680	39,552	75.1	11,496	21.8	—		799	1.5	833	1.6	28,056	R
Virginia	137,065	52,572	38.4	82,946	60.5	255	0.2	1,111	0.8	181	0.1	30,374	D
Washington	183,570	106,062	57.8	58,383	31.8	14,177	7.7	4,700	2.6	248	0.1	47,679	R
West Virginia	258,098	137,869	53.4	111,410	43.2	3,679	1.4	5,140	2.0	—		26,459	R
Wisconsin	454,438	247,744	54.5	166,662	36.7	28,147	6.2	11,565	2.5	320	0.1	81,082	R
Wyoming	37,608	20,846	55.4	14,918	39.7	1,715	4.6	66	0.2	63	0.2	5,928	R
Totals	14,882,734	7,676,258	51.6	6,406,801	43.0	420,380	2.8	252,821	1.7	126,474	0.8	1,269,457	R

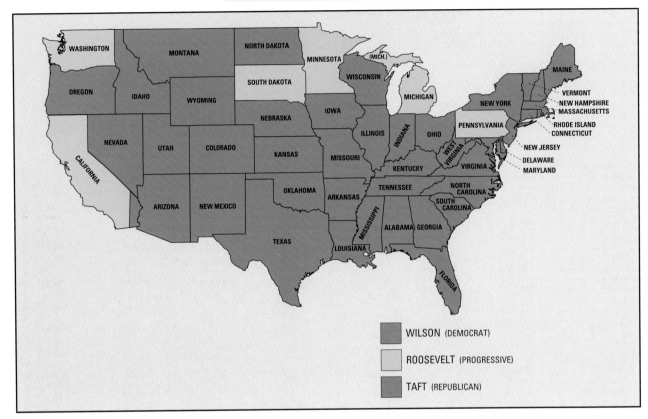

WILSON (DEMOCRAT)

ROOSEVELT (PROGRESSIVE)

TAFT (REPUBLICAN)

States	Electoral Votes	Wilson	Roosevelt	Taft	States	Electoral Votes	Wilson	Roosevelt	Taft
Alabama	(12)	12	-	-	Nebraska	(8)	8	-	-
Arizona	(3)	3	-	-	Nevada	(3)	3	-	-
Arkansas	(9)	9	-	-	New Hampshire	(4)	4	-	-
California	(13)	2	11	-	New Jersey	(14)	14	-	-
Colorado	(6)	6	-	-	New Mexico	(3)	3	-	-
Connecticut	(7)	7	-	-	New York	(45)	45	-	-
Delaware	(3)	3	-	-	North Carolina	(12)	12	-	-
Florida	(6)	6	-	-	North Dakota	(5)	5	-	-
Georgia	(14)	14	-	-	Ohio	(24)	24	-	-
Idaho	(4)	4	-	-	Oklahoma	(10)	10	-	-
Illinois	(29)	29	-	-	Oregon	(5)	5	-	-
Indiana	(15)	15	-	-	Pennsylvania	(38)	-	38	-
Iowa	(13)	13	-	-	Rhode Island	(5)	5	-	-
Kansas	(10)	10	-	-	South Carolina	(9)	9	-	-
Kentucky	(13)	13	-	-	South Dakota	(5)	-	5	-
Louisiana	(10)	10	-	-	Tennessee	(12)	12	-	-
Maine	(6)	6	-	-	Texas	(20)	20	-	-
Maryland	(8)	8	-	-	Utah	(4)	-	-	4
Massachusetts	(18)	18	-	-	Vermont	(4)	-	-	4
Michigan	(15)	-	15	-	Virginia	(12)	12	-	-
Minnesota	(12)	-	12	-	Washington	(7)	-	7	-
Mississippi	(10)	10	-	-	West Virginia	(8)	8	-	-
Missouri	(18)	18	-	-	Wisconsin	(13)	13	-	-
Montana	(4)	4	-	-	Wyoming	(3)	3	-	-
					Totals	**(531)**	**435**	**88**	**8**

1912
PRESIDENTIAL ELECTION RETURNS

STATE	TOTAL VOTE	WOODROW WILSON (Democrat)		THEODORE ROOSEVELT (Progressive)		WILLIAM H. TAFT (Republican)		EUGENE V. DEBS (Socialist)		OTHER		PLURALITY	
		Votes	%	Votes	%	Votes	%	Votes	%	Votes	%		
Alabama	117,959	82,438	69.9	22,680	19.2	9,807	8.3	3,029	2.6	5		59,758	D
Arizona	23,687	10,324	43.6	6,949	29.3	2,986	12.6	3,163	13.4	265	1.1	3,375	D
Arkansas	125,104	68,814	55.0	21,644	17.3	25,585	20.5	8,153	6.5	908	0.7	43,229	D
California	677,877	283,436	41.8	283,610	41.8	3,847	0.6	79,201	11.7	27,783	4.1	174	P
Colorado	265,954	113,912	42.8	71,752	27.0	58,386	22.0	16,366	6.2	5,538	2.1	42,160	D
Connecticut	190,404	74,561	39.2	34,129	17.9	68,324	35.9	10,056	5.3	3,334	1.8	6,237	D
Delaware	48,690	22,631	46.5	8,886	18.3	15,997	32.9	556	1.1	620	1.3	6,634	D
Florida	50,837	35,343	69.5	4,555	9.0	4,279	8.4	4,806	9.5	1,854	3.6	30,788	D
Georgia	121,470	93,087	76.6	21,985	18.1	5,191	4.3	1,058	0.9	149	0.1	71,102	D
Idaho	105,754	33,921	32.1	25,527	24.1	32,810	31.0	11,960	11.3	1,536	1.5	1,111	D
Illinois	1,146,173	405,048	35.3	386,478	33.7	253,593	22.1	81,278	7.1	19,776	1.7	18,570	D
Indiana	654,474	281,890	43.1	162,007	24.8	151,267	23.1	36,931	5.6	22,379	3.4	119,883	D
Iowa	492,353	185,322	37.6	161,819	32.9	119,805	24.3	16,967	3.4	8,440	1.7	23,503	D
Kansas	365,560	143,663	39.3	120,210	32.9	74,845	20.5	26,779	7.3	63		23,453	D
Kentucky	452,714	219,484	48.5	101,766	22.5	115,510	25.5	11,646	2.6	4,308	1.0	103,974	D
Louisiana	79,248	60,871	76.8	9,283	11.7	3,833	4.8	5,261	6.6	—		51,588	D
Maine	129,641	51,113	39.4	48,495	37.4	26,545	20.5	2,541	2.0	947	0.7	2,618	D
Maryland	231,981	112,674	48.6	57,789	24.9	54,956	23.7	3,996	1.7	2,566	1.1	54,885	D
Massachusetts	488,056	173,408	35.5	142,228	29.1	155,948	32.0	12,616	2.6	3,856	0.8	17,460	D
Michigan	547,971	150,201	27.4	213,243	38.9	151,434	27.6	23,060	4.2	10,033	1.8	61,809	P
Minnesota	334,219	106,426	31.8	125,856	37.7	64,334	19.2	27,505	8.2	10,098	3.0	19,430	P
Mississippi	64,483	57,324	88.9	3,549	5.5	1,560	2.4	2,050	3.2	—		53,775	D
Missouri	698,566	330,746	47.3	124,375	17.8	207,821	29.7	28,466	4.1	7,158	1.0	122,925	D
Montana	80,256	28,129	35.0	22,709	28.3	18,575	23.1	10,811	13.5	32		5,420	D
Nebraska	249,483	109,008	43.7	72,681	29.1	54,226	21.7	10,185	4.1	3,383	1.4	36,327	D
Nevada	20,115	7,986	39.7	5,620	27.9	3,196	15.9	3,313	16.5	—		2,366	D
New Hampshire	87,961	34,724	39.5	17,794	20.2	32,927	37.4	1,981	2.3	535	0.6	1,797	D
New Jersey	433,663	178,638	41.2	145,679	33.6	89,066	20.5	15,948	3.7	4,332	1.0	32,959	D
New Mexico	48,807	20,437	41.9	8,347	17.1	17,164	35.2	2,859	5.9	—		3,273	D
New York	1,588,315	655,573	41.3	390,093	24.6	455,487	28.7	63,434	4.0	23,728	1.5	200,086	D
North Carolina	243,776	144,407	59.2	69,135	28.4	29,129	11.9	987	0.4	118		75,272	D
North Dakota	86,474	29,549	34.2	25,726	29.7	22,990	26.6	6,966	8.1	1,243	1.4	3,823	D
Ohio	1,037,114	424,834	41.0	229,807	22.2	278,168	26.8	90,164	8.7	14,141	1.4	146,666	D
Oklahoma	253,694	119,143	47.0	—		90,726	35.8	41,630	16.4	2,195	0.9	28,417	D
Oregon	137,040	47,064	34.3	37,600	27.4	34,673	25.3	13,343	9.7	4,360	3.2	9,464	D
Pennsylvania	1,217,736	395,637	32.5	444,894	36.5	273,360	22.4	83,614	6.9	20,231	1.7	49,257	P
Rhode Island	77,894	30,412	39.0	16,878	21.7	27,703	35.6	2,049	2.6	852	1.1	2,709	D
South Carolina	50,403	48,355	95.9	1,293	2.6	536	1.1	164	0.3	55	0.1	47,062	D
South Dakota	116,327	48,942	42.1	58,811	50.6	—		4,664	4.0	3,910	3.4	9,869	P
Tennessee	251,933	133,021	52.8	54,041	21.5	60,475	24.0	3,564	1.4	832	0.3	72,546	D
Texas	300,961	218,921	72.7	26,715	8.9	28,310	9.4	24,884	8.3	2,131	0.7	190,611	D
Utah	112,272	36,576	32.6	24,174	21.5	42,013	37.4	8,999	8.0	510	0.5	5,437	R
Vermont	62,804	15,350	24.4	22,129	35.2	23,303	37.1	928	1.5	1,094	1.7	1,174	R
Virginia	136,975	90,332	65.9	21,776	15.9	23,288	17.0	820	0.6	759	0.6	67,044	D
Washington	322,799	86,840	26.9	113,698	35.2	70,445	21.8	40,134	12.4	11,682	3.6	26,858	P
West Virginia	268,728	113,097	42.1	79,112	29.4	56,754	21.1	15,248	5.7	4,517	1.7	33,985	D
Wisconsin	399,975	164,230	41.1	62,448	15.6	130,596	32.7	33,476	8.4	9,225	2.3	33,634	D
Wyoming	42,283	15,310	36.2	9,232	21.8	14,560	34.4	2,760	6.5	421	1.0	750	D
Totals	15,040,963	6,293,152	41.8	4,119,207	27.4	3,486,333	23.2	900,369	6.0	241,902	1.6	2,173,945	D

PRESIDENTIAL ELECTION OF
1916

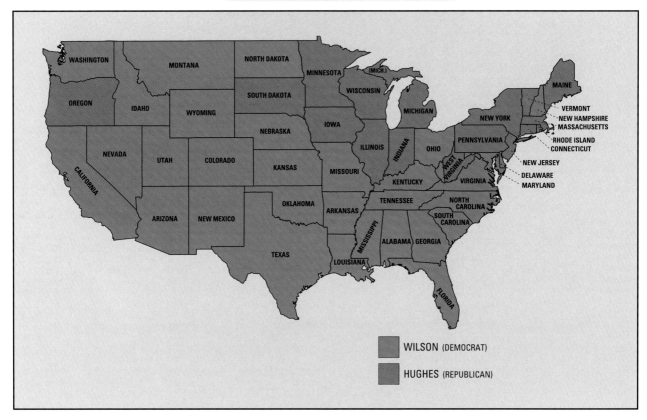

States	Electoral Votes	Wilson	Hughes	States	Electoral Votes	Wilson	Hughes
Alabama	(12)	12	-	Nebraska	(8)	8	-
Arizona	(3)	3	-	Nevada	(3)	3	-
Arkansas	(9)	9	-	New Hampshire	(4)	4	-
California	(13)	13	-	New Jersey	(14)	-	14
Colorado	(6)	6	-	New Mexico	(3)	3	-
Connecticut	(7)	-	7	New York	(45)	-	45
Delaware	(3)	-	3	North Carolina	(12)	12	-
Florida	(6)	6	-	North Dakota	(5)	5	-
Georgia	(14)	14	-	Ohio	(24)	24	-
Idaho	(4)	4	-	Oklahoma	(10)	10	-
Illinois	(29)	-	29	Oregon	(5)	-	5
Indiana	(15)	-	15	Pennsylvania	(38)	-	38
Iowa	(13)	-	13	Rhode Island	(5)	-	5
Kansas	(10)	10	-	South Carolina	(9)	9	-
Kentucky	(13)	13	-	South Dakota	(5)	-	5
Louisiana	(10)	10	-	Tennessee	(12)	12	-
Maine	(6)	-	6	Texas	(20)	20	-
Maryland	(8)	8	-	Utah	(4)	4	-
Massachusetts	(18)	-	18	Vermont	(4)	-	4
Michigan	(15)	-	15	Virginia	(12)	12	-
Minnesota	(12)	-	12	Washington	(7)	7	-
Mississippi	(10)	10	-	West Virginia	(8)	1	7
Missouri	(18)	18	-	Wisconsin	(13)	-	13
Montana	(4)	4	-	Wyoming	(3)	3	-
				Totals	**(531)**	**277**	**254**

1916

PRESIDENTIAL ELECTION RETURNS

STATE	TOTAL VOTE	WOODROW WILSON (Democrat)		CHARLES E. HUGHES (Republican)		ALLAN L. BENSON (Socialist)		J. FRANK HANLY (Prohibition)		OTHER		PLURALITY	
		Votes	%	Votes	%	Votes	%	Votes	%	Votes	%		
Alabama	130,435	99,116	76.0	28,662	22.0	1,916	1.5	741	0.6	—		70,454	D
Arizona	58,019	33,170	57.2	20,522	35.4	3,174	5.5	1,153	2.0	—		12,648	D
Arkansas	170,104	112,211	66.0	48,879	28.7	6,999	4.1	2,015	1.2	—		63,332	D
California	999,250	465,936	46.6	462,516	46.3	42,898	4.3	27,713	2.8	187		3,420	D
Colorado	292,037	177,496	60.8	101,388	34.7	9,951	3.4	2,793	1.0	409	0.1	76,108	D
Connecticut	213,874	99,786	46.7	106,514	49.8	5,179	2.4	1,789	0.8	606	0.3	6,728	R
Delaware	51,810	24,753	47.8	26,011	50.2	480	0.9	566	1.1	—		1,258	R
Florida	80,734	55,984	69.3	14,611	18.1	5,353	6.6	4,786	5.9	—		41,373	D
Georgia	160,681	127,754	79.5	11,294	7.0	941	0.6	—		20,692	12.9	107,062	D
Idaho	134,615	70,054	52.0	55,368	41.1	8,066	6.0	1,127	0.8	—		14,686	D
Illinois	2,192,707	950,229	43.3	1,152,549	52.6	61,394	2.8	26,047	1.2	2,488	0.1	202,320	R
Indiana	718,853	334,063	46.5	341,005	47.4	21,860	3.0	16,368	2.3	5,557	0.8	6,942	R
Iowa	518,738	221,699	42.7	280,439	54.1	10,976	2.1	3,371	0.6	2,253	0.4	58,740	R
Kansas	629,813	314,588	49.9	277,658	44.1	24,685	3.9	12,882	2.0	—		36,930	D
Kentucky	520,078	269,990	51.9	241,854	46.5	4,734	0.9	3,039	0.6	461	0.1	28,136	D
Louisiana	92,974	79,875	85.9	6,466	7.0	284	0.3	—		6,349	6.8	73,409	D
Maine	136,314	64,033	47.0	69,508	51.0	2,177	1.6	596	0.4	—		5,475	R
Maryland	262,039	138,359	52.8	117,347	44.8	2,674	1.0	2,903	1.1	756	0.3	21,012	D
Massachusetts	531,822	247,885	46.6	268,784	50.5	11,058	2.1	2,993	0.6	1,102	0.2	20,899	R
Michigan	646,873	283,993	43.9	337,952	52.2	16,012	2.5	8,085	1.2	831	0.1	53,959	R
Minnesota	387,367	179,155	46.2	179,544	46.3	20,117	5.2	7,793	2.0	758	0.2	389	R
Mississippi	86,679	80,422	92.8	4,253	4.9	1,484	1.7	—		520	0.6	76,169	D
Missouri	786,773	398,032	50.6	369,339	46.9	14,612	1.9	3,887	0.5	903	0.1	28,693	D
Montana	178,009	101,104	56.8	66,933	37.6	9,634	5.4	—		338	0.2	34,171	D
Nebraska	287,315	158,827	55.3	117,771	41.0	7,141	2.5	2,952	1.0	624	0.2	41,056	D
Nevada	33,314	17,776	53.4	12,127	36.4	3,065	9.2	346	1.0	—		5,649	D
New Hampshire	89,127	43,781	49.1	43,725	49.1	1,318	1.5	303	0.3	—		56	D
New Jersey	494,442	211,018	42.7	268,982	54.4	10,405	2.1	3,182	0.6	855	0.2.	57,964	R
New Mexico	66,879	33,693	50.4	31,097	46.5	1,977	3.0	112	0.2	—		2,596	D
New York	1,706,305	759,426	44.5	879,238	51.5	45,944	2.7	19,031	1.1	2,666	0.2	119,812	R
North Carolina	289,837	168,383	58.1	120,890	41.7	509	0.2	55		—		47,493	D
North Dakota	115,390	55,206	47.8	53,471	46.3	5,716	5.0	997	0.9	—		1,735	D
Ohio	1,165,091	604,161	51.9	514,753	44.2	38,092	3.3	8,085	0.7	—		89,408	D
Oklahoma	292,327	148,123	50.7	97,233	33.3	45,091	15.4	1,646	0.6	234	0.1	50,890	D
Oregon	261,650	120,087	45.9	126,813	48.5	9,711	3.7	4,729	1.8	310	0.1	6,726	R
Pennsylvania	1,297,189	521,784	40.2	703,823	54.3	42,638	3.3	28,525	2.2	419		182,039	R
Rhode Island	87,816	40,394	46.0	44,858	51.1	1,914	2.2	470	0.5	180	0.2	4,464	R
South Carolina	63,950	61,845	96.7	1,550	2.4	135	0.2	—		420	0.7	60,295	D
South Dakota	128,942	59,191	45.9	64,217	49.8	3,760	2.9	1,774	1.4	—		5,026	R
Tennessee	272,190	153,280	56.3	116,223	42.7	2,542	0.9	145	0.1	—		37,057	D
Texas	373,310	287,415	77.0	64,999	17.4	18,960	5.1	1,936	0.5	—		222,416	D
Utah	143,145	84,145	58.8	54,137	37.8	4,460	3.1	149	0.1	254	0.2	30,008	D
Vermont	64,475	22,708	35.2	40,250	62.4	798	1.2	709	1.1	10		17,542	R
Virginia	152,025	101,840	67.0	48,384	31.8	1,056	0.7	678	0.4	67		53,456	D
Washington	380,994	183,388	48.1	167,208	43.9	22,800	6.0	6,868	1.8	730	0.2	16,180	D
West Virginia	289,671	140,403	48.5	143,124	49.4	6,144	2.1	—		—		2,721	R
Wisconsin	447,134	191,363	42.8	220,822	49.4	27,631	6.2	7,318	1.6	—		29,459	R
Wyoming	51,906	28,376	54.7	21,698	41.8	1,459	2.8	373	0.7	—		6,678	D
Totals	**18,535,022**	**9,126,300**	**49.2**	**8,546,789**	**46.1**	**589,924**	**3.2**	**221,030**	**1.2**	**50,979**	**0.3**	**579,511**	**D**

PRESIDENTIAL ELECTION OF
1920

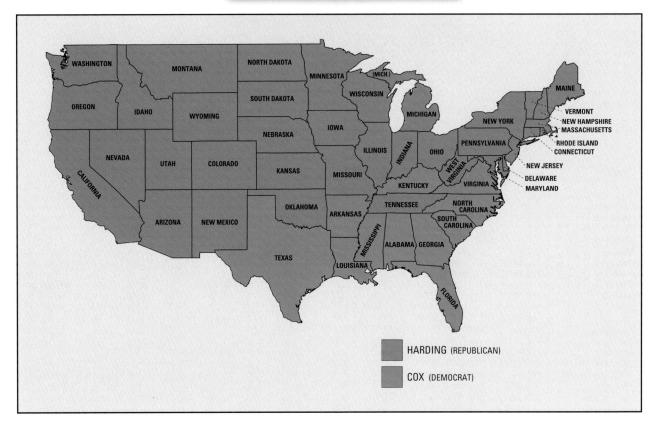

Congressional Quarterly's Guide to U.S. Elections, 3rd. edition, copyright ©1994. Used with permission. All rights reserved.

States	Electoral Votes	Harding	Cox	States	Electoral Votes	Harding	Cox
Alabama	(12)	-	12	Nebraska	(8)	8	-
Arizona	(3)	3	-	Nevada	(3)	3	-
Arkansas	(9)	-	9	New Hampshire	(4)	4	-
California	(13)	13	-	New Jersey	(14)	14	-
Colorado	(6)	6	-	New Mexico	(3)	3	-
Connecticut	(7)	7	-	New York	(45)	45	-
Delaware	(3)	3	-	North Carolina	(12)	-	12
Florida	(6)	-	6	North Dakota	(5)	5	-
Georgia	(14)	-	14	Ohio	(24)	24	-
Idaho	(4)	4	-	Oklahoma	(10)	10	-
Illinois	(29)	29	-	Oregon	(5)	5	-
Indiana	(15)	15	-	Pennsylvania	(38)	38	-
Iowa	(13)	13	-	Rhode Island	(5)	5	-
Kansas	(10)	10	-	South Carolina	(9)	-	9
Kentucky	(13)	-	13	South Dakota	(5)	5	-
Louisiana	(10)	-	10	Tennessee	(12)	12	-
Maine	(6)	6	-	Texas	(20)	-	20
Maryland	(8)	8	-	Utah	(4)	4	-
Massachusetts	(18)	18	-	Vermont	(4)	4	-
Michigan	(15)	15	-	Virginia	(12)	-	12
Minnesota	(12)	12	-	Washington	(7)	7	-
Mississippi	(10)	-	10	West Virginia	(8)	8	-
Missouri	(18)	18	-	Wisconsin	(13)	13	-
Montana	(4)	4	-	Wyoming	(3)	3	-
				Totals	**(531)**	**404**	**127**

1920

PRESIDENTIAL ELECTION RETURNS

STATE	TOTAL VOTE	WARREN G. HARDING (Republican)		JAMES M. COX (Democrat)		EUGENE V. DEBS (Socialist)		PARLEY P. CHRISTENSEN (Farmer-Labor)		OTHER		PLURALITY	
		Votes	%	Votes	%	Votes	%	Votes	%	Votes	%		
Alabama	233,951	74,719	31.9	156,064	66.7	2,402	1.0	—		766	0.3	81,345	D
Arizona	66,803	37,016	55.4	29,546	44.2	222	0.3	15		4		7,470	R
Arkansas	183,871	72,316	39.3	106,427	57.9	5,128	2.8	—		—		34,111	D
California	943,463	624,992	66.2	229,191	24.3	64,076	6.8	—		25,204	2.7	395,801	R
Colorado	292,053	173,248	59.3	104,936	35.9	8,046	2.8	3,016	1.0	2,807	1.0	68,312	R
Connecticut	365,518	229,238	62.7	120,721	33.0	10,350	2.8	1,947	0.5	3,262	0.9	108,517	R
Delaware	94,875	52,858	55.7	39,911	42.1	988	1.0	93	0.1	1,025	1.1	12,947	R
Florida	145,684	44,853	30.8	90,515	62.1	5,189	3.6	—		5,127	3.5	45,662	D
Georgia	149,558	42,981	28.7	106,112	71.0	465	0.3	—		—		63,131	D
Idaho	138,281	91,351	66.1	46,930	33.9	—		—		—		44,421	R
Illinois	2,094,714	1,420,480	67.8	534,395	25.5	74,747	3.6	49,630	2.4	15,462	0.7	886,085	R
Indiana	1,262,974	696,370	55.1	511,364	40.5	24,713	2.0	16,499	1.3	14,028	1.1	185,006	R
Iowa	894,959	634,674	70.9	227,804	25.5	16,981	1.9	10,321	1.2	5,179	0.6	406,870	R
Kansas	570,243	369,268	64.8	185,464	32.5	15,511	2.7	—		—		183,804	R
Kentucky	918,636	452,480	49.3	456,497	49.7	6,409	0.7	—		3,250	0.4	4,017	D
Louisiana	126,397	38,539	30.5	87,519	69.2	—		—		339	0.3	48,980	D
Maine	197,840	136,355	68.9	58,961	29.8	2,214	1.1	—		310	0.2	77,394	R
Maryland	428,443	236,117	55.1	180,626	42.2	8,876	2.1	1,645	0.4	1,179	0.3	55,491	R
Massachusetts	993,718	681,153	68.5	276,691	27.8	32,267	3.2	—		3,607	0.4	404,462	R
Michigan	1,048,411	762,865	72.8	233,450	22.3	28,947	2.8	10,480	1.0	12,669	1.2	529,415	R
Minnesota	735,838	519,421	70.6	142,994	19.4	56,106	7.6	—		17,317	2.4	376,427	R
Mississippi	82,351	11,576	14.1	69,136	84.0	1,639	2.0	—		—		57,560	D
Missouri	1,332,140	727,252	54.6	574,699	43.1	20,342	1.5	3,108	0.2	6,739	0.5	152,553	R
Montana	179,006	109,430	61.1	57,372	32.1	—		12,204	6.8	—		52,058	R
Nebraska	382,743	247,498	64.7	119,608	31.3	9,600	2.5	—		6,037	1.6	127,890	R
Nevada	27,194	15,479	56.9	9,851	36.2	1,864	6.9	—		—		5,628	R
New Hampshire	159,092	95,196	59.8	62,662	39.4	1,234	0.8	—		—		32,534	R
New Jersey	910,251	615,333	67.6	258,761	28.4	27,385	3.0	2,264	0.2	6,508	0.7	356,572	R
New Mexico	105,412	57,634	54.7	46,668	44.3	2		1,104	1.0	4		10,966	R
New York	2,898,513	1,871,167	64.6	781,238	27.0	203,201	7.0	18,413	0.6	24,494	0.8	1,089,929	R
North Carolina	538,649	232,819	43.2	305,367	56.7	446	0.1	—		17		72,548	D
North Dakota	205,786	160,082	77.8	37,422	18.2	8,282	4.0	—		—		122,660	R
Ohio	2,021,653	1,182,022	58.5	780,037	38.6	57,147	2.8	—		2,447	0.1	401,985	R
Oklahoma	485,678	243,840	50.2	216,122	44.5	25,716	5.3	—		—		27,718	R
Oregon	238,522	143,592	60.2	80,019	33.5	9,801	4.1	—		5,110	2.1	63,573	R
Pennsylvania	1,851,248	1,218,215	65.8	503,202	27.2	70,021	3.8	15,642	0.8	44,168	2.4	715,013	R
Rhode Island	167,981	107,463	64.0	55,062	32.8	4,351	2.6	—		1,105	0.7	52,401	R
South Carolina	66,808	2,610	3.9	64,170	96.1	28		—		—		61,560	D
South Dakota	182,237	110,692	60.7	35,938	19.7	—		34,707	19.0	900	0.5	74,754	R
Tennessee	428,036	219,229	51.2	206,558	48.3	2,249	0.5	—		—		12,671	R
Texas	486,109	114,658	23.6	287,920	59.2	8,124	1.7	—		75,407	15.5	173,262	D
Utah	145,828	81,555	55.9	56,639	38.8	3,159	2.2	4,475	3.1	—		24,916	R
Vermont	89,961	68,212	75.8	20,919	23.3	—		—		830	0.9	47,293	R
Virginia	231,000	87,456	37.9	141,670	61.3	808	0.3	240	0.1	826	0.4	54,214	D
Washington	398,715	223,137	56.0	84,298	21.1	8,913	2.2	77,246	19.4	5,121	1.3	138,839	R
West Virginia	509,936	282,007	55.3	220,785	43.3	5,618	1.1	—		1,526	0.3	61,222	R
Wisconsin	701,281	498,576	71.1	113,422	16.2	80,635	11.5	—		8,648	1.2	385,154	R
Wyoming	56,253	35,091	62.4	17,429	31.0	1,288	2.3	2,180	3.9	265	0.5	17,662	R
Totals	26,768,613	16,153,115	60.3	9,133,092	34.1	915,490	3.4	265,229	1.0	301,687	1.1	7,020,023	R

PRESIDENTIAL ELECTION OF
1924

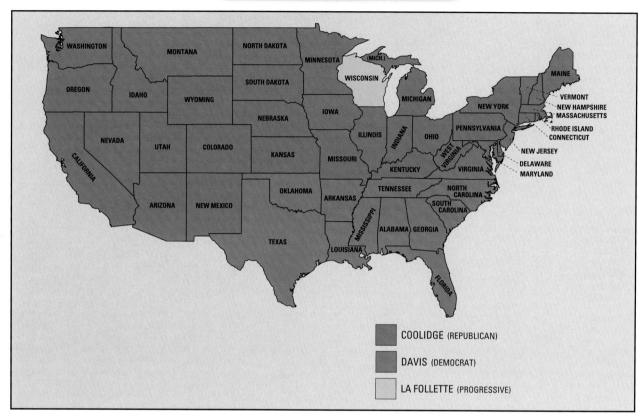

COOLIDGE (REPUBLICAN)

DAVIS (DEMOCRAT)

LA FOLLETTE (PROGRESSIVE)

Congressional Quarterly's Guide to U.S. Elections, 3rd. edition, copyright ©1994. Used with permission. All rights reserved.

States	Electoral Votes	Coolidge	Davis	La Follette	States	Electoral Votes	Coolidge	Davis	La Follette
Alabama	(12)	-	12	-	Nebraska	(8)	8	-	-
Arizona	(3)	3	-	-	Nevada	(3)	3	-	-
Arkansas	(9)	-	9	-	New Hampshire	(4)	4	-	-
California	(13)	13	-	-	New Jersey	(14)	14	-	-
Colorado	(6)	6	-	-	New Mexico	(3)	3	-	-
Connecticut	(7)	7	-	-	New York	(45)	45	-	-
Delaware	(3)	3	-	-	North Carolina	(12)	-	12	-
Florida	(6)	-	6	-	North Dakota	(5)	5	-	-
Georgia	(14)	-	14	-	Ohio	(24)	24	-	-
Idaho	(4)	4	-	-	Oklahoma	(10)	-	10	-
Illinois	(29)	29	-	-	Oregon	(5)	5	-	-
Indiana	(15)	15	-	-	Pennsylvania	(38)	38	-	-
Iowa	(13)	13	-	-	Rhode Island	(5)	5	-	-
Kansas	(10)	10	-	-	South Carolina	(9)	-	9	-
Kentucky	(13)	13	-	-	South Dakota	(5)	5	-	-
Louisiana	(10)	-	10	-	Tennessee	(12)	-	12	-
Maine	(6)	6	-	-	Texas	(20)	-	20	-
Maryland	(8)	8	-	-	Utah	(4)	4	-	-
Massachusetts	(18)	18	-	-	Vermont	(4)	4	-	-
Michigan	(15)	15	-	-	Virginia	(12)	-	12	-
Minnesota	(12)	12	-	-	Washington	(7)	7	-	-
Mississippi	(10)	-	10	-	West Virginia	(8)	8	-	-
Missouri	(18)	18	-	-	Wisconsin	(13)	-	-	13
Montana	(4)	4	-	-	Wyoming	(3)	3	-	-
					Totals	**(531)**	**382**	**136**	**13**

1924

PRESIDENTIAL ELECTION RETURNS

STATE	TOTAL VOTE	CALVIN COOLIDGE (Republican)		JOHN W. DAVIS (Democrat)		ROBERT M. LA FOLLETTE (Progressive)		HERMAN P. FARIS (Prohibition)		OTHER		PLURALITY
		Votes	%	Votes	%	Votes	%	Votes	%	Votes	%	
Alabama	164,563	42,823	26.0	113,138	68.8	8,040	4.9	562	0.3	—		70,315 D
Arizona	73,961	30,516	41.3	26,235	35.5	17,210	23.3	—		—		4,281 R
Arkansas	138,540	40,583	29.3	84,790	61.2	13,167	9.5	—		—		44,207 D
California	1,281,778	733,250	57.2	105,514	8.2	424,649	33.1	18,365	1.4	—		308,601 R
Colorado	342,261	195,171	57.0	75,238	22.0	69,946	20.4	966	0.3	940	0.3	119,933 R
Connecticut	400,396	246,322	61.5	110,184	27.5	42,416	10.6	—		1,474	0.4	136,138 R
Delaware	90,885	52,441	57.7	33,445	36.8	4,979	5.5	—		20		18,996 R
Florida	109,158	30,633	28.1	62,083	56.9	8,625	7.9	5,498	5.0	2,319	2.1	31,450 D
Georgia	166,635	30,300	18.2	123,262	74.0	12,687	7.6	231	0.1	155	0.1	92,962 D
Idaho	147,690	69,791	47.3	23,951	16.2	53,948	36.5			—		15,843 R
Illinois	2,470,067	1,453,321	58.8	576,975	23.4	432,027	17.5	2,367	0.1	5,377	0.2	876,346 R
Indiana	1,272,390	703,042	55.3	492,245	38.7	71,700	5.6	4,416	0.3	987	0.1	210,797 R
Iowa	976,770	537,458	55.0	160,382	16.4	274,448	28.1	—		4,482	0.5	263,010 R
Kansas	662,456	407,671	61.5	156,320	23.6	98,461	14.9	—		4		251,351 R
Kentucky	813,843	396,758	48.8	375,593	46.2	38,465	4.7	—		3,027	0.4	21,165 R
Louisiana	121,951	24,670	20.2	93,218	76.4	—		—		4,063	3.3	68,548 D
Maine	192,192	138,440	72.0	41,964	21.8	11,382	5.9	—		406	0.2	96,476 R
Maryland	358,630	162,414	45.3	148,072	41.3	47,157	13.1	—		987	0.3	14,342 R
Massachusetts	1,129,837	703,476	62.3	280,831	24.9	141,225	12.5	—		4,305	0.4	422,645 R
Michigan	1,160,419	874,631	75.4	152,359	13.1	122,014	10.5	6,085	0.5	5,330	0.5	722,272 R
Minnesota	822,146	420,759	51.2	55,913	6.8	339,192	41.3	—		6,282	0.8	81,567 R
Mississippi	112,442	8,494	7.6	100,474	89.4	3,474	3.1	—		—		91,980 D
Missouri	1,310,095	648,488	49.5	574,962	43.9	83,996	6.4	1,418	0.1	1,231	0.1	73,526 R
Montana	174,425	74,138	42.5	33,805	19.4	66,124	37.9	—		358	0.2	8,014 R
Nebraska	463,559	218,985	47.2	137,299	29.6	105,681	22.8	1,594	0.3	—		81,686 R
Nevada	26,921	11,243	41.8	5,909	21.9	9,769	36.3	—		—		1,474 R
New Hampshire	164,769	98,575	59.8	57,201	34.7	8,993	5.5	—		—		41,374 R
New Jersey	1,088,054	676,277	62.2	298,043	27.4	109,028	10.0	1,660	0.2	3,046	0.3	378,234 R
New Mexico	112,830	54,745	48.5	48,542	43.0	9,543	8.5	—		—		6,203 R
New York	3,263,939	1,820,058	55.8	950,796	29.1	474,913	14.6	—		18,172	0.6	869,262 R
North Carolina	481,608	190,754	39.6	284,190	59.0	6,651	1.4	13		—		93,436 D
North Dakota	199,081	94,931	47.7	13,858	7.0	89,922	45.2	—		370	0.2	5,009 R
Ohio	2,016,296	1,176,130	58.3	477,887	23.7	358,008	17.8	—		4,271	0.2	698,243 R
Oklahoma	527,828	225,756	42.8	255,798	48.5	46,274	8.8	—		—		30,042 D
Oregon	279,488	142,579	51.0	67,589	24.2	68,403	24.5	—		917	0.3	74,176 R
Pennsylvania	2,144,850	1,401,481	65.3	409,192	19.1	307,567	14.3	9,779	0.5	16,831	0.8	992,289 R
Rhode Island	210,115	125,286	59.6	76,606	36.5	7,628	3.6	—		595	0.3	48,680 R
South Carolina	50,755	1,123	2.2	49,008	96.6	623	1.2	—		1		47,885 D
South Dakota	203,868	101,299	49.7	27,214	13.3	75,355	37.0	—		—		25,944 R
Tennessee	301,030	130,831	43.5	159,339	52.9	10,666	3.5	94		100		28,508 D
Texas	657,054	130,794	19.9	483,381	73.6	42,879	6.5	—		—		352,587 D
Utah	156,990	77,327	49.3	47,001	29.9	32,662	20.8	—		—		30,326 R
Vermont	102,917	80,498	78.2	16,124	15.7	5,964	5.8	326	0.3	5		64,374 R
Virginia	223,603	73,328	32.8	139,717	62.5	10,369	4.6	—		189	0.1	66,389 D
Washington	421,549	220,224	52.2	42,842	10.2	150,727	35.8	—		7,756	1.8	69,497 R
West Virginia	583,662	288,635	49.5	257,232	44.1	36,723	6.3	—		1,072	0.2	31,403 R
Wisconsin	840,827	311,614	37.1	68,115	8.1	453,678	54.0	2,918	0.3	4,502	0.5	142,064 P
Wyoming	79,900	41,858	52.4	12,868	16.1	25,174	31.5	—		—		16,684 R
Totals	29,095,023	15,719,921	54.0	8,386,704	28.8	4,832,532	16.6	56,292	0.2	99,574	0.3	7,333,217 R

PRESIDENTIAL ELECTION OF

1928

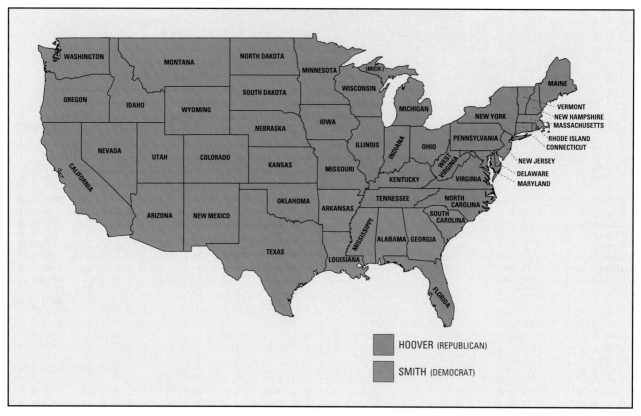

WASHINGTON

MONTANA

NORTH DAKOTA

MINNESOTA

(MICH.)

MAINE

OREGON

IDAHO

WYOMING

SOUTH DAKOTA

WISCONSIN

VERMONT

NEW HAMPSHIRE

MASSACHUSETTS

NEBRASKA

IOWA

MICHIGAN

NEW YORK

RHODE ISLAND

CONNECTICUT

NEVADA

UTAH

COLORADO

KANSAS

MISSOURI

ILLINOIS

INDIANA

OHIO

PENNSYLVANIA

NEW JERSEY

DELAWARE

MARYLAND

CALIFORNIA

KENTUCKY

WEST VIRGINIA

VIRGINIA

OKLAHOMA

ARKANSAS

TENNESSEE

NORTH CAROLINA

ARIZONA

NEW MEXICO

MISSISSIPPI

ALABAMA GEORGIA

SOUTH CAROLINA

TEXAS

LOUISIANA

FLORIDA

HOOVER (REPUBLICAN)

SMITH (DEMOCRAT)

Congressional Quarterly's Guide to U.S. Elections, 3rd. edition, copyright ©1994. Used with permission. All rights reserved.

States	Electoral Votes	Hoover	Smith	States	Electoral Votes	Hoover	Smith
Alabama	(12)	-	12	Nebraska	(8)	8	-
Arizona	(3)	3	-	Nevada	(3)	3	-
Arkansas	(9)	-	9	New Hampshire	(4)	4	-
California	(13)	13	-	New Jersey	(14)	14	-
Colorado	(6)	6	-	New Mexico	(3)	3	-
Connecticut	(7)	7	-	New York	(45)	45	-
Delaware	(3)	3	-	North Carolina	(12)	12	-
Florida	(6)	6	-	North Dakota	(5)	5	-
Georgia	(14)	-	14	Ohio	(24)	24	-
Idaho	(4)	4	-	Oklahoma	(10)	10	-
Illinois	(29)	29	-	Oregon	(5)	5	-
Indiana	(15)	15	-	Pennsylvania	(38)	38	-
Iowa	(13)	13	-	Rhode Island	(5)	-	5
Kansas	(10)	10	-	South Carolina	(9)	-	9
Kentucky	(13)	13	-	South Dakota	(5)	5	-
Louisiana	(10)	-	10	Tennessee	(12)	12	-
Maine	(6)	6	-	Texas	(20)	20	-
Maryland	(8)	8	-	Utah	(4)	4	-
Massachusetts	(18)	-	18	Vermont	(4)	4	-
Michigan	(15)	15	-	Virginia	(12)	12	-
Minnesota	(12)	12	-	Washington	(7)	7	-
Mississippi	(10)	-	10	West Virginia	(8)	8	-
Missouri	(18)	18	-	Wisconsin	(13)	13	-
Montana	(4)	4	-	Wyoming	(3)	3	-
				Totals	(531)	444	87

1928

PRESIDENTIAL ELECTION RETURNS

STATE	TOTAL VOTE	HERBERT C. HOOVER (Republican)		ALFRED E. SMITH (Democrat)		NORMAN M. THOMAS (Socialist)		WILLIAM Z. FOSTER (Communist)		OTHER		PLURALITY
		Votes	%	Votes	%	Votes	%	Votes	%	Votes	%	
Alabama	248,981	120,725	48.5	127,796	51.3	460	0.2	—		—		7,071 D
Arizona	91,254	52,533	57.6	38,537	42.2	—		184	0.2	—		13,996 R
Arkansas	197,726	77,784	39.3	119,196	60.3	429	0.2	317	0.2	—		41,412 D
California	1,796,656	1,162,323	64.7	614,365	34.2	19,595	1.1	—		373		547,958 R
Colorado	392,242	253,872	64.7	133,131	33.9	3,472	0.9	675	0.2	1,092	0.3	120,741 R
Connecticut	553,118	296,641	53.6	252,085	45.6	3,029	0.5	738	0.1	625	0.1	44,556 R
Delaware	104,602	68,860	65.8	35,354	33.8	329	0.3	59	0.1	—		33,506 R
Florida	252,068	145,860	57.9	101,764	40.4	2,284	0.9	2,160	0.9	—		44,096 R
Georgia	231,592	101,800	44.0	129,604	56.0	124	0.1	64		—		27,804 D
Idaho	151,541	97,322	64.2	52,926	34.9	1,293	0.9	—		—		44,396 R
Illinois	3,107,489	1,769,141	56.9	1,313,817	42.3	19,138	0.6	3,581	0.1	1,812	0.1	455,324 R
Indiana	1,421,314	848,290	59.7	562,691	39.6	3,871	0.3	321		6,141	0.4	285,599 R
Iowa	1,009,189	623,570	61.8	379,011	37.6	2,960	0.3	328		3,320	0.3	244,559 R
Kansas	713,200	513,672	72.0	193,003	27.1	6,205	0.9	320		—		320,669 R
Kentucky	940,521	558,064	59.3	381,070	40.5	783	0.1	288		316		176,994 R
Louisiana	215,833	51,160	23.7	164,655	76.3	—		—		18		113,495 D
Maine	262,170	179,923	68.6	81,179	31.0	1,068	0.4	—		—		98,744 R
Maryland	528,348	301,479	57.1	223,626	42.3	1,701	0.3	636	0.1	906	0.2	77,853 R
Massachusetts	1,577,823	775,566	49.2	792,758	50.2	6,262	0.4	2,461	0.2	776		17,192 D
Michigan	1,372,082	965,396	70.4	396,762	28.9	3,516	0.3	2,881	0.2	3,527	0.3	568,634 R
Minnesota	970,976	560,977	57.8	396,451	40.8	6,774	0.7	4,853	0.5	1,921	0.2	164,526 R
Mississippi	151,568	27,030	17.8	124,538	82.2	—		—		—		97,508 D
Missouri	1,500,845	834,080	55.6	662,684	44.2	3,739	0.2	—		342		171,396 R
Montana	194,108	113,300	58.4	78,578	40.5	1,667	0.9	563	0.3	—		34,722 R
Nebraska	547,128	345,745	63.2	197,950	36.2	3,433	0.6	—		—		147,795 R
Nevada	32,417	18,327	56.5	14,090	43.5	—		—		—		4,237 R
New Hampshire	196,757	115,404	58.7	80,715	41.0	465	0.2	173	0.1	—		34,689 R
New Jersey	1,549,381	926,050	59.8	616,517	39.8	4,897	0.3	1,257	0.1	660		309,533 R
New Mexico	118,077	69,708	59.0	48,211	40.8	—		158	0.1	—		21,497 R
New York	4,405,626	2,193,344	49.8	2,089,863	47.4	107,332	2.4	10,876	0.2	4,211	0.1	103,481 R
North Carolina	635,150	348,923	54.9	286,227	45.1	—		—		—		62,696 R
North Dakota	239,845	131,419	54.8	106,648	44.5	936	0.4	842	0.4	—		24,771 R
Ohio	2,508,346	1,627,546	64.9	864,210	34.5	8,683	0.3	2,836	0.1	5,071	0.2	763,336 R
Oklahoma	618,427	394,046	63.7	219,174	35.4	3,924	0.6	—		1,283	0.2	174,872 R
Oregon	319,942	205,341	64.2	109,223	34.1	2,720	0.9	1,094	0.3	1,564	0.5	96,118 R
Pennsylvania	3,150,612	2,055,382	65.2	1,067,586	33.9	18,647	0.6	4,726	0.2	4,271	0.1	987,796 R
Rhode Island	237,194	117,522	49.5	118,973	50.2	—		283	0.1	416	0.2	1,451 D
South Carolina	68,605	5,858	8.5	62,700	91.4	47	0.1	—		—		56,842 D
South Dakota	261,857	157,603	60.2	102,660	39.2	443	0.2	224	0.1	927	0.4	54,943 R
Tennessee	353,192	195,388	55.3	157,143	44.5	567	0.2	94		—		38,245 R
Texas	717,733	372,324	51.9	344,542	48.0	658	0.1	209		—		27,782 R
Utah	176,603	94,618	53.6	80,985	45.9	954	0.5	46		—		13,633 R
Vermont	135,191	90,404	66.9	44,440	32.9	—		—		347	0.3	45,964 R
Virginia	305,364	164,609	53.9	140,146	45.9	249	0.1	179	0.1	181	0.1	24,463 R
Washington	500,840	335,844	67.1	156,772	31.3	2,615	0.5	1,541	0.3	4,068	0.8	179,072 R
West Virginia	642,752	375,551	58.4	263,784	41.0	1,313	0.2	401	0.1	1,703	0.3	111,767 R
Wisconsin	1,016,831	544,205	53.5	450,259	44.3	18,213	1.8	1,528	0.2	2,626	0.3	93,946 R
Wyoming	82,835	52,748	63.7	29,299	35.4	788	1.0	—		—		23,449 R
Totals	36,805,951	21,437,277	58.2	15,007,698	40.8	265,583	0.7	46,896	0.1	48,497	0.1	6,429,579 R

PRESIDENTIAL ELECTION OF
1932

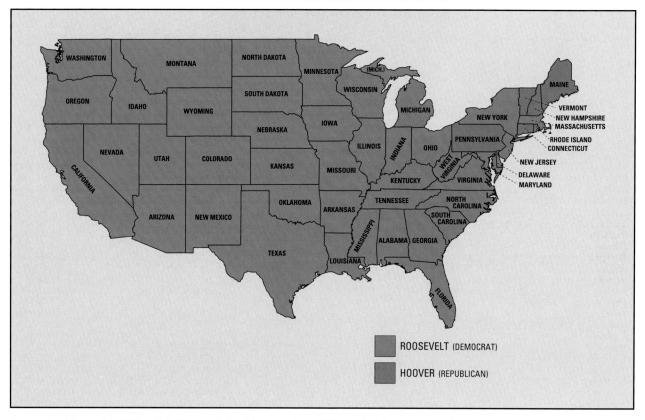

ROOSEVELT (DEMOCRAT)

HOOVER (REPUBLICAN)

Congressional Quarterly's Guide to U.S. Elections, 3rd. edition, copyright ©1994. Used with permission. All rights reserved.

States	Electoral Votes	Roosevelt	Hoover	States	Electoral Votes	Roosevelt	Hoover
Alabama	(11)	11	-	Nebraska	(7)	7	-
Arizona	(3)	3	-	Nevada	(3)	3	-
Arkansas	(9)	9	-	New Hampshire	(4)	-	4
California	(22)	22	-	New Jersey	(16)	16	-
Colorado	(6)	6	-	New Mexico	(3)	3	-
Connecticut	(8)	-	8	New York	(47)	47	-
Delaware	(3)	-	3	North Carolina	(13)	13	-
Florida	(7)	7	-	North Dakota	(4)	4	-
Georgia	(12)	12	-	Ohio	(26)	26	-
Idaho	(4)	4	-	Oklahoma	(11)	11	-
Illinois	(29)	29	-	Oregon	(5)	5	-
Indiana	(14)	14	-	Pennsylvania	(36)	-	36
Iowa	(11)	11	-	Rhode Island	(4)	4	-
Kansas	(9)	9	-	South Carolina	(8)	8	-
Kentucky	(11)	11	-	South Dakota	(4)	4	-
Louisiana	(10)	10	-	Tennessee	(11)	11	-
Maine	(5)	-	5	Texas	(23)	23	-
Maryland	(8)	8	-	Utah	(4)	4	-
Massachusetts	(17)	17	-	Vermont	(3)	-	3
Michigan	(19)	19	-	Virginia	(11)	11	-
Minnesota	(11)	11	-	Washington	(8)	8	-
Mississippi	(9)	9	-	West Virginia	(8)	8	-
Missouri	(15)	15	-	Wisconsin	(12)	12	-
Montana	(4)	4	-	Wyoming	(3)	3	-
				Totals	**(531)**	**472**	**59**

1932

PRESIDENTIAL ELECTION RETURNS

STATE	TOTAL VOTE	FRANKLIN D. ROOSEVELT (Democrat)		HERBERT C. HOOVER (Republican)		NORMAN M. THOMAS (Socialist)		WILLIAM Z. FOSTER (Communist)		OTHER		PLURALITY	
		Votes	%	Votes	%	Votes	%	Votes	%	Votes	%		
Alabama	245,303	207,910	84.8	34,675	14.1	2,030	0.8	675	0.3	13		173,235	D
Arizona	118,251	79,264	67.0	36,104	30.5	2,618	2.2	256	0.2	9		43,160	D
Arkansas	216,569	186,829	86.3	27,465	12.7	1,166	0.5	157	0.1	952	0.4	159,364	D
California	2,266,972	1,324,157	58.4	847,902	37.4	63,299	2.8	1,023		30,591	1.3	476,255	D
Colorado	457,696	250,877	54.8	189,617	41.4	13,591	3.0	787	0.2	2,824	0.6	61,260	D
Connecticut	594,183	281,632	47.4	288,420	48.5	20,480	3.4	1,364	0.2	2,287	0.4	6,788	R
Delaware	112,901	54,319	48.1	57,073	50.6	1,376	1.2	133	0.1	—		2,754	R
Florida	276,943	206,307	74.5	69,170	25.0	775	0.3	—		691	0.2	137,137	D
Georgia	255,590	234,118	91.6	19,863	7.8	461	0.2	23		1,125	0.4	214,255	D
Idaho	186,520	109,479	58.7	71,312	38.2	526	0.3	491	0.3	4,712	2.5	38,167	D
Illinois	3,407,926	1,882,304	55.2	1,432,756	42.0	67,258	2.0	15,582	0.5	10,026	0.3	449,548	D
Indiana	1,576,927	862,054	54.7	677,184	42.9	21,388	1.4	2,187	0.1	14,114	0.9	184,870	D
Iowa	1,036,687	598,019	57.7	414,433	40.0	20,467	2.0	559	0.1	3,209	0.3	183,586	D
Kansas	791,978	424,204	53.6	349,498	44.1	18,276	2.3	—		—		74,706	D
Kentucky	983,059	580,574	59.1	394,716	40.2	3,853	0.4	271		3,645	0.4	185,858	D
Louisiana	268,804	249,418	92.8	18,853	7.0	—		—		533	0.2	230,565	D
Maine	298,444	128,907	43.2	166,631	55.8	2,489	0.8	162	0.1	255	0.1	37,724	R
Maryland	511,054	314,314	61.5	184,184	36.0	10,489	2.1	1,031	0.2	1,036	0.2	130,130	D
Massachusetts	1,580,114	800,148	50.6	736,959	46.6	34,305	2.2	4,821	0.3	3,881	0.2	63,189	D
Michigan	1,664,765	871,700	52.4	739,894	44.4	39,205	2.4	9,318	0.6	4,648	0.3	131,806	D
Minnesota	1,002,843	600,806	59.9	363,959	36.3	25,476	2.5	6,101	0.6	6,501	0.6	236,847	D
Mississippi	146,034	140,168	96.0	5,180	3.5	686	0.5	—		—		134,988	D
Missouri	1,609,894	1,025,406	63.7	564,713	35.1	16,374	1.0	568		2,833	0.2	460,693	D
Montana	216,479	127,286	58.8	78,078	36.1	7,891	3.6	1,775	0.8	1,449	0.7	49,208	D
Nebraska	570,135	359,082	63.0	201,177	35.3	9,876	1.7	—		—		157,905	D
Nevada	41,430	28,756	69.4	12,674	30.6	—		—		—		16,082	D
New Hampshire	205,520	100,680	49.0	103,629	50.4	947	0.5	264	0.1	—		2,949	R
New Jersey	1,630,063	806,630	49.5	775,684	47.6	42,998	2.6	2,915	0.2	1,836	0.1	30,946	D
New Mexico	151,606	95,089	62.7	54,217	35.8	1,776	1.2	135	0.1	389	0.3	40,872	D
New York	4,688,614	2,534,959	54.1	1,937,963	41.3	177,397	3.8	27,956	0.6	10,339	0.2	596,996	D
North Carolina	711,498	497,566	69.9	208,344	29.3	5,588	0.8	—		—		289,222	D
North Dakota	256,290	178,350	69.6	71,772	28.0	3,521	1.4	830	0.3	1,817	0.7	106,578	D
Ohio	2,609,728	1,301,695	49.9	1,227,319	47.0	64,094	2.5	7,231	0.3	9,389	0.4	74,376	D
Oklahoma	704,633	516,468	73.3	188,165	26.7	—		—		—		328,303	D
Oregon	368,751	213,871	58.0	136,019	36.9	15,450	4.2	1,681	0.5	1,730	0.5	77,852	D
Pennsylvania	2,859,021	1,295,948	45.3	1,453,540	50.8	91,119	3.2	5,658	0.2	12,756	0.4	157,592	R
Rhode Island	266,170	146,604	55.1	115,266	43.3	3,138	1.2	546	0.2	616	0.2	31,338	D
South Carolina	104,407	102,347	98.0	1,978	1.9	82	0.1	—		—		100,369	D
South Dakota	288,438	183,515	63.6	99,212	34.4	1,551	0.5	364	0.1	3,796	1.3	84,303	D
Tennessee	390,273	259,473	66.5	126,752	32.5	1,796	0.5	254	0.1	1,998	0.5	132,721	D
Texas	874,382	771,109	88.2	98,218	11.2	4,414	0.5	207		434		672,891	D
Utah	206,578	116,750	56.5	84,795	41.0	4,087	2.0	946	0.5	—		31,955	D
Vermont	136,980	56,266	41.1	78,984	57.7	1,533	1.1	195	0.1	2		22,718	R
Virginia	297,942	203,979	68.5	89,637	30.1	2,382	0.8	86		1,858	0.6	114,342	D
Washington	614,814	353,260	57.5	208,645	33.9	17,080	2.8	2,972	0.5	32,857	5.3	144,615	D
West Virginia	743,774	405,124	54.5	330,731	44.5	5,133	0.7	444	0.1	2,342	0.3	74,393	D
Wisconsin	1,114,814	707,410	63.5	347,741	31.2	53,379	4.8	3,105	0.3	3,179	0.3	359,669	D
Wyoming	96,962	54,370	56.1	39,583	40.8	2,829	2.9	180	0.2	—		14,787	D
Totals	**39,758,759**	**22,829,501**	**57.4**	**15,760,684**	**39.6**	**884,649**	**2.2**	**103,253**	**0.3**	**180,672**	**0.5**	**7,068,817**	**D**

PRESIDENTIAL ELECTION OF

1936

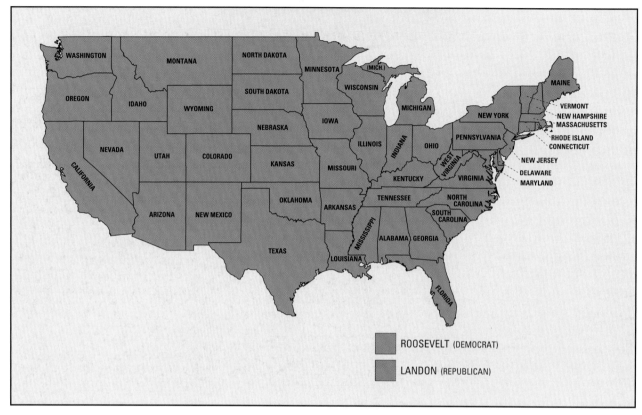

Congressional Quarterly's Guide to U.S. Elections, 3rd. edition, copyright ©1994. Used with permission. All rights reserved.

States	Electoral Votes	Roosevelt	Landon	States	Electoral Votes	Roosevelt	Landon
Alabama	(11)	11	-	Nebraska	(7)	7	-
Arizona	(3)	3	-	Nevada	(3)	3	-
Arkansas	(9)	9	-	New Hampshire	(4)	4	-
California	(22)	22	-	New Jersey	(16)	16	-
Colorado	(6)	6	-	New Mexico	(3)	3	-
Connecticut	(8)	8	-	New York	(47)	47	-
Delaware	(3)	3	-	North Carolina	(13)	13	-
Florida	(7)	7	-	North Dakota	(4)	4	-
Georgia	(12)	12	-	Ohio	(26)	26	-
Idaho	(4)	4	-	Oklahoma	(11)	11	-
Illinois	(29)	29	-	Oregon	(5)	5	-
Indiana	(14)	14	-	Pennsylvania	(36)	36	-
Iowa	(11)	11	-	Rhode Island	(4)	4	-
Kansas	(9)	9	-	South Carolina	(8)	8	-
Kentucky	(11)	11	-	South Dakota	(4)	4	-
Louisiana	(10)	10	-	Tennessee	(11)	11	-
Maine	(5)	-	5	Texas	(23)	23	-
Maryland	(8)	8	-	Utah	(4)	4	-
Massachusetts	(17)	17	-	Vermont	(3)	-	3
Michigan	(19)	19	-	Virginia	(11)	11	-
Minnesota	(11)	11	-	Washington	(8)	8	-
Mississippi	(9)	9	-	West Virginia	(8)	8	-
Missouri	(15)	15	-	Wisconsin	(12)	12	-
Montana	(4)	4	-	Wyoming	(3)	3	-
				Totals	**(531)**	**523**	**8**

1936

PRESIDENTIAL ELECTION RETURNS

STATE	TOTAL VOTE	FRANKLIN D. ROOSEVELT (Democrat)		ALFRED M. LANDON (Republican)		WILLIAM LEMKE (Union)		NORMAN M. THOMAS (Socialist)		OTHER		PLURALITY	
		Votes	%	Votes	%	Votes	%	Votes	%	Votes	%		
Alabama	275,744	238,196	86.4	35,358	12.8	551	0.2	242	0.1	1,397	0.5	202,838	D
Arizona	124,163	86,722	69.8	33,433	26.9	3,307	2.7	317	0.3	384	0.3	53,289	D
Arkansas	179,431	146,765	81.8	32,049	17.9	4		446	0.2	167	0.1	114,716	D
California	2,638,882	1,766,836	67.0	836,431	31.7	—		11,331	0.4	24,284	0.9	930,405	D
Colorado	488,685	295,021	60.4	181,267	37.1	9,962	2.0	1,594	0.3	841	0.2	113,754	D
Connecticut	690,723	382,129	55.3	278,685	40.3	21,805	3.2	5,683	0.8	2,421	0.4	103,444	D
Delaware	127,603	69,702	54.6	57,236	44.9	442	0.3	172	0.1	51		12,466	D
Florida	327,436	249,117	76.1	78,248	23.9	—		—		71		170,869	D
Georgia	293,170	255,363	87.1	36,943	12.6	136		68		660	0.2	218,420	D
Idaho	199,617	125,683	63.0	66,256	33.2	7,678	3.8	—		—		59,427	D
Illinois	3,956,522	2,282,999	57.7	1,570,393	39.7	89,439	2.3	7,530	0.2	6,161	0.2	712,606	D
Indiana	1,650,897	934,974	56.6	691,570	41.9	19,407	1.2	3,856	0.2	1,090	0.1	243,404	D
Iowa	1,142,737	621,756	54.4	487,977	42.7	29,687	2.6	1,373	0.1	1,944	0.2	133,779	D
Kansas	865,507	464,520	53.7	397,727	46.0	494	0.1	2,766	0.3	—		66,793	D
Kentucky	926,214	541,944	58.5	369,702	39.9	12,501	1.3	627	0.1	1,440	0.2	172,242	D
Louisiana	329,778	292,894	88.8	36,791	11.2	—		—		93		256,103	D
Maine	304,240	126,333	41.5	168,823	55.5	7,581	2.5	783	0.3	720	0.2	42,490	R
Maryland	624,896	389,612	62.3	231,435	37.0	—		1,629	0.3	2,220	0.4	158,177	D
Massachusetts	1,840,357	942,716	51.2	768,613	41.8	118,639	6.4	5,111	0.3	5,278	0.3	174,103	D
Michigan	1,805,098	1,016,794	56.3	699,733	38.8	75,795	4.2	8,208	0.5	4,568	0.3	317,061	D
Minnesota	1,129,975	698,811	61.8	350,461	31.0	74,296	6.6	2,872	0.3	3,535	0.3	348,350	D
Mississippi	162,142	157,333	97.0	4,467	2.8	—		342	0.2	—		152,866	D
Missouri	1,828,635	1,111,043	60.8	697,891	38.2	14,630	0.8	3,454	0.2	1,617	0.1	413,152	D
Montana	230,502	159,690	69.3	63,598	27.6	5,539	2.4	1,066	0.5	609	0.3	96,092	D
Nebraska	608,023	347,445	57.1	247,731	40.7	12,847	2.1	—		—		99,714	D
Nevada	43,848	31,925	72.8	11,923	27.2	—		—		—		20,002	D
New Hampshire	218,114	108,460	49.7	104,642	48.0	4,819	2.2	—		193	0.1	3,818	D
New Jersey	1,820,437	1,083,850	59.5	720,322	39.6	9,407	0.5	3,931	0.2	2,927	0.2	363,528	D
New Mexico	169,135	106,037	62.7	61,727	36.5	924	0.5	343	0.2	104	0.1	44,310	D
New York	5,596,398	3,293,222	58.8	2,180,670	39.0	—		86,897	1.6	35,609	0.6	1,112,552	D
North Carolina	839,475	616,141	73.4	223,294	26.6	2		21		17		392,847	D
North Dakota	273,716	163,148	59.6	72,751	26.6	36,708	13.4	552	0.2	557	0.2	90,397	D
Ohio	3,012,660	1,747,140	58.0	1,127,855	37.4	132,212	4.4	167		5,286	0.2	619,285	D
Oklahoma	749,740	501,069	66.8	245,122	32.7	—		2,221	0.3	1,328	0.2	255,947	D
Oregon	414,021	266,733	64.4	122,706	29.6	21,831	5.3	2,143	0.5	608	0.1	144,027	D
Pennsylvania	4,138,105	2,353,788	56.9	1,690,300	40.8	67,467	1.6	14,375	0.3	12,175	0.3	663,488	D
Rhode Island	310,278	164,338	53.0	125,031	40.3	19,569	6.3	—		1,340	0.4	39,307	D
South Carolina	115,437	113,791	98.6	1,646	1.4	—		—		—		112,145	D
South Dakota	296,452	160,137	54.0	125,977	42.5	10,338	3.5	—		—		34,160	D
Tennessee	477,086	328,083	68.8	147,055	30.8	296	0.1	692	0.1	960	0.2	181,028	D
Texas	849,701	739,952	87.1	104,661	12.3	3,187	0.4	1,122	0.1	779	0.1	635,291	D
Utah	216,679	150,248	69.3	64,555	29.8	1,121	0.5	432	0.2	323	0.1	85,693	D
Vermont	143,689	62,124	43.2	81,023	56.4	—		—		542	0.4	18,899	R
Virginia	334,590	234,980	70.2	98,336	29.4	233	0.1	313	0.1	728	0.2	136,644	D
Washington	692,338	459,579	66.4	206,892	29.9	17,463	2.5	3,496	0.5	4,908	0.7	252,687	D
West Virginia	829,945	502,582	60.6	325,358	39.2	—		832	0.1	1,173	0.1	177,224	D
Wisconsin	1,258,560	802,984	63.8	380,828	30.3	60,297	4.8	10,626	0.8	3,825	0.3	422,156	D
Wyoming	103,382	62,624	60.6	38,739	37.5	1,653	1.6	200	0.2	166	0.2	23,885	D
Totals	45,654,763	27,757,333	60.8	16,684,231	36.5	892,267	2.0	187,833	0.4	133,099	0.3	11,073,102	D

PRESIDENTIAL ELECTION OF

1940

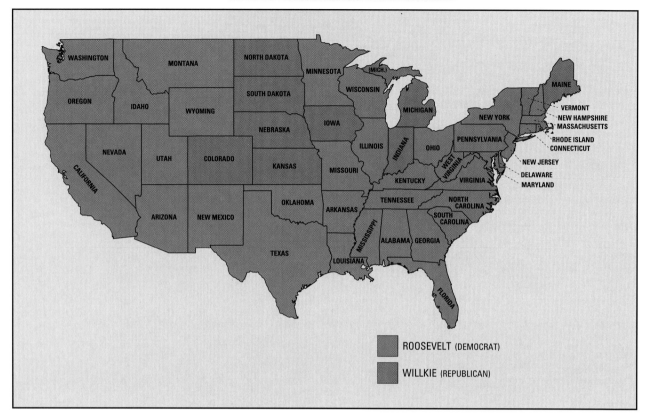

ROOSEVELT (DEMOCRAT)

WILLKIE (REPUBLICAN)

Congressional Quarterly's Guide to U.S. Elections, 3rd. edition, copyright ©1994. Used with permission. All rights reserved.

States	Electoral Votes	Roosevelt	Willkie	States	Electoral Votes	Roosevelt	Willkie
Alabama	(11)	11	-	Nebraska	(7)	-	7
Arizona	(3)	3	-	Nevada	(3)	3	-
Arkansas	(9)	9	-	New Hampshire	(4)	4	-
California	(22)	22	-	New Jersey	(16)	16	-
Colorado	(6)	-	6	New Mexico	(3)	3	-
Connecticut	(8)	8	-	New York	(47)	47	-
Delaware	(3)	3	-	North Carolina	(13)	13	-
Florida	(7)	7	-	North Dakota	(4)	-	4
Georgia	(12)	12	-	Ohio	(26)	26	-
Idaho	(4)	4	-	Oklahoma	(11)	11	-
Illinois	(29)	29	-	Oregon	(5)	5	-
Indiana	(14)	-	14	Pennsylvania	(36)	36	-
Iowa	(11)	-	11	Rhode Island	(4)	4	-
Kansas	(9)	-	9	South Carolina	(8)	8	-
Kentucky	(11)	11	-	South Dakota	(4)	-	4
Louisiana	(10)	10	-	Tennessee	(11)	11	-
Maine	(5)	-	5	Texas	(23)	23	-
Maryland	(8)	8	-	Utah	(4)	4	-
Massachusetts	(17)	17	-	Vermont	(3)	-	3
Michigan	(19)	-	19	Virginia	(11)	11	-
Minnesota	(11)	11	-	Washington	(8)	8	-
Mississippi	(9)	9	-	West Virginia	(8)	8	-
Missouri	(15)	15	-	Wisconsin	(12)	12	-
Montana	(4)	4	-	Wyoming	(3)	3	-
				Totals	**(531)**	**449**	**82**

1940

PRESIDENTIAL ELECTION RETURNS

STATE	TOTAL VOTE	FRANKLIN D. ROOSEVELT (Democrat)		WENDELL WILLKIE (Republican)		NORMAN M. THOMAS (Socialist)		ROGER W. BABSON (Prohibition)		OTHER		PLURALITY	
		Votes	%	Votes	%	Votes	%	Votes	%	Votes	%		
Alabama	294,219	250,726	85.2	42,184	14.3	100		700	0.2	509	0.2	208,542	D
Arizona	150,039	95,267	63.5	54,030	36.0	—		742	0.5	—		41,237	D
Arkansas	200,429	157,213	78.4	42,122	21.0	301	0.2	793	0.4	—		115,091	D
California	3,268,791	1,877,618	57.4	1,351,419	41.3	16,506	0.5	9,400	0.3	13,848	0.4	526,199	D
Colorado	549,004	265,554	48.4	279,576	50.9	1,899	0.3	1,597	0.3	378	0.1	14,022	R
Connecticut	781,502	417,621	53.4	361,819	46.3	—		—		2,062	0.3	55,802	D
Delaware	136,374	74,599	54.7	61,440	45.1	115	0.1	220	0.2	—		13,159	D
Florida	485,640	359,334	74.0	126,158	26.0	—		—		148		233,176	D
Georgia	312,686	265,194	84.8	46,495	14.9	—		983	0.3	14		218,699	D
Idaho	235,168	127,842	54.4	106,553	45.3	497	0.2	—		276	0.1	21,289	D
Illinois	4,217,935	2,149,934	51.0	2,047,240	48.5	10,914	0.3	9,190	0.2	657		102,694	D
Indiana	1,782,747	874,063	49.0	899,466	50.5	2,075	0.1	6,437	0.4	706		25,403	R
Iowa	1,215,432	578,802	47.6	632,370	52.0	—		2,284	0.2	1,976	0.2	53,568	R
Kansas	860,297	364,725	42.4	489,169	56.9	2,347	0.3	4,056	0.5	—		124,444	R
Kentucky	970,163	557,322	57.4	410,384	42.3	1,014	0.1	1,443	0.1	—		146,938	D
Louisiana	372,305	319,751	85.9	52,446	14.1	—		—		108		267,305	D
Maine	320,840	156,478	48.8	163,951	51.1	—		—		411	0.1	7,473	R
Maryland	660,104	384,546	58.3	269,534	40.8	4,093	0.6	—		1,931	0.3	115,012	D
Massachusetts	2,026,993	1,076,522	53.1	939,700	46.4	4,091	0.2	1,370	0.1	5,310	0.3	136,822	D
Michigan	2,085,929	1,032,991	49.5	1,039,917	49.9	7,593	0.4	1,795	0.1	3,633	0.2	6,926	R
Minnesota	1,251,188	644,196	51.5	596,274	47.7	5,454	0.4	—		5,264	0.4	47,922	D
Mississippi	175,824	168,267	95.7	7,364	4.2	193	0.1	—		—		160,903	D
Missouri	1,833,729	958,476	52.3	871,009	47.5	2,226	0.1	1,809	0.1	209		87,467	D
Montana	247,873	145,698	58.8	99,579	40.2	1,443	0.6	664	0.3	489	0.2	46,119	D
Nebraska	615,878	263,677	42.8	352,201	57.2	—		—		—		88,524	R
Nevada	53,174	31,945	60.1	21,229	39.9	—		—		—		10,716	D
New Hampshire	235,419	125,292	53.2	110,127	46.8	—		—		—		15,165	D
New Jersey	1,972,552	1,016,808	51.5	945,475	47.9	2,433	0.1	873		6,963	0.4	71,333	D
New Mexico	183,258	103,699	56.6	79,315	43.3	144	0.1	100	0.1	—		24,384	D
New York	6,301,596	3,251,918	51.6	3,027,478	48.0	18,950	0.3	3,250	0.1	—		224,440	D
North Carolina	822,648	609,015	74.0	213,633	26.0	—		—		—		395,382	D
North Dakota	280,775	124,036	44.2	154,590	55.1	1,279	0.5	325	0.1	545	0.2	30,554	R
Ohio	3,319,912	1,733,139	52.2	1,586,773	47.8	—		—		—		146,366	D
Oklahoma	826,212	474,313	57.4	348,872	42.2	—		3,027	0.4	—		125,441	D
Oregon	481,240	258,415	53.7	219,555	45.6	398	0.1	154		2,718	0.6	38,860	D
Pennsylvania	4,078,714	2,171,035	53.2	1,889,848	46.3	10,967	0.3	—		6,864	0.2	281,187	D
Rhode Island	321,152	182,181	56.7	138,654	43.2	—		74		243	0.1	43,527	D
South Carolina	99,830	95,470	95.6	4,360	4.4	—		—		—		91,110	D
South Dakota	308,427	131,362	42.6	177,065	57.4	—		—		—		45,703	R
Tennessee	522,823	351,601	67.3	169,153	32.4	463	0.1	1,606	0.3	—		182,448	D
Texas	1,124,437	909,974	80.9	212,692	18.9	628	0.1	928	0.1	215		697,282	D
Utah	247,819	154,277	62.3	93,151	37.6	200	0.1	—		191	0.1	61,126	D
Vermont	143,062	64,269	44.9	78,371	54.8	—		—		422	0.3	14,102	R
Virginia	346,608	235,961	68.1	109,363	31.6	282	0.1	882	0.3	120		126,598	D
Washington	793,833	462,145	58.2	322,123	40.6	4,586	0.6	1,686	0.2	3,293	0.4	140,022	D
West Virginia	868,076	495,662	57.1	372,414	42.9	—		—		—		123,248	D
Wisconsin	1,405,522	704,821	50.1	679,206	48.3	15,071	1.1	2,148	0.2	4,276	0.3	25,615	D
Wyoming	112,240	59,287	52.8	52,633	46.9	148	0.1	172	0.2	—		6,654	D
Totals	49,900,418	27,313,041	54.7	22,348,480	44.8	116,410	0.2	58,708	0.1	63,779	0.1	4,964,561	D

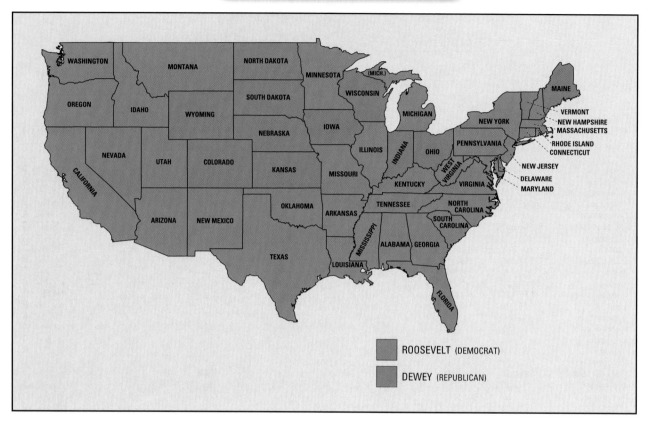

PRESIDENTIAL ELECTION OF

1944

States	Electoral Votes	Roosevelt	Dewey	States	Electoral Votes	Roosevelt	Dewey
Alabama	(11)	11	-	Nebraska	(6)	-	6
Arizona	(4)	4	-	Nevada	(3)	3	-
Arkansas	(9)	9	-	New Hampshire	(4)	4	-
California	(25)	25	-	New Jersey	(16)	16	-
Colorado	(6)	-	6	New Mexico	(4)	4	-
Connecticut	(8)	8	-	New York	(47)	47	-
Delaware	(3)	3	-	North Carolina	(14)	14	-
Florida	(8)	8	-	North Dakota	(4)	-	4
Georgia	(12)	12	-	Ohio	(25)	-	25
Idaho	(4)	4	-	Oklahoma	(10)	10	-
Illinois	(28)	28	-	Oregon	(6)	6	-
Indiana	(13)	-	13	Pennsylvania	(35)	35	-
Iowa	(10)	-	10	Rhode Island	(4)	4	-
Kansas	(8)	-	8	South Carolina	(8)	8	-
Kentucky	(11)	11	-	South Dakota	(4)	-	4
Louisiana	(10)	10	-	Tennessee	(12)	12	-
Maine	(5)	-	5	Texas	(23)	23	-
Maryland	(8)	8	-	Utah	(4)	4	-
Massachusetts	(16)	16	-	Vermont	(3)	-	3
Michigan	(19)	19	-	Virginia	(11)	11	-
Minnesota	(11)	11	-	Washington	(8)	8	-
Mississippi	(9)	9	-	West Virginia	(8)	8	-
Missouri	(15)	15	-	Wisconsin	(12)	-	12
Montana	(4)	4	-	Wyoming	(3)	-	3
				Totals	**(531)**	**432**	**99**

1944

PRESIDENTIAL ELECTION RETURNS

STATE	TOTAL VOTE	FRANKLIN D. ROOSEVELT (Democrat)		THOMAS E. DEWEY (Republican)		NORMAN M. THOMAS (Socialist)		CLAUDE A. WATSON (Prohibition)		OTHER		PLURALITY	
		Votes	%	Votes	%	Votes	%	Votes	%	Votes	%		
Alabama	244,743	198,918	81.3	44,540	18.2	190	0.1	1,095	0.4	—		154,378	D
Arizona	137,634	80,926	58.8	56,287	40.9	—		421	0.3	—		24,639	D
Arkansas	212,954	148,965	70.0	63,551	29.8	438	0.2	—		—		85,414	D
California	3,520,875	1,988,564	56.5	1,512,965	43.0	2,515	0.1	14,770	0.4	2,061	0.1	475,599	D
Colorado	505,039	234,331	46.4	268,731	53.2	1,977	0.4	—		—		34,400	R
Connecticut	831,990	435,146	52.3	390,527	46.9	5,097	0.6	—		1,220	0.1	44,619	D
Delaware	125,361	68,166	54.4	56,747	45.3	154	0.1	294	0.2	—		11,419	D
Florida	482,803	339,377	70.3	143,215	29.7	—		—		211		196,162	D
Georgia	328,129	268,187	81.7	59,900	18.3	6		36		—		208,287	D
Idaho	208,321	107,399	51.6	100,137	48.1	282	0.1	503	0.2	—		7,262	D
Illinois	4,036,061	2,079,479	51.5	1,939,314	48.0	180		7,411	0.2	9,677	0.2	140,165	D
Indiana	1,672,091	781,403	46.7	875,891	52.4	2,223	0.1	12,574	0.8	—		94,488	R
Iowa	1,052,599	499,876	47.5	547,267	52.0	1,511	0.1	3,752	0.4	193		47,391	R
Kansas	733,776	287,458	39.2	442,096	60.2	1,613	0.2	2,609	0.4	—		154,638	R
Kentucky	867,924	472,589	54.5	392,448	45.2	535	0.1	2,023	0.2	329		80,141	D
Louisiana	349,383	281,564	80.6	67,750	19.4	—		—		69		213,814	D
Maine	296,400	140,631	47.4	155,434	52.4	—		—		335	0.1	14,803	R
Maryland	608,439	315,490	51.9	292,949	48.1	—		—		—		22,541	D
Massachusetts	1,960,665	1,035,296	52.8	921,350	47.0	—		973		3,046	0.2	113,946	D
Michigan	2,205,223	1,106,899	50.2	1,084,423	49.2	4,598	0.2	6,503	0.3	2,800	0.1	22,476	D
Minnesota	1,125,504	589,864	52.4	527,416	46.9	5,048	0.4	—		3,176	0.3	62,448	D
Mississippi	180,234	168,621	93.6	11,613	6.4	—		—		—		157,008	D
Missouri	1,571,697	807,356	51.4	761,175	48.4	1,751	0.1	1,195	0.1	220		46,181	D
Montana	207,355	112,556	54.3	93,163	44.9	1,296	0.6	340	0.2	—		19,393	D
Nebraska	563,126	233,246	41.4	329,880	58.6	—		—		—		96,634	R
Nevada	54,234	29,623	54.6	24,611	45.4	—		—		—		5,012	D
New Hampshire	229,625	119,663	52.1	109,916	47.9	46		—		—		9,747	D
New Jersey	1,963,761	987,874	50.3	961,335	49.0	3,358	0.2	4,255	0.2	6,939	0.4	26,539	D
New Mexico	152,225	81,389	53.5	70,688	46.4	—		148	0.1	—		10,701	D
New York	6,316,790	3,304,238	52.3	2,987,647	47.3	10,553	0.2	—		14,352	0.2	316,591	D
North Carolina	790,554	527,399	66.7	263,155	33.3	—		—		—		264,244	D
North Dakota	220,182	100,144	45.5	118,535	53.8	954	0.4	549	0.2	—		18,391	R
Ohio	3,153,056	1,570,763	49.8	1,582,293	50.2	—		—		—		11,530	R
Oklahoma	722,636	401,549	55.6	319,424	44.2	—		1,663	0.2	—		82,125	D
Oregon	480,147	248,635	51.8	225,365	46.9	3,785	0.8	2,362	0.5	—		23,270	D
Pennsylvania	3,794,793	1,940,479	51.1	1,835,054	48.4	11,721	0.3	5,750	0.2	1,789		105,425	D
Rhode Island	299,276	175,356	58.6	123,487	41.3	—		433	0.1	—		51,869	D
South Carolina	103,382	90,601	87.6	4,617	4.5	—		365	0.4	7,799	7.5	82,802	D
South Dakota	232,076	96,711	41.7	135,365	58.3	—		—		—		38,654	R
Tennessee	510,692	308,707	60.4	200,311	39.2	792	0.2	882	0.2	—		108,396	D
Texas	1,150,334	821,605	71.4	191,423	16.6	594	0.1	1,018	0.1	135,694	11.8	630,182	D
Utah	248,319	150,088	60.4	97,891	39.4	340	0.1	—		—		52,197	D
Vermont	125,361	53,820	42.9	71,527	57.1	—		—		14		17,707	R
Virginia	388,485	242,276	62.4	145,243	37.4	417	0.1	459	0.1	90		97,033	D
Washington	856,328	486,774	56.8	361,689	42.2	3,824	0.4	2,396	0.3	1,645	0.2	125,085	D
West Virginia	715,596	392,777	54.9	322,819	45.1	—		—		—		69,958	D
Wisconsin	1,339,152	650,413	48.6	674,532	50.4	13,205	1.0	—		1,002	0.1	24,119	R
Wyoming	101,340	49,419	48.8	51,921	51.2	—		—		—		2,502	R
Totals	47,976,670	25,612,610	53.4	22,017,617	45.9	79,003	0.2	74,779	0.2	192,661	0.4	3,594,993	D

PRESIDENTIAL ELECTION OF

1948

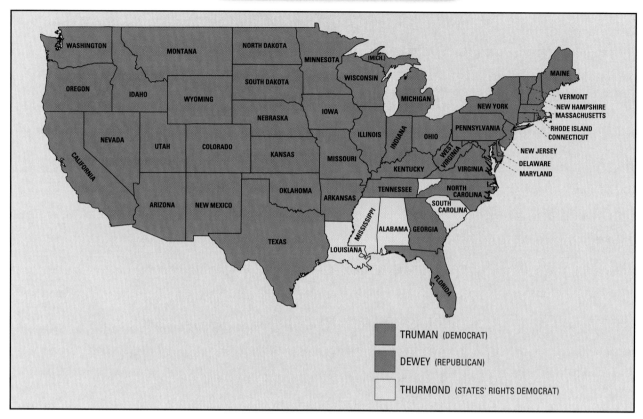

TRUMAN (DEMOCRAT)

DEWEY (REPUBLICAN)

THURMOND (STATES' RIGHTS DEMOCRAT)

Congressional Quarterly's Guide to U.S. Elections, 3rd. edition, copyright ©1994. Used with permission. All rights reserved.

States	Electoral Votes	Truman	Dewey	Thurmond	States	Electoral Votes	Truman	Dewey	Thurmond
Alabama	(11)	-	-	11	Nebraska	(6)	-	6	-
Arizona	(4)	4	-	-	Nevada	(3)	3	-	-
Arkansas	(9)	9	-	-	New Hampshire	(4)	-	4	-
California	(25)	25	-	-	New Jersey	(16)	-	16	-
Colorado	(6)	6	-	-	New Mexico	(4)	4	-	-
Connecticut	(8)	-	8	-	New York	(47)	-	47	-
Delaware	(3)	-	3	-	North Carolina	(14)	14	-	-
Florida	(8)	8	-	-	North Dakota	(4)	-	4	-
Georgia	(12)	12	-	-	Ohio	(25)	25	-	-
Idaho	(4)	4	-	-	Oklahoma	(10)	10	-	-
Illinois	(28)	28	-	-	Oregon	(6)	-	6	-
Indiana	(13)	-	13	-	Pennsylvania	(35)	-	35	-
Iowa	(10)	10	-	-	Rhode Island	(4)	4	-	-
Kansas	(8)	-	8	-	South Carolina	(8)	-	-	8
Kentucky	(11)	11	-	-	South Dakota	(4)	-	4	-
Louisiana	(10)	-	-	10	Tennessee	(12)	11	-	1
Maine	(5)	-	5	-	Texas	(23)	23	-	-
Maryland	(8)	-	8	-	Utah	(4)	4	-	-
Massachusetts	(16)	16	-	-	Vermont	(3)	-	3	-
Michigan	(19)	-	19	-	Virginia	(11)	11	-	-
Minnesota	(11)	11	-	-	Washington	(8)	8	-	-
Mississippi	(9)	-	-	9	West Virginia	(8)	8	-	-
Missouri	(15)	15	-	-	Wisconsin	(12)	12	-	-
Montana	(4)	4	-	-	Wyoming	(3)	3	-	-
					Totals	**(531)**	**303**	**189**	**39**

1948

PRESIDENTIAL ELECTION RETURNS

STATE	TOTAL VOTE	HARRY S. TRUMAN (Democrat)		THOMAS E. DEWEY (Republican)		J. STROM THURMOND (States' Rights Democrat)		HENRY A. WALLACE (Progressive)		OTHER		PLURALITY	
		Votes	%	Votes	%	Votes	%	Votes	%	Votes	%		
Alabama	214,980	—		40,930	19.0	171,443	79.7	1,522	0.7	1,085	0.5	130,513	SR
Arizona	177,065	95,251	53.8	77,597	43.8	—		3,310	1.9	907	0.5	17,654	D
Arkansas	242,475	149,659	61.7	50,959	21.0	40,068	16.5	751	0.3	1,038	0.4	98,700	D
California	4,021,538	1,913,134	47.6	1,895,269	47.1	1,228		190,381	4.7	21,526	0.5	17,865	D
Colorado	515,237	267,288	51.9	239,714	46.5	—		6,115	1.2	2,120	0.4	27,574	D
Connecticut	883,518	423,297	47.9	437,754	49.5	—		13,713	1.6	8,754	1.0	14,457	R
Delaware	139,073	67,813	48.8	69,588	50.0	—		1,050	0.8	622	0.4	1,775	R
Florida	577,643	281,988	48.8	194,280	33.6	89,755	15.5	11,620	2.0	—		87,708	D
Georgia	418,844	254,646	60.8	76,691	18.3	85,135	20.3	1,636	0.4	736	0.2	169,511	D
Idaho	214,816	107,370	50.0	101,514	47.3	—		4,972	2.3	960	0.4	5,856	D
Illinois	3,984,046	1,994,715	50.1	1,961,103	49.2	—		—		28,228	0.7	33,612	D
Indiana	1,656,212	807,831	48.8	821,079	49.6	—		9,649	0.6	17,653	1.1	13,248	R
Iowa	1,038,264	522,380	50.3	494,018	47.6	—		12,125	1.2	9,741	0.9	28,362	D
Kansas	788,819	351,902	44.6	423,039	53.6	—		4,603	0.6	9,275	1.2	71,137	R
Kentucky	822,658	466,756	56.7	341,210	41.5	10,411	1.3	1,567	0.2	2,714	0.3	125,546	D
Louisiana	416,336	136,344	32.7	72,657	17.5	204,290	49.1	3,035	0.7	10		67,946	SR
Maine	264,787	111,916	42.3	150,234	56.7	—		1,884	0.7	753	0.3	38,318	R
Maryland	596,748	286,521	48.0	294,814	49.4	2,489	0.4	9,983	1.7	2,941	0.5	8,293	R
Massachusetts	2,107,146	1,151,788	54.7	909,370	43.2	—		38,157	1.8	7,831	0.4	242,418	D
Michigan	2,109,609	1,003,448	47.6	1,038,595	49.2	—		46,515	2.2	21,051	1.0	35,147	R
Minnesota	1,212,226	692,966	57.2	483,617	39.9	—		27,866	2.3	7,777	0.6	209,349	D
Mississippi	192,190	19,384	10.1	5,043	2.6	167,538	87.2	225	0.1	—		148,154	SR
Missouri	1,578,628	917,315	58.1	655,039	41.5	—		3,998	0.3	2,276	0.1	262,276	D
Montana	224,278	119,071	53.1	96,770	43.1	—		7,313	3.3	1,124	0.5	22,301	D
Nebraska	488,940	224,165	45.8	264,774	54.2	—		—		1		40,609	R
Nevada	62,117	31,291	50.4	29,357	47.3	—		1,469	2.4	—		1,934	D
New Hampshire	231,440	107,995	46.7	121,299	52.4	7		1,970	0.9	169	0.1	13,304	R
New Jersey	1,949,555	895,455	45.9	981,124	50.3	—		42,683	2.2	30,293	1.6	85,669	R
New Mexico	187,063	105,464	56.4	80,303	42.9	—		1,037	0.6	259	0.1	25,161	D
New York	6,177,337	2,780,204	45.0	2,841,163	46.0	—		509,559	8.2	46,411	0.8	60,959	R
North Carolina	791,209	459,070	58.0	258,572	32.7	69,652	8.8	3,915	0.5	—		200,498	D
North Dakota	220,716	95,812	43.4	115,139	52.2	374	0.2	8,391	3.8	1,000	0.5	19,327	R
Ohio	2,936,071	1,452,791	49.5	1,445,684	49.2	—		37,596	1.3	—		7,107	D
Oklahoma	721,599	452,782	62.7	268,817	37.3	—		—		—		183,965	D
Oregon	524,080	243,147	46.4	260,904	49.8	—		14,978	2.9	5,051	1.0	17,757	R
Pennsylvania	3,735,348	1,752,426	46.9	1,902,197	50.9	—		55,161	1.5	25,564	0.7	149,771	R
Rhode Island	327,702	188,736	57.6	135,787	41.4	—		2,619	0.8	560	0.2	52,949	D
South Carolina	142,571	34,423	24.1	5,386	3.8	102,607	72.0	154	0.1	1		68,184	SR
South Dakota	250,105	117,653	47.0	129,651	51.8	—		2,801	1.1	—		11,998	R
Tennessee	550,283	270,402	49.1	202,914	36.9	73,815	13.4	1,864	0.3	1,288	0.2	67,488	D
Texas	1,249,577	824,235	66.0	303,467	24.3	113,920	9.1	3,918	0.3	4,037	0.3	520,768	D
Utah	276,306	149,151	54.0	124,402	45.0	—		2,679	1.0	74		24,749	D
Vermont	123,382	45,557	36.9	75,926	61.5	—		1,279	1.0	620	0.5	30,369	R
Virginia	419,256	200,786	47.9	172,070	41.0	43,393	10.4	2,047	0.5	960	0.2	28,716	D
Washington	905,058	476,165	52.6	386,314	42.7	—		31,692	3.5	10,887	1.2	89,851	D
West Virginia	748,750	429,188	57.3	316,251	42.2	—		3,311	0.4	—		112,937	D
Wisconsin	1,276,800	647,310	50.7	590,959	46.3	—		25,282	2.0	13,249	1.0	56,351	D
Wyoming	101,425	52,354	51.6	47,947	47.3	—		931	0.9	193	0.2	4,407	D
Totals	48,793,826	24,179,345	49.6	21,991,291	45.1	1,176,125	2.4	1,157,326	2.4	289,739	0.6	2,188,054	D

PRESIDENTIAL ELECTION OF
1952

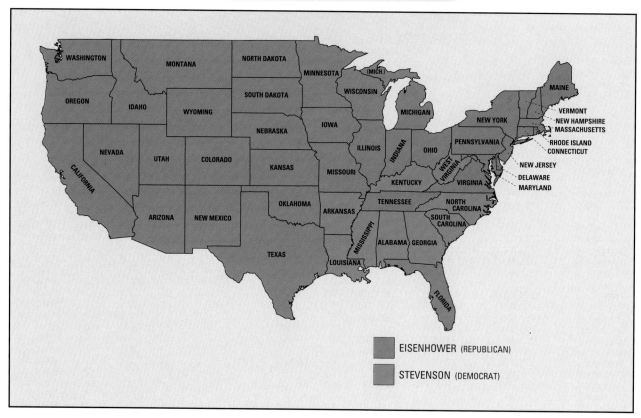

EISENHOWER (REPUBLICAN)

STEVENSON (DEMOCRAT)

States	Electoral Votes	Eisenhower	Stevenson	States	Electoral Votes	Eisenhower	Stevenson
Alabama	(11)	-	11	Nebraska	(6)	6	-
Arizona	(4)	4	-	Nevada	(3)	3	-
Arkansas	(8)	-	8	New Hampshire	(4)	4	-
California	(32)	32	-	New Jersey	(16)	16	-
Colorado	(6)	6	-	New Mexico	(4)	4	-
Connecticut	(8)	8	-	New York	(45)	45	-
Delaware	(3)	3	-	North Carolina	(14)	-	14
Florida	(10)	10	-	North Dakota	(4)	4	-
Georgia	(12)	-	12	Ohio	(25)	25	-
Idaho	(4)	4	-	Oklahoma	(8)	8	-
Illinois	(27)	27	-	Oregon	(6)	6	-
Indiana	(13)	13	-	Pennsylvania	(32)	32	-
Iowa	(10)	10	-	Rhode Island	(4)	4	-
Kansas	(8)	8	-	South Carolina	(8)	-	8
Kentucky	(10)	-	10	South Dakota	(4)	4	-
Louisiana	(10)	-	10	Tennessee	(11)	11	-
Maine	(5)	5	-	Texas	(24)	24	-
Maryland	(9)	9	-	Utah	(4)	4	-
Massachusetts	(16)	16	-	Vermont	(3)	3	-
Michigan	(20)	20	-	Virginia	(12)	12	-
Minnesota	(11)	11	-	Washington	(9)	9	-
Mississippi	(8)	-	8	West Virginia	(8)	-	8
Missouri	(13)	13	-	Wisconsin	(12)	12	-
Montana	(4)	4	-	Wyoming	(3)	3	-
				Totals	**(531)**	**442**	**89**

1952

PRESIDENTIAL ELECTION RETURNS

STATE	TOTAL VOTE	DWIGHT D. EISENHOWER (Republican)		ADLAI E. STEVENSON (Democrat)		VINCENT HALLINAN (Progressive)		STUART HAMBLEN (Prohibition)		OTHER		PLURALITY	
		Votes	%	Votes	%	Votes	%	Votes	%	Votes	%		
Alabama	426,120	149,231	35.0	275,075	64.6	—		1,814	0.4	—		125,844	D
Arizona	260,570	152,042	58.3	108,528	41.7	—		—		—		43,514	R
Arkansas	404,800	177,155	43.8	226,300	55.9	—		886	0.2	459	0.1	49,145	D
California	5,141,849	2,897,310	56.3	2,197,548	42.7	24,106	0.5	15,653	0.3	7,232	0.1	699,762	R
Colorado	630,103	379,782	60.3	245,504	39.0	1,919	0.3	—		2,898	0.5	134,278	R
Connecticut	1,096,911	611,012	55.7	481,649	43.9	1,466	0.1	—		2,784	0.3	129,363	R
Delaware	174,025	90,059	51.8	83,315	47.9	155	0.1	234	0.1	262	0.2	6,744	R
Florida	989,337	544,036	55.0	444,950	45.0	—		—		351		99,086	R
Georgia	655,785	198,961	30.3	456,823	69.7	—		—		1		257,862	D
Idaho	276,254	180,707	65.4	95,081	34.4	443	0.2	—		23		85,626	R
Illinois	4,481,058	2,457,327	54.8	2,013,920	44.9	—		—		9,811	0.2	443,407	R
Indiana	1,955,049	1,136,259	58.1	801,530	41.0	1,085	0.1	15,335	0.8	840		334,729	R
Iowa	1,268,773	808,906	63.8	451,513	35.6	5,085	0.4	2,882	0.2	387		357,393	R
Kansas	896,166	616,302	68.8	273,296	30.5	—		6,038	0.7	530	0.1	343,006	R
Kentucky	993,148	495,029	49.8	495,729	49.9	336		1,161	0.1	893	0.1	700	D
Louisiana	651,952	306,925	47.1	345,027	52.9	—		—		—		38,102	D
Maine	351,786	232,353	66.0	118,806	33.8	332	0.1	—		295	0.1	113,547	R
Maryland	902,074	499,424	55.4	395,337	43.8	7,313	0.8	—		—		104,087	R
Massachusetts	2,383,398	1,292,325	54.2	1,083,525	45.5	4,636	0.2	886		2,026	0.1	208,800	R
Michigan	2,798,592	1,551,529	55.4	1,230,657	44.0	3,922	0.1	10,331	0.4	2,153	0.1	320,872	R
Minnesota	1,379,483	763,211	55.3	608,458	44.1	2,666	0.2	2,147	0.2	3,001	0.2	154,753	R
Mississippi	285,532	112,966	39.6	172,566	60.4	—		—		—		59,600	D
Missouri	1,892,062	959,429	50.7	929,830	49.1	987	0.1	885		931		29,599	R
Montana	265,037	157,394	59.4	106,213	40.1	723	0.3	548	0.2	159	0.1	51,181	R
Nebraska	609,660	421,603	69.2	188,057	30.8	—		—		—		233,546	R
Nevada	82,190	50,502	61.4	31,688	38.6	—		—		—		18,814	R
New Hampshire	272,950	166,287	60.9	106,663	39.1	—		—		—		59,624	R
New Jersey	2,418,554	1,373,613	56.8	1,015,902	42.0	5,589	0.2	989		22,461	0.9	357,711	R
New Mexico	238,608	132,170	55.4	105,661	44.3	225	0.1	297	0.1	255	0.1	26,509	R
New York	7,128,239	3,952,813	55.5	3,104,601	43.6	64,211	0.9	—		6,614	0.1	848,212	R
North Carolina	1,210,910	558,107	46.1	652,803	53.9	—		—		—		94,696	D
North Dakota	270,127	191,712	71.0	76,694	28.4	344	0.1	302	0.1	1,075	0.4	115,018	R
Ohio	3,700,758	2,100,391	56.8	1,600,367	43.2	—		—		—		500,024	R
Oklahoma	948,984	518,045	54.6	430,939	45.4	—		—		—		87,106	R
Oregon	695,059	420,815	60.5	270,579	38.9	3,665	0.5	—		—		150,236	R
Pennsylvania	4,580,969	2,415,789	52.7	2,146,269	46.9	4,222	0.1	8,951	0.2	5,738	0.1	269,520	R
Rhode Island	414,498	210,935	50.9	203,293	49.0	187		—		83		7,642	R
South Carolina	341,087	168,082	49.3	173,004	50.7	—		1		—		4,922	D
South Dakota	294,283	203,857	69.3	90,426	30.7	—		—		—		113,431	R
Tennessee	892,553	446,147	50.0	443,710	49.7	885	0.1	1,432	0.2	379		2,437	R
Texas	2,075,946	1,102,878	53.1	969,228	46.7	294		1,983	0.1	1,563	0.1	133,650	R
Utah	329,554	194,190	58.9	135,364	41.1	—		—		—		58,826	R
Vermont	153,557	109,717	71.5	43,355	28.2	282	0.2	—		203	0.1	66,362	R
Virginia	619,689	349,037	56.3	268,677	43.4	311	0.1	—		1,664	0.3	80,360	R
Washington	1,102,708	599,107	54.3	492,845	44.7	2,460	0.2	—		8,296	0.8	106,262	R
West Virginia	873,548	419,970	48.1	453,578	51.9	—		—		—		33,608	D
Wisconsin	1,607,370	979,744	61.0	622,175	38.7	2,174	0.1	—		3,277	0.2	357,569	R
Wyoming	129,253	81,049	62.7	47,934	37.1	—		194	0.2	76	0.1	33,115	R
Totals	61,550,918	33,936,234	55.1	27,314,992	44.4	140,023	0.2	72,949	0.1	86,720	0.1	6,621,242	R

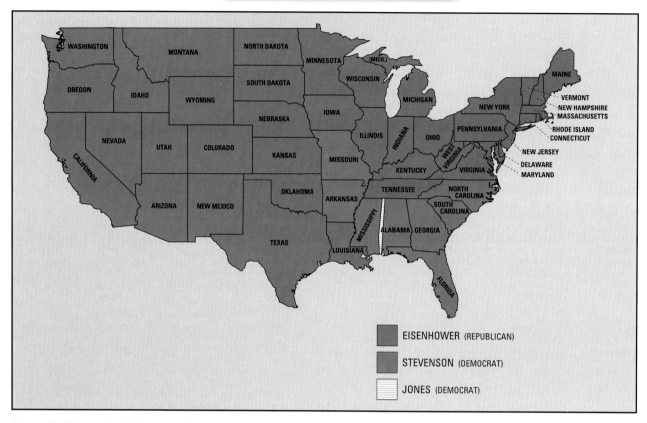

PRESIDENTIAL ELECTION OF
1956

EISENHOWER (REPUBLICAN)

STEVENSON (DEMOCRAT)

JONES (DEMOCRAT)

Congressional Quarterly's Guide to U.S. Elections, 3rd. edition, copyright ©1994. Used with permission. All rights reserved.

States	Electoral Votes	Eisenhower	Stevenson	Jones	States	Electoral Votes	Eisenhower	Stevenson	Jones
Alabama	(11)	-	10	1	Nebraska	(6)	6	-	-
Arizona	(4)	4	-	-	Nevada	(3)	3	-	-
Arkansas	(8)	-	8	-	New Hampshire	(4)	4	-	-
California	(32)	32	-	-	New Jersey	(16)	16	-	-
Colorado	(6)	6	-	-	New Mexico	(4)	4	-	-
Connecticut	(8)	8	-	-	New York	(45)	45	-	-
Delaware	(3)	3	-	-	North Carolina	(14)	-	14	-
Florida	(10)	10	-	-	North Dakota	(4)	4	-	-
Georgia	(12)	-	12	-	Ohio	(25)	25	-	-
Idaho	(4)	4	-	-	Oklahoma	(8)	8	-	-
Illinois	(27)	27	-	-	Oregon	(6)	6	-	-
Indiana	(13)	13	-	-	Pennsylvania	(32)	32	-	-
Iowa	(10)	10	-	-	Rhode Island	(4)	4	-	-
Kansas	(8)	8	-	-	South Carolina	(8)	-	8	-
Kentucky	(10)	10	-	-	South Dakota	(4)	4	-	-
Louisiana	(10)	10	-	-	Tennessee	(11)	11	-	-
Maine	(5)	5	-	-	Texas	(24)	24	-	-
Maryland	(9)	9	-	-	Utah	(4)	4	-	-
Massachusetts	(16)	16	-	-	Vermont	(3)	3	-	-
Michigan	(20)	20	-	-	Virginia	(12)	12	-	-
Minnesota	(11)	11	-	-	Washington	(9)	9	-	-
Mississippi	(8)	-	8	-	West Virginia	(8)	8	-	-
Missouri	(13)	-	13	-	Wisconsin	(12)	12	-	-
Montana	(4)	4	-	-	Wyoming	(3)	3	-	-
					Totals	**(531)**	**457**	**73**	**1**

1956

PRESIDENTIAL ELECTION RETURNS

STATE	TOTAL VOTE	DWIGHT D. EISENHOWER (Republican)		ADLAI E. STEVENSON (Democrat)		T. COLEMAN ANDREWS (Constitution)		ERIC HASS (Socialist Labor)		OTHER		PLURALITY	
		Votes	%	Votes	%	Votes	%	Votes	%	Votes	%		
Alabama	496,861	195,694	39.4	280,844	56.5	—		—		20,323	4.1	85,150	D
Arizona	290,173	176,990	61.0	112,880	38.9	303	0.1	—		—		64,110	R
Arkansas	406,572	186,287	45.8	213,277	52.5	7,008	1.7	—		—		26,990	D
California	5,466,355	3,027,668	55.4	2,420,135	44.3	6,087	0.1	300		12,165	0.2	607,533	R
Colorado	657,074	394,479	60.0	257,997	39.3	759	0.1	3,308	0.5	531	0.1	136,482	R
Connecticut	1,117,121	711,837	63.7	405,079	36.3	—		—		205		306,758	R
Delaware	177,988	98,057	55.1	79,421	44.6	—		110	0.1	400	0.2	18,636	R
Florida	1,125,762	643,849	57.2	480,371	42.7	—		—		1,542	0.1	163,478	R
Georgia	669,655	222,778	33.3	444,688	66.4	2,096	0.3	—		93		221,910	D
Idaho	272,989	166,979	61.2	105,868	38.8	126		—		16		61,111	R
Illinois	4,407,407	2,623,327	59.5	1,775,682	40.3	—		8,342	0.2	56		847,645	R
Indiana	1,974,607	1,182,811	59.9	783,908	39.7	—		1,334	0.1	6,554	0.3	398,903	R
Iowa	1,234,564	729,187	59.1	501,858	40.7	3,202	0.3	125		192		227,329	R
Kansas	866,243	566,878	65.4	296,317	34.2	—		—		3,048	0.4	270,561	R
Kentucky	1,053,805	572,192	54.3	476,453	45.2	—		358		4,802	0.5	95,739	R
Louisiana	617,544	329,047	53.3	243,977	39.5	—		—		44,520	7.2	85,070	R
Maine	351,706	249,238	70.9	102,468	29.1	—		—		—		146,770	R
Maryland	932,827	559,738	60.0	372,613	39.9	—		—		476	0.1	187,125	R
Massachusetts	2,348,506	1,393,197	59.3	948,190	40.4	—		5,573	0.2	1,546	0.1	445,007	R
Michigan	3,080,468	1,713,647	55.6	1,359,898	44.1	—		—		6,923	0.2	353,749	R
Minnesota	1,340,005	719,302	53.7	617,525	46.1	—		2,080	0.2	1,098	0.1	101,777	R
Mississippi	248,104	60,685	24.5	144,453	58.2	—		—		42,966	17.3	83,768	D
Missouri	1,832,562	914,289	49.9	918,273	50.1	—		—		—		3,984	D
Montana	271,171	154,933	57.1	116,238	42.9	—		—		—		38,695	R
Nebraska	577,137	378,108	65.5	199,029	34.5	—		—		—		179,079	R
Nevada	96,689	56,049	58.0	40,640	42.0	—		—		—		15,409	R
New Hampshire	266,994	176,519	66.1	90,364	33.8	111		—		—		86,155	R
New Jersey	2,484,312	1,606,942	64.7	850,337	34.2	5,317	0.2	6,736	0.3	14,980	0.6	756,605	R
New Mexico	253,926	146,788	57.8	106,098	41.8	364	0.1	69		607	0.2	40,690	R
New York	7,095,971	4,345,506	61.2	2,747,944	38.7	1,027		150		1,344		1,597,562	R
North Carolina	1,165,592	575,062	49.3	590,530	50.7	—		—		—		15,468	D
North Dakota	253,991	156,766	61.7	96,742	38.1	483	0.2	—		—		60,024	R
Ohio	3,702,265	2,262,610	61.1	1,439,655	38.9	—		—		—		822,955	R
Oklahoma	859,350	473,769	55.1	385,581	44.9	—		—		—		88,188	R
Oregon	736,132	406,393	55.2	329,204	44.7	—		—		535	0.1	77,189	R
Pennsylvania	4,576,503	2,585,252	56.5	1,981,769	43.3	—		7,447	0.2	2,035		603,483	R
Rhode Island	387,609	225,819	58.3	161,790	41.7	—		—		—		64,029	R
South Carolina	300,583	75,700	25.2	136,372	45.4	2		—		88,509	29.4	47,863	D
South Dakota	293,857	171,569	58.4	122,288	41.6	—		—		—		49,281	R
Tennessee	939,404	462,288	49.2	456,507	48.6	19,820	2.1	—		789	0.1	5,781	R
Texas	1,955,168	1,080,619	55.3	859,958	44.0	14,591	0.7	—		—		220,661	R
Utah	333,995	215,631	64.6	118,364	35.4	—		—		—		97,267	R
Vermont	152,978	110,390	72.2	42,549	27.8	—		—		39		67,841	R
Virginia	697,978	386,459	55.4	267,760	38.4	42,964	6.2	351	0.1	444	0.1	118,699	R
Washington	1,150,889	620,430	53.9	523,002	45.4	—		7,457	0.6	—		97,428	R
West Virginia	830,831	449,297	54.1	381,534	45.9	—		—		—		67,763	R
Wisconsin	1,550,558	954,844	61.6	586,768	37.8	6,918	0.4	710		1,318	0.1	368,076	R
Wyoming	124,127	74,573	60.1	49,554	39.9	—		—		—		25,019	R
Totals	62,026,908	35,590,472	57.4	26,022,752	42.0	111,178	0.2	44,450	0.1	258,056	0.4	9,567,720	R

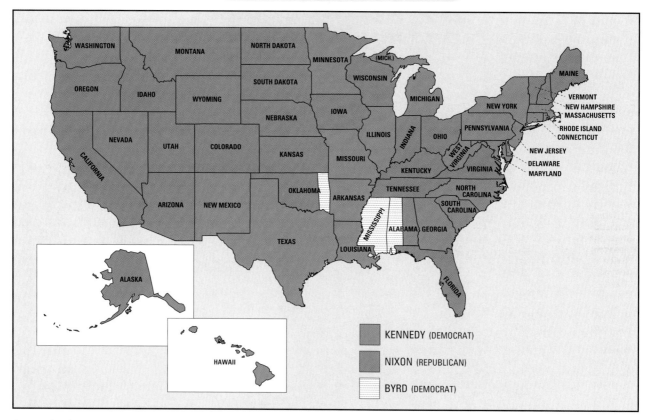

PRESIDENTIAL ELECTION OF
1960

KENNEDY (DEMOCRAT)

NIXON (REPUBLICAN)

BYRD (DEMOCRAT)

States	Electoral Votes	Kennedy	Nixon	Byrd	States	Electoral Votes	Kennedy	Nixon	Byrd
Alabama	(11)	5	-	6	Montana	(4)	-	4	-
Alaska	(3)	-	3	-	Nebraska	(6)	-	6	-
Arizona	(4)	-	4	-	Nevada	(3)	3	-	-
Arkansas	(8)	8	-	-	New Hampshire	(4)	-	4	-
California	(32)	-	32	-	New Jersey	(16)	16	-	-
Colorado	(6)	-	6	-	New Mexico	(4)	4	-	-
Connecticut	(8)	8	-	-	New York	(45)	45	-	-
Delaware	(3)	3	-	-	North Carolina	(14)	14	-	-
Florida	(10)	-	10	-	North Dakota	(4)	-	4	-
Georgia	(12)	12	-	-	Ohio	(25)	-	25	-
Hawaii	(3)	3	-	-	Oklahoma	(8)	-	7	1
Idaho	(4)	-	4	-	Oregon	(6)	-	6	-
Illinois	(27)	27	-	-	Pennsylvania	(32)	32	-	-
Indiana	(13)	-	13	-	Rhode Island	(4)	4	-	-
Iowa	(10)	-	10	-	South Carolina	(8)	8	-	-
Kansas	(8)	-	8	-	South Dakota	(4)	-	4	-
Kentucky	(10)	-	10	-	Tennessee	(11)	-	11	-
Louisiana	(10)	10	-	-	Texas	(24)	24	-	-
Maine	(5)	-	5	-	Utah	(4)	-	4	-
Maryland	(9)	9	-	-	Vermont	(3)	-	3	-
Massachusetts	(16)	16	-	-	Virginia	(12)	-	12	-
Michigan	(20)	20	-	-	Washington	(9)	-	9	-
Minnesota	(11)	11	-	-	West Virginia	(8)	8	-	-
Mississippi	(8)	-	-	8	Wisconsin	(12)	-	12	-
Missouri	(13)	13	-	-	Wyoming	(3)	-	3	-
					Totals	**(537)**	**303**	**219**	**15**

1960

PRESIDENTIAL ELECTION RETURNS

STATE	TOTAL VOTE	JOHN F. KENNEDY (Democrat)		RICHARD M. NIXON (Republican)		ERIC HASS (Socialist Labor)		UNPLEDGED		OTHER		PLURALITY	
		Votes	%	Votes	%	Votes	%	Votes	%	Votes	%		
Alabama	570,225	324,050	56.8	237,981	41.7	—		—		8,194	1.4	86,069	D
Alaska	60,762	29,809	49.1	30,953	50.9	—		—		—		1,144	R
Arizona	398,491	176,781	44.4	221,241	55.5	469	0.1	—		—		44,460	R
Arkansas	428,509	215,049	50.2	184,508	43.1	—		—		28,952	6.8	30,541	D
California	6,506,578	3,224,099	49.6	3,259,722	50.1	1,051		—		21,706	0.3	35,623	R
Colorado	736,236	330,629	44.9	402,242	54.6	2,803	0.4	—		562	0.1	71,613	R
Connecticut	1,222,883	657,055	53.7	565,813	46.3	—		—		15		91,242	D
Delaware	196,683	99,590	50.6	96,373	49.0	82		—		638	0.3	3,217	D
Florida	1,544,176	748,700	48.5	795,476	51.5	—		—		—		46,776	R
Georgia	733,349	458,638	62.5	274,472	37.4	—		—		239		184,166	D
Hawaii	184,705	92,410	50.0	92,295	50.0	—		—		—		115	D
Idaho	300,450	138,853	46.2	161,597	53.8	—		—		—		22,744	R
Illinois	4,757,409	2,377,846	50.0	2,368,988	49.8	10,560	0.2	—		15		8,858	D
Indiana	2,135,360	952,358	44.6	1,175,120	55.0	1,136	0.1	—		6,746	0.3	222,762	R
Iowa	1,273,810	550,565	43.2	722,381	56.7	230		—		634		171,816	R
Kansas	928,825	363,213	39.1	561,474	60.4	—		—		4,138	0.4	198,261	R
Kentucky	1,124,462	521,855	46.4	602,607	53.6	—		—		—		80,752	R
Louisiana	807,891	407,339	50.4	230,980	28.6	—		—		169,572	21.0	176,359	D
Maine	421,767	181,159	43.0	240,608	57.0	—		—		—		59,449	R
Maryland	1,055,349	565,808	53.6	489,538	46.4	—		—		3		76,270	D
Massachusetts	2,469,480	1,487,174	60.2	976,750	39.6	3,892	0.2	—		1,664	0.1	510,424	D
Michigan	3,318,097	1,687,269	50.9	1,620,428	48.8	1,718	0.1	—		8,682	0.3	66,841	D
Minnesota	1,541,887	779,933	50.6	757,915	49.2	962	0.1	—		3,077	0.2	22,018	D
Mississippi	298,171	108,362	36.3	73,561	24.7	—		116,248	39.0	—		7,886	U
Missouri	1,934,422	972,201	50.3	962,221	49.7	—		—		—		9,980	D
Montana	277,579	134,891	48.6	141,841	51.1	—		—		847	0.3	6,950	R
Nebraska	613,095	232,542	37.9	380,553	62.1	—		—		—		148,011	R
Nevada	107,267	54,880	51.2	52,387	48.8	—		—		—		2,493	D
New Hampshire	295,761	137,772	46.6	157,989	53.4	—		—		—		20,217	R
New Jersey	2,773,111	1,385,415	50.0	1,363,324	49.2	4,262	0.2	—		20,110	0.7	22,091	D
New Mexico	311,107	156,027	50.2	153,733	49.4	570	0.2	—		777	0.2	2,294	D
New York	7,291,079	3,830,085	52.5	3,446,419	47.3	—		—		14,575	0.2	383,666	D
North Carolina	1,368,556	713,136	52.1	655,420	47.9	—		—		—		57,716	D
North Dakota	278,431	123,963	44.5	154,310	55.4	—		—		158	0.1	30,347	R
Ohio	4,161,859	1,944,248	46.7	2,217,611	53.3	—		—		—		273,363	R
Oklahoma	903,150	370,111	41.0	533,039	59.0	—		—		—		162,928	R
Oregon	776,421	367,402	47.3	408,060	52.6	—		—		959	0.1	40,658	R
Pennsylvania	5,006,541	2,556,282	51.1	2,439,956	48.7	7,185	0.1	—		3,118	0.1	116,326	D
Rhode Island	405,535	258,032	63.6	147,502	36.4	—		—		1		110,530	D
South Carolina	386,688	198,129	51.2	188,558	48.8	—		—		1		9,571	D
South Dakota	306,487	128,070	41.8	178,417	58.2	—		—		—		50,347	R
Tennessee	1,051,792	481,453	45.8	556,577	52.9	—		—		13,762	1.3	75,124	R
Texas	2,311,084	1,167,567	50.5	1,121,310	48.5	—		—		22,207	1.0	46,257	D
Utah	374,709	169,248	45.2	205,361	54.8	—		—		100		36,113	R
Vermont	167,324	69,186	41.3	98,131	58.6	—		—		7		28,945	R
Virginia	771,449	362,327	47.0	404,521	52.4	397	0.1	—		4,204	0.5	42,194	R
Washington	1,241,572	599,298	48.3	629,273	50.7	10,895	0.9	—		2,106	0.2	29,975	R
West Virginia	837,781	441,786	52.7	395,995	47.3	—		—		—		45,791	D
Wisconsin	1,729,082	830,805	48.0	895,175	51.8	1,310	0.1	—		1,792	0.1	64,370	R
Wyoming	140,782	63,331	45.0	77,451	55.0	—		—		—		14,120	R
Totals	68,838,219	34,226,731	49.7	34,108,157	49.5	47,522	0.1	116,248	0.2	339,561	0.5	118,574	D

PRESIDENTIAL ELECTION OF
1964

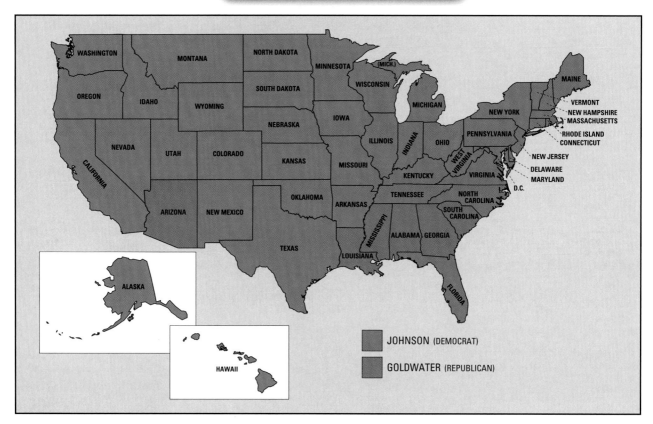

States	Electoral Votes	Johnson	Goldwater	States	Electoral Votes	Johnson	Goldwater
Alabama	(10)	-	10	Montana	(4)	4	-
Alaska	(3)	3	-	Nebraska	(5)	5	-
Arizona	(5)	-	5	Nevada	(3)	3	-
Arkansas	(6)	6	-	New Hampshire	(4)	4	-
California	(40)	40	-	New Jersey	(17)	17	-
Colorado	(6)	6	-	New Mexico	(4)	4	-
Connecticut	(8)	8	-	New York	(43)	43	-
Delaware	(3)	3	-	North Carolina	(13)	13	-
District of Columbia	(3)	3	-	North Dakota	(4)	4	-
Florida	(14)	14	-	Ohio	(26)	26	-
Georgia	(12)	-	12	Oklahoma	(8)	8	-
Hawaii	(4)	4	-	Oregon	(6)	6	-
Idaho	(4)	4	-	Pennsylvania	(29)	29	-
Illinois	(26)	26	-	Rhode Island	(4)	4	-
Indiana	(13)	13	-	South Carolina	(8)	-	8
Iowa	(9)	9	-	South Dakota	(4)	4	-
Kansas	(7)	7	-	Tennessee	(11)	11	-
Kentucky	(9)	9	-	Texas	(25)	25	-
Louisiana	(10)	-	10	Utah	(4)	4	-
Maine	(4)	4	-	Vermont	(3)	3	-
Maryland	(10)	10	-	Virginia	(12)	12	-
Massachusetts	(14)	14	-	Washington	(9)	9	-
Michigan	(21)	21	-	West Virginia	(7)	7	-
Minnesota	(10)	10	-	Wisconsin	(12)	12	-
Mississippi	(7)	-	7	Wyoming	(3)	3	-
Missouri	(12)	12	-	**Totals**	**(538)**	**486**	**52**

1964

PRESIDENTIAL ELECTION RETURNS

STATE	TOTAL VOTE	LYNDON B. JOHNSON (Democrat)		BARRY M. GOLDWATER (Republican)		ERIC HASS (Socialist Labor)		CLIFTON DeBERRY (Socialist Workers)		OTHER		PLURALITY	
		Votes	%	Votes	%	Votes	%	Votes	%	Votes	%		
Alabama	689,818	—		479,085	69.5	—		—		210,733	30.5	268,353	R
Alaska	67,259	44,329	65.9	22,930	34.1	—		—		—		21,399	D
Arizona	480,770	237,753	49.5	242,535	50.4	482	0.1	—		—		4,782	R
Arkansas	560,426	314,197	56.1	243,264	43.4	—		—		2,965	0.5	70,933	D
California	7,057,586	4,171,877	59.1	2,879,108	40.8	489		378		5,734	0.1	1,292,769	D
Colorado	776,986	476,024	61.3	296,767	38.2	302		2,537	0.3	1,356	0.2	179,257	D
Connecticut	1,218,578	826,269	67.8	390,996	32.1	—		—		1,313	0.1	435,273	D
Delaware	201,320	122,704	60.9	78,078	38.8	113	0.1	—		425	0.2	44,626	D
Florida	1,854,481	948,540	51.1	905,941	48.9	—		—		—		42,599	D
Georgia	1,139,335	522,556	45.9	616,584	54.1					195		94,028	R
Hawaii	207,271	163,249	78.8	44,022	21.2	—		—		—		119,227	D
Idaho	292,477	148,920	50.9	143,557	49.1	—		—		—		5,363	D
Illinois	4,702,841	2,796,833	59.5	1,905,946	40.5	—		—		62		890,887	D
Indiana	2,091,606	1,170,848	56.0	911,118	43.6	1,374	0.1	—		8,266	0.4	259,730	D
Iowa	1,184,539	733,030	61.9	449,148	37.9	182		159		2,020	0.2	283,882	D
Kansas	857,901	464,028	54.1	386,579	45.1	1,901	0.2	—		5,393	0.6	77,449	D
Kentucky	1,046,105	669,659	64.0	372,977	35.7	—		—		3,469	0.3	296,682	D
Louisiana	896,293	387,068	43.2	509,225	56.8	—		—		—		122,157	R
Maine	380,965	262,264	68.8	118,701	31.2	—		—		—		143,563	D
Maryland	1,116,457	730,912	65.5	385,495	34.5	—		—		50		345,417	D
Massachusetts	2,344,798	1,786,422	76.2	549,727	23.4	4,755	0.2	—		3,894	0.2	1,236,695	D
Michigan	3,203,102	2,136,615	66.7	1,060,152	33.1	1,704	0.1	3,817	0.1	814		1,076,463	D
Minnesota	1,554,462	991,117	63.8	559,624	36.0	2,544	0.2	1,177	0.1	—		431,493	D
Mississippi	409,146	52,618	12.9	356,528	87.1	—		—		—		303,910	R
Missouri	1,817,879	1,164,344	64.0	653,535	36.0	—		—		—		510,809	D
Montana	278,628	164,246	58.9	113,032	40.6	—		332	0.1	1,018	0.4	51,214	D
Nebraska	584,154	307,307	52.6	276,847	47.4	—		—		—		30,460	D
Nevada	135,433	79,339	58.6	56,094	41.4	—		—		—		23,245	D
New Hampshire	288,093	184,064	63.9	104,029	36.1	—		—		—		80,035	D
New Jersey	2,847,663	1,868,231	65.6	964,174	33.9	7,075	0.2	8,183	0.3	—		904,057	D
New Mexico	328,645	194,015	59.0	132,838	40.4	1,217	0.4	—		575	0.2	61,177	D
New York	7,166,275	4,913,102	68.6	2,243,559	31.3	6,118	0.1	3,228		268		2,669,543	D
North Carolina	1,424,983	800,139	56.2	624,844	43.8	—		—		—		175,295	D
North Dakota	258,389	149,784	58.0	108,207	41.9	—		224	0.1	174	0.1	41,577	D
Ohio	3,969,196	2,498,331	62.9	1,470,865	37.1	—		—		—		1,027,466	D
Oklahoma	932,499	519,834	55.7	412,665	44.3	—		—		—		107,169	D
Oregon	786,305	501,017	63.7	282,779	36.0	—		—		2,509	0.3	218,238	D
Pennsylvania	4,822,690	3,130,954	64.9	1,673,657	34.7	5,092	0.1	10,456	0.2	2,531	0.1	1,457,297	D
Rhode Island	390,091	315,463	80.9	74,615	19.1	—		—		13		240,848	D
South Carolina	524,779	215,723	41.1	309,048	58.9	—		—		8		93,325	R
South Dakota	293,118	163,010	55.6	130,108	44.4	—		—		—		32,902	D
Tennessee	1,143,946	634,947	55.5	508,965	44.5	—		—		34		125,982	D
Texas	2,626,811	1,663,185	63.3	958,566	36.5	—		—		5,060	0.2	704,619	D
Utah	401,413	219,628	54.7	181,785	45.3	—		—		—		37,843	D
Vermont	163,089	108,127	66.3	54,942	33.7	—		—		20		53,185	D
Virginia	1,042,267	558,038	53.5	481,334	46.2	2,895	0.3	—		—		76,704	D
Washington	1,258,556	779,881	62.0	470,366	37.4	7,772	0.6	537		—		309,515	D
West Virginia	792,040	538,087	67.9	253,953	32.1	—		—		—		284,134	D
Wisconsin	1,691,815	1,050,424	62.1	638,495	37.7	1,204	0.1	1,692	0.1	—		411,929	D
Wyoming	142,716	80,718	56.6	61,998	43.4	—		—		—		18,720	D
Dist. of Col.	198,597	169,796	85.5	28,801	14.5	—		—		—		140,995	D
Totals	70,644,592	43,129,566	61.1	27,178,188	38.5	45,219	0.1	32,720		258,899	0.4	15,951,378	D

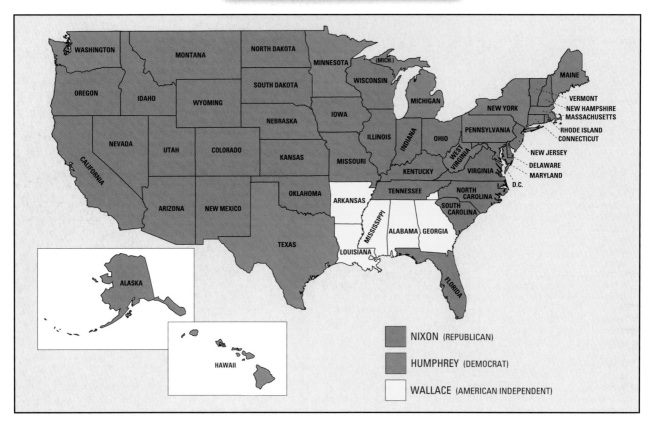

PRESIDENTIAL ELECTION OF
1968

NIXON (REPUBLICAN)

HUMPHREY (DEMOCRAT)

WALLACE (AMERICAN INDEPENDENT)

States	Electoral Votes	Nixon	Humphrey	Wallace	States	Electoral Votes	Nixon	Humphrey	Wallace
Alabama	(10)	-	-	10	Montana	(4)	4	-	-
Alaska	(3)	3	-	-	Nebraska	(5)	5	-	-
Arizona	(5)	5	-	-	Nevada	(3)	3	-	-
Arkansas	(6)	-	-	6	New Hampshire	(4)	4	-	-
California	(40)	40	-	-	New Jersey	(17)	17	-	-
Colorado	(6)	6	-	-	New Mexico	(4)	4	-	-
Connecticut	(8)	-	8	-	New York	(43)	-	43	-
Delaware	(3)	3	-	-	North Carolina	(13)	12	-	1
District of Columbia	(3)	-	3	-	North Dakota	(4)	4	-	-
Florida	(14)	14	-	-	Ohio	(26)	26	-	-
Georgia	(12)	-	-	12	Oklahoma	(8)	8	-	-
Hawaii	(4)	-	4	-	Oregon	(6)	6	-	-
Idaho	(4)	4	-	-	Pennsylvania	(29)	-	29	-
Illinois	(26)	26	-	-	Rhode Island	(4)	-	4	-
Indiana	(13)	13	-	-	South Carolina	(8)	8	-	-
Iowa	(9)	9	-	-	South Dakota	(4)	4	-	-
Kansas	(7)	7	-	-	Tennessee	(11)	11	-	-
Kentucky	(9)	9	-	-	Texas	(25)	-	25	-
Louisiana	(10)	-	-	10	Utah	(4)	4	-	-
Maine	(4)	-	4	-	Vermont	(3)	3	-	-
Maryland	(10)	-	10	-	Virginia	(12)	12	-	-
Massachusetts	(14)	-	14	-	Washington	(9)	-	9	-
Michigan	(21)	-	21	-	West Virginia	(7)	-	7	-
Minnesota	(10)	-	10	-	Wisconsin	(12)	12	-	-
Mississippi	(7)	-	-	7	Wyoming	(3)	3	-	-
Missouri	(12)	12	-	-	**Totals**	**(538)**	**301**	**191**	**46**

1968

PRESIDENTIAL ELECTION RETURNS

STATE	TOTAL VOTE	RICHARD M. NIXON (Republican)		HUBERT H. HUMPHREY (Democrat)		GEORGE C. WALLACE (American Independent)		HENNING A. BLOMEN (Socialist Labor)		OTHER		PLURALITY	
		Votes	%	Votes	%	Votes	%	Votes	%	Votes	%		
Alabama	1,049,922	146,923	14.0	196,579	18.7	691,425	65.9	—		14,995	1.4	494,846	A
Alaska	83,035	37,600	45.3	35,411	42.6	10,024	12.1	—		—		2,189	R
Arizona	486,936	266,721	54.8	170,514	35.0	46,573	9.6	75		3,053	0.6	96,207	R
Arkansas	619,969	190,759	30.8	188,228	30.4	240,982	38.9	—		—		50,223	A
California	7,251,587	3,467,664	47.8	3,244,318	44.7	487,270	6.7	341		51,994	0.7	223,346	R
Colorado	811,199	409,345	50.5	335,174	41.3	60,813	7.5	3,016	0.4	2,851	0.4	74,171	R
Connecticut	1,256,232	556,721	44.3	621,561	49.5	76,650	6.1	—		1,300	0.1	64,840	D
Delaware	214,367	96,714	45.1	89,194	41.6	28,459	13.3	—		—		7,520	R
Florida	2,187,805	886,804	40.5	676,794	30.9	624,207	28.5	—		—		210,010	R
Georgia	1,250,266	380,111	30.4	334,440	26.7	535,550	42.8	—		165		155,439	A
Hawaii	236,218	91,425	38.7	141,324	59.8	3,469	1.5	—		—		49,899	D
Idaho	291,183	165,369	56.8	89,273	30.7	36,541	12.5	—		—		76,096	R
Illinois	4,619,749	2,174,774	47.1	2,039,814	44.2	390,958	8.5	13,878	0.3	325		134,960	R
Indiana	2,123,597	1,067,885	50.3	806,659	38.0	243,108	11.4	—		5,945	0.3	261,226	R
Iowa	1,167,931	619,106	53.0	476,699	40.8	66,422	5.7	241		5,463	0.5	142,407	R
Kansas	872,783	478,674	54.8	302,996	34.7	88,921	10.2	—		2,192	0.3	175,678	R
Kentucky	1,055,893	462,411	43.8	397,541	37.6	193,098	18.3	—		2,843	0.3	64,870	R
Louisiana	1,097,450	257,535	23.5	309,615	28.2	530,300	48.3	—		—		220,685	A
Maine	392,936	169,254	43.1	217,312	55.3	6,370	1.6	—		—		48,058	D
Maryland	1,235,039	517,995	41.9	538,310	43.6	178,734	14.5	—		—		20,315	D
Massachusetts	2,331,752	766,844	32.9	1,469,218	63.0	87,088	3.7	6,180	0.3	2,422	0.1	702,374	D
Michigan	3,306,250	1,370,665	41.5	1,593,082	48.2	331,968	10.0	1,762	0.1	8,773	0.3	222,417	D
Minnesota	1,588,506	658,643	41.5	857,738	54.0	68,931	4.3	285		2,909	0.2	199,095	D
Mississippi	654,509	88,516	13.5	150,644	23.0	415,349	63.5	—		—		264,705	A
Missouri	1,809,502	811,932	44.9	791,444	43.7	206,126	11.4	—		—		20,488	R
Montana	274,404	138,835	50.6	114,117	41.6	20,015	7.3	—		1,437	0.5	24,718	R
Nebraska	536,851	321,163	59.8	170,784	31.8	44,904	8.4	—		—		150,379	R
Nevada	154,218	73,188	47.5	60,598	39.3	20,432	13.2	—		—		12,590	R
New Hampshire	297,298	154,903	52.1	130,589	43.9	11,173	3.8	—		633	0.2	24,314	R
New Jersey	2,875,395	1,325,467	46.1	1,264,206	44.0	262,187	9.1	6,784	0.2	16,751	0.6	61,261	R
New Mexico	327,350	169,692	51.8	130,081	39.7	25,737	7.9	—		1,840	0.6	39,611	R
New York	6,791,688	3,007,932	44.3	3,378,470	49.7	358,864	5.3	8,432	0.1	37,990	0.6	370,538	D
North Carolina	1,587,493	627,192	39.5	464,113	29.2	496,188	31.3	—		—		131,004	R
North Dakota	247,882	138,669	55.9	94,769	38.2	14,244	5.7	—		200	0.1	43,900	R
Ohio	3,959,698	1,791,014	45.2	1,700,586	42.9	467,495	11.8	120		483		90,428	R
Oklahoma	943,086	449,697	47.7	301,658	32.0	191,731	20.3	—		—		148,039	R
Oregon	819,622	408,433	49.8	358,866	43.8	49,683	6.1	—		2,640	0.3	49,567	R
Pennsylvania	4,747,928	2,090,017	44.0	2,259,405	47.6	378,582	8.0	4,977	0.1	14,947	0.3	169,388	D
Rhode Island	385,000	122,359	31.8	246,518	64.0	15,678	4.1	—		445	0.1	124,159	D
South Carolina	666,978	254,062	38.1	197,486	29.6	215,430	32.3	—		—		38,632	R
South Dakota	281,264	149,841	53.3	118,023	42.0	13,400	4.8	—		—		31,818	R
Tennessee	1,248,617	472,592	37.8	351,233	28.1	424,792	34.0	—		—		47,800	R
Texas	3,079,216	1,227,844	39.9	1,266,804	41.1	584,269	19.0	—		299		38,960	D
Utah	422,568	238,728	56.5	156,665	37.1	26,906	6.4	—		269	0.1	82,063	R
Vermont	161,404	85,142	52.8	70,255	43.5	5,104	3.2	—		903	0.6	14,887	R
Virginia	1,361,491	590,319	43.4	442,387	32.5	321,833	23.6	4,671	0.3	2,281	0.2	147,932	R
Washington	1,304,281	588,510	45.1	616,037	47.2	96,990	7.4	488		2,256	0.2	27,527	D
West Virginia	754,206	307,555	40.8	374,091	49.6	72,560	9.6	—		—		66,536	D
Wisconsin	1,691,538	809,997	47.9	748,804	44.3	127,835	7.6	1,338	0.1	3,564	0.2	61,193	R
Wyoming	127,205	70,927	55.8	45,173	35.5	11,105	8.7	—		—		25,754	R
Dist. of Col.	170,578	31,012	18.2	139,566	81.8	—		—		—		108,554	D
Totals	73,211,875	31,785,480	43.4	31,275,166	42.7	9,906,473	13.5	52,588	0.1	192,168	0.3	510,314	R

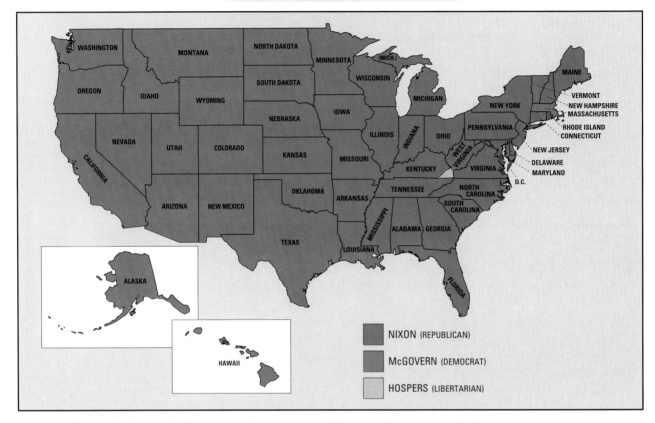

PRESIDENTIAL ELECTION OF
1972

States	Electoral Votes	Nixon	McGovern	Hospers	States	Electoral Votes	Nixon	McGovern	Hospers
Alabama	(9)	9	-	-	Montana	(4)	4	-	-
Alaska	(3)	3	-	-	Nebraska	(5)	5	-	-
Arizona	(6)	6	-	-	Nevada	(3)	3	-	-
Arkansas	(6)	6	-	-	New Hampshire	(4)	4	-	-
California	(45)	45	-	-	New Jersey	(17)	17	-	-
Colorado	(7)	7	-	-	New Mexico	(4)	4	-	-
Connecticut	(8)	8	-	-	New York	(41)	41	-	-
Delaware	(3)	3	-	-	North Carolina	(13)	13	-	-
District of Columbia	(3)	-	3	-	North Dakota	(3)	3	-	-
Florida	(17)	17	-	-	Ohio	(25)	25	-	-
Georgia	(12)	12	-	-	Oklahoma	(8)	8	-	-
Hawaii	(4)	4	-	-	Oregon	(6)	6	-	-
Idaho	(4)	4	-	-	Pennsylvania	(27)	27	-	-
Illinois	(26)	26	-	-	Rhode Island	(4)	4	-	-
Indiana	(13)	13	-	-	South Carolina	(8)	8	-	-
Iowa	(8)	8	-	-	South Dakota	(4)	4	-	-
Kansas	(7)	7	-	-	Tennessee	(10)	10	-	-
Kentucky	(9)	9	-	-	Texas	(26)	26	-	-
Louisiana	(10)	10	-	-	Utah	(4)	4	-	-
Maine	(4)	4	-	-	Vermont	(3)	3	-	-
Maryland	(10)	10	-	-	Virginia [1]	(12)	11	-	1
Massachusetts	(14)	-	14	-	Washington	(9)	9	-	-
Michigan	(21)	21	-	-	West Virginia	(6)	6	-	-
Minnesota	(10)	10	-	-	Wisconsin	(11)	11	-	-
Mississippi	(7)	7	-	-	Wyoming	(3)	3	-	-
Missouri	(12)	12	-	-	**Totals**	**(538)**	**520**	**17**	**1**

1972

PRESIDENTIAL ELECTION RETURNS

STATE	TOTAL VOTE	RICHARD M. NIXON (Republican)		GEORGE S. McGOVERN (Democrat)		JOHN G. SCHMITZ (American)		BENJAMIN SPOCK (People's)		OTHER		PLURALITY	
		Votes	%	Votes	%	Votes	%	Votes	%	Votes	%		
Alabama	1,006,111	728,701	72.4	256,923	25.5	11,928	1.2	—		8,559	0.9	471,778	R
Alaska	95,219	55,349	58.1	32,967	34.6	6,903	7.2	—		—		22,382	R
Arizona	622,926	402,812	64.7	198,540	31.9	21,208	3.4	—		366	0.1	204,272	R
Arkansas	651,320	448,541	68.9	199,892	30.7	2,887	0.4	—		—		248,649	R
California	8,367,862	4,602,096	55.0	3,475,847	41.5	232,554	2.8	55,167	0.7	2,198		1,126,249	R
Colorado	953,884	597,189	62.6	329,980	34.6	17,269	1.8	2,403	0.3	7,043	0.7	267,209	R
Connecticut	1,384,277	810,763	58.6	555,498	40.1	17,239	1.2	—		777	0.1	255,265	R
Delaware	235,516	140,357	59.6	92,283	39.2	2,638	1.1	—		238	0.1	48,074	R
Florida	2,583,283	1,857,759	71.9	718,117	27.8	—		—		7,4C7	0.3	1,139,642	R
Georgia	1,174,772	881,496	75.0	289,529	24.6	812	0.1	—		2,935	0.2	591,967	R
Hawaii	270,274	168,865	62.5	101,409	37.5	—		—		—		67,456	R
Idaho	310,379	199,384	64.2	80,826	26.0	28,869	9.3	903	0.3	397	0.1	118,558	R
Illinois	4,723,236	2,788,179	59.0	1,913,472	40.5	2,471	0.1	—		19,114	0.4	874,707	R
Indiana	2,125,529	1,405,154	66.1	708,568	33.3	—		4,544	0.2	7,263	0.3	696,586	R
Iowa	1,225,944	706,207	57.6	496,206	40.5	22,056	1.8	—		1,475	0.1	210,001	R
Kansas	916,095	619,812	67.7	270,287	29.5	21,808	2.4	—		4,188	0.5	349,525	R
Kentucky	1,067,499	676,446	63.4	371,159	34.8	17,627	1.7	1,118	0.1	1,149	0.1	305,287	R
Louisiana	1,051,491	686,852	65.3	298,142	28.4	52,099	5.0	—		14,398	1.4	388,710	R
Maine	417,042	256,458	61.5	160,584	38.5	—		—		—		95,874	R
Maryland	1,353,812	829,305	61.3	505,781	37.4	18,726	1.4	—		—		323,524	R
Massachusetts	2,458,756	1,112,078	45.2	1,332,540	54.2	2,877	0.1	101		11,160	0.5	220,462	D
Michigan	3,489,727	1,961,721	56.2	1,459,435	41.8	63,321	1.8	—		5,250	0.2	502,286	R
Minnesota	1,741,652	898,269	51.6	802,346	46.1	31,407	1.8	2,805	0.2	6,825	0.4	95,923	R
Mississippi	645,963	505,125	78.2	126,782	19.6	11,598	1.8	—		2,458	0.4	378,343	R
Missouri	1,855,803	1,153,852	62.2	697,147	37.6	—		—		4,804	0.3	456,705	R
Montana	317,603	183,976	57.9	120,197	37.8	13,430	4.2	—		—		63,779	R
Nebraska	576,289	406,298	70.5	169,991	29.5	—		—		—		236,307	R
Nevada	181,766	115,750	63.7	66,016	36.3	—		—		—		49,734	R
New Hampshire	334,055	213,724	64.0	116,435	34.9	3,386	1.0	—		510	0.2	97,289	R
New Jersey	2,997,229	1,845,502	61.6	1,102,211	36.8	34,378	1.1	5,355	0.2	9,783	0.3	743,291	R
New Mexico	386,241	235,606	61.0	141,084	36.5	8,767	2.3	—		784	0.2	94,522	R
New York	7,165,919	4,192,778	58.5	2,951,084	41.2	—		—		22,057	0.3	1,241,694	R
North Carolina	1,518,612	1,054,889	69.5	438,705	28.9	25,018	1.6	—		—		616,184	R
North Dakota	280,514	174,109	62.1	100,384	35.8	5,646	2.0	—		375	0.1	73,725	R
Ohio	4,094,787	2,441,827	59.6	1,558,889	38.1	80,067	2.0	—		14,004	0.3	882,938	R
Oklahoma	1,029,900	759,025	73.7	247,147	24.0	23,728	2.3	—		—		511,878	R
Oregon	927,946	486,686	52.4	392,760	42.3	46,211	5.0	—		2,289	0.2	93,926	R
Pennsylvania	4,592,106	2,714,521	59.1	1,796,951	39.1	70,593	1.5	—		10,041	0.2	917,570	R
Rhode Island	415,808	220,383	53.0	194,645	46.8	25		5		750	0.2	25,738	R
South Carolina	673,960	477,044	70.8	186,824	27.7	10,075	1.5	—		17		290,220	R
South Dakota	307,415	166,476	54.2	139,945	45.5	—		—		994	0.3	26,531	R
Tennessee	1,201,182	813,147	67.7	357,293	29.7	30,373	2.5	—		369		455,854	R
Texas	3,471,281	2,298,896	66.2	1,154,289	33.3	6,039	0.2	—		12,057	0.3	1,144,607	R
Utah	478,476	323,643	67.6	126,284	26.4	28,549	6.0	—		—		197,359	R
Vermont	186,947	117,149	62.7	68,174	36.5	—		1,010	0.5	614	0.3	48,975	R
Virginia	1,457,019	988,493	67.8	438,887	30.1	19,721	1.4	—		9,918	0.7	549,606	R
Washington	1,470,847	837,135	56.9	568,334	38.6	58,906	4.0	2,644	0.2	3,828	0.3	268,801	R
West Virginia	762,399	484,964	63.6	277,435	36.4	—		—		—		207,529	R
Wisconsin	1,852,890	989,430	53.4	810,174	43.7	47,525	2.6	2,701	0.1	3,060	0.2	179,256	R
Wyoming	145,570	100,464	69.0	44,358	30.5	748	0.5	—		—		56,106	R
Dist. of Col.	163,421	35,226	21.6	127,627	78.1	—		—		568	0.3	92,401	D
Totals	77,718,554	47,169,911	60.7	29,170,383	37.5	1,099,482	1.4	78,756	0.1	200,022	0.3	17,999,528	R

PRESIDENTIAL ELECTION OF
1976

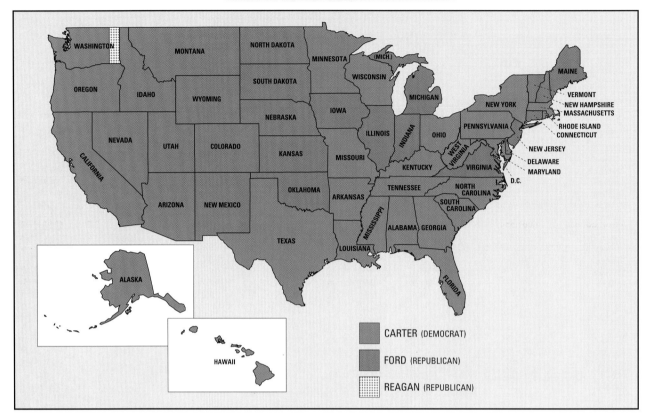

Congressional Quarterly's Guide to U.S. Elections, 3rd. edition, copyright ©1994. Used with permission. All rights reserved.

States	Electoral Votes	Carter	Ford	Reagan	States	Electoral Votes	Carter	Ford	Reagan
Alabama	(9)	9	-	-	Montana	(4)	-	4	-
Alaska	(3)	-	3	-	Nebraska	(5)	-	5	-
Arizona	(6)	-	6	-	Nevada	(3)	-	3	-
Arkansas	(6)	6	-	-	New Hampshire	(4)	-	4	-
California	(45)	-	45	-	New Jersey	(17)	-	17	-
Colorado	(7)	-	7	-	New Mexico	(4)	-	4	-
Connecticut	(8)	-	8	-	New York	(41)	41	-	-
Delaware	(3)	3	-	-	North Carolina	(13)	13	-	-
District of Columbia	(3)	3	-	-	North Dakota	(3)	-	3	-
Florida	(17)	17	-	-	Ohio	(25)	25	-	-
Georgia	(12)	12	-	-	Oklahoma	(8)	-	8	-
Hawaii	(4)	4	-	-	Oregon	(6)	-	6	-
Idaho	(4)	-	4	-	Pennsylvania	(27)	27	-	-
Illinois	(26)	-	26	-	Rhode Island	(4)	4	-	-
Indiana	(13)	-	13	-	South Carolina	(8)	8	-	-
Iowa	(8)	-	8	-	South Dakota	(4)	-	4	-
Kansas	(7)	-	7	-	Tennessee	(10)	10	-	-
Kentucky	(9)	9	-	-	Texas	(26)	26	-	-
Louisiana	(10)	10	-	-	Utah	(4)	-	4	-
Maine	(4)	-	4	-	Vermont	(3)	-	3	-
Maryland	(10)	10	-	-	Virginia	(12)	-	12	-
Massachusetts	(14)	14	-	-	Washington	(9)	-	8	1
Michigan	(21)	-	21	-	West Virginia	(6)	6	-	-
Minnesota	(10)	10	-	-	Wisconsin	(11)	11	-	-
Mississippi	(7)	7	-	-	Wyoming	(3)	-	3	-
Missouri	(12)	12	-	-	**Totals**	**(538)**	**297**	**240**	**1**

1976
PRESIDENTIAL ELECTION RETURNS

STATE	TOTAL VOTE	JIMMY CARTER (Democrat)		GERALD R. FORD (Republican)		EUGENE J. McCARTHY (Independent)		ROGER MacBRIDE (Libertarian)		OTHER		PLURALITY
		Votes	%	Votes	%	Votes	%	Votes	%	Votes	%	
Alabama	1,182,850	659,170	55.7	504,070	42.6	99		1,481	0.1	18,030	1.5	155,100 D
Alaska	123,574	44,058	35.7	71,555	57.9	—		6,785	5.5	1,176	1.0	27,497 R
Arizona	742,719	295,602	39.8	418,642	56.4	19,229	2.6	7,647	1.0	1,599	0.2	123,040 R
Arkansas	767,535	498,604	65.0	267,903	34.9	639	0.1	—		389	0.1	230,701 D
California	7,867,117	3,742,284	47.6	3,882,244	49.3	58,412	0.7	56,388	0.7	127,789	1.6	139,960 R
Colorado	1,081,554	460,353	42.6	584,367	54.0	26,107	2.4	5,330	0.5	5,397	0.5	124,014 R
Connecticut	1,381,526	647,895	46.9	719,261	52.1	3,759	0.3	209		10,402	0.8	71,366 R
Delaware	235,834	122,596	52.0	109,831	46.6	2,437	1.0	—		970	0.4	12,765 D
Florida	3,150,631	1,636,000	51.9	1,469,531	46.6	23,643	0.8	103		21,354	0.7	166,469 D
Georgia	1,467,458	979,409	66.7	483,743	33.0	991	0.1	175		3,140	0.2	495,666 D
Hawaii	291,301	147,375	50.6	140,003	48.1	—		3,923	1.3	—		7,372 D
Idaho	344,071	126,549	36.8	204,151	59.3	1,194	0.3	3,558	1.0	8,619	2.5	77,602 R
Illinois	4,718,914	2,271,295	48.1	2,364,269	50.1	55,939	1.2	8,057	0.2	19,354	0.4	92,974 R
Indiana	2,220,362	1,014,714	45.7	1,183,958	53.3	—		—		21,690	1.0	169,244 R
Iowa	1,279,306	619,931	48.5	632,863	49.5	20,051	1.6	1,452	0.1	5,009	0.4	12,932 R
Kansas	957,845	430,421	44.9	502,752	52.5	13,185	1.4	3,242	0.3	8,245	0.9	72,331 R
Kentucky	1,167,142	615,717	52.8	531,852	45.6	6,837	0.6	814	0.1	11,922	1.0	83,865 D
Louisiana	1,278,439	661,365	51.7	587,446	46.0	6,588	0.5	3,325	0.3	19,715	1.5	73,919 D
Maine	483,216	232,279	48.1	236,320	48.9	10,874	2.3	11		3,732	0.8	4,041 R
Maryland	1,439,897	759,612	52.8	672,661	46.7	4,541	0.3	255		2,828	0.2	86,951 D
Massachusetts	2,547,558	1,429,475	56.1	1,030,276	40.4	65,637	2.6	135		22,035	0.9	399,199 D
Michigan	3,653,749	1,696,714	46.4	1,893,742	51.8	47,905	1.3	5,406	0.1	9,982	0.3	197,028 R
Minnesota	1,949,931	1,070,440	54.9	819,395	42.0	35,490	1.8	3,529	0.2	21,077	1.1	251,045 D
Mississippi	769,361	381,309	49.6	366,846	47.7	4,074	0.5	2,788	0.4	14,344	1.9	14,463 D
Missouri	1,953,600	998,387	51.1	927,443	47.5	24,029	1.2	—		3,741	0.2	70,944 D
Montana	328,734	149,259	45.4	173,703	52.8	—		—		5,772	1.8	24,444 R
Nebraska	607,668	233,692	38.5	359,705	59.2	9,409	1.5	1,482	0.2	3,380	0.6	126,013 R
Nevada	201,876	92,479	45.8	101,273	50.2	—		1,519	0.8	6,605	3.3	8,794 R
New Hampshire	339,618	147,635	43.5	185,935	54.7	4,095	1.2	936	0.3	1,017	0.3	38,300 R
New Jersey	3,014,472	1,444,653	47.9	1,509,688	50.1	32,717	1.1	9,449	0.3	17,965	0.6	65,035 R
New Mexico	418,409	201,148	48.1	211,419	50.5	1,161	0.3	1,110	0.3	3,571	0.9	10,271 R
New York	6,534,170	3,389,558	51.9	3,100,791	47.5	4,303	0.1	12,197	0.2	27,321	0.4	288,767 D
North Carolina	1,678,914	927,365	55.2	741,960	44.2	780		2,219	0.1	6,590	0.4	185,405 D
North Dakota	297,188	136,078	45.8	153,470	51.6	2,952	1.0	253	0.1	4,435	1.5	17,392 R
Ohio	4,111,873	2,011,621	48.9	2,000,505	48.7	58,258	1.4	8,961	0.2	32,528	0.8	11,116 D
Oklahoma	1,092,251	532,442	48.7	545,708	50.0	14,101	1.3	—		—		13,266 R
Oregon	1,029,876	490,407	47.6	492,120	47.8	40,207	3.9	—		7,142	0.7	1,713 R
Pennsylvania	4,620,787	2,328,677	50.4	2,205,604	47.7	50,584	1.1	—		35,922	0.8	123,073 D
Rhode Island	411,170	227,636	55.4	181,249	44.1	479	0.1	715	0.2	1,091	0.3	46,387 D
South Carolina	802,583	450,807	56.2	346,149	43.1	289		53		5,285	0.7	104,658 D
South Dakota	300,678	147,068	48.9	151,505	50.4	—		1,619	0.5	486	0.2	4,437 R
Tennessee	1,476,345	825,879	55.9	633,969	42.9	5,004	0.3	1,375	0.1	10,118	0.7	191,910 D
Texas	4,071,884	2,082,319	51.1	1,953,300	48.0	20,118	0.5	189		15,958	0.4	129,019 D
Utah	541,198	182,110	33.6	337,908	62.4	3,907	0.7	2,438	0.5	14,835	2.7	155,798 R
Vermont	187,765	80,954	43.1	102,085	54.4	4,001	2.1	—		725	0.4	21,131 R
Virginia	1,697,094	813,896	48.0	836,554	49.3	—		4,648	0.3	41,996	2.5	22,658 R
Washington	1,555,534	717,323	46.1	777,732	50.0	36,986	2.4	5,042	0.3	18,451	1.2	60,409 R
West Virginia	750,964	435,914	58.0	314,760	41.9	113		16		161		121,154 D
Wisconsin	2,104,175	1,040,232	49.4	1,004,987	47.8	34,943	1.7	3,814	0.2	20,199	1.0	35,245 D
Wyoming	156,343	62,239	39.8	92,717	59.3	624	0.4	89	0.1	674	0.4	30,478 R
Dist. of Col.	168,830	137,818	81.6	27,873	16.5	—		274	0.2	2,865	1.7	109,945 D
Totals	81,555,889	40,830,763	50.1	39,147,793	48.0	756,691	0.9	173,011	0.2	647,631	0.8	1,682,970 D

PRESIDENTIAL ELECTION OF

1980

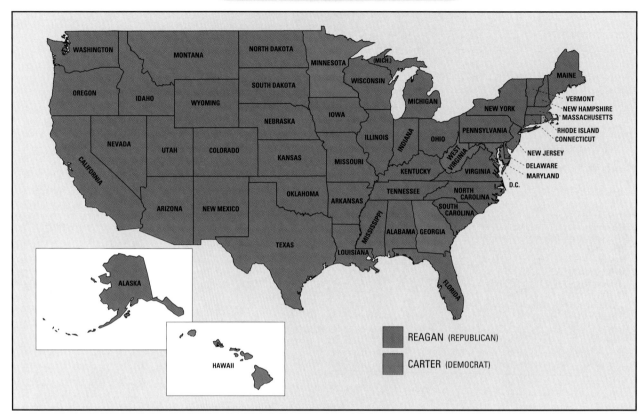

REAGAN (REPUBLICAN)

CARTER (DEMOCRAT)

Congressional Quarterly's Guide to U.S. Elections, 3rd. edition, copyright ©1994. Used with permission. All rights reserved.

States	Electoral Votes	Reagan	Carter	States	Electoral Votes	Reagan	Carter
Alabama	(9)	9	-	Montana	(4)	4	-
Alaska	(3)	3	-	Nebraska	(5)	5	-
Arizona	(6)	6	-	Nevada	(3)	3	-
Arkansas	(6)	6	-	New Hampshire	(4)	4	-
California	(45)	45	-	New Jersey	(17)	17	-
Colorado	(7)	7	-	New Mexico	(4)	4	-
Connecticut	(8)	8	-	New York	(41)	41	-
Delaware	(3)	3	-	North Carolina	(13)	13	-
District of Columbia	(3)	-	3	North Dakota	(3)	3	-
Florida	(17)	17	-	Ohio	(25)	25	-
Georgia	(12)	-	12	Oklahoma	(8)	8	-
Hawaii	(4)	-	4	Oregon	(6)	6	-
Idaho	(4)	4	-	Pennsylvania	(27)	27	-
Illinois	(26)	26	-	Rhode Island	(4)	-	4
Indiana	(13)	13	-	South Carolina	(8)	8	-
Iowa	(8)	8	-	South Dakota	(4)	4	-
Kansas	(7)	7	-	Tennessee	(10)	10	-
Kentucky	(9)	9	-	Texas	(26)	26	-
Louisiana	(10)	10	-	Utah	(4)	4	-
Maine	(4)	4	-	Vermont	(3)	3	-
Maryland	(10)	-	10	Virginia	(12)	12	-
Massachusetts	(14)	14	-	Washington	(9)	9	-
Michigan	(21)	21	-	West Virginia	(6)	-	6
Minnesota	(10)	-	10	Wisconsin	(11)	11	-
Mississippi	(7)	7	-	Wyoming	(3)	3	-
Missouri	(12)	12	-	**Totals**	**(538)**	**489**	**49**

1980

PRESIDENTIAL ELECTION RETURNS

STATE	TOTAL VOTE	RONALD REAGAN (Republican)		JIMMY CARTER (Democrat)		JOHN B. ANDERSON (Independent)		ED CLARK (Libertarian)		OTHER		PLURALITY	
		Votes	%	Votes	%	Votes	%	Votes	%	Votes	%		
Alabama	1,341,929	654,192	48.8	636,730	47.4	16,481	1.2	13,318	1.0	21,208	1.6	17,462	R
Alaska	158,445	86,112	54.3	41,842	26.4	11,155	7.0	18,479	11.7	857	0.5	44,270	R
Arizona	873,945	529,688	60.6	246,843	28.2	76,952	8.8	18,784	2.1	1,678	0.2	282,845	R
Arkansas	837,582	403,164	48.1	398,041	47.5	22,468	2.7	8,970	1.1	4,939	0.6	5,123	R
California	8,587,063	4,524,858	52.7	3,083,661	35.9	739,833	8.6	148,434	1.7	90,277	1.1	1,441,197	R
Colorado	1,184,415	652,264	55.1	367,973	31.1	130,633	11.0	25,744	2.2	7,801	0.7	284,291	R
Connecticut	1,406,285	677,210	48.2	541,732	38.5	171,807	12.2	8,570	0.6	6,966	0.5	135,478	R
Delaware	235,900	111,252	47.2	105,754	44.8	16,288	6.9	1,974	0.8	632	0.3	5,498	R
Florida	3,686,930	2,046,951	55.5	1,419,475	38.5	189,692	5.1	30,524	0.8	288		627,476	R
Georgia	1,596,695	654,168	41.0	890,733	55.8	36,055	2.3	15,627	1.0	112		236,565	D
Hawaii	303,287	130,112	42.9	135,879	44.8	32,021	10.6	3,269	1.1	2,006	0.7	5,767	R
Idaho	437,431	290,699	66.5	110,192	25.2	27,058	6.2	8,425	1.9	1,057	0.2	180,507	R
Illinois	4,749,721	2,358,049	49.6	1,981,413	41.7	346,754	7.3	38,939	0.8	24,566	0.5	376,636	R
Indiana	2,242,033	1,255,656	56.0	844,197	37.7	111,639	5.0	19,627	0.9	10,914	0.5	411,459	R
Iowa	1,317,661	676,026	51.3	508,672	38.6	115,633	8.8	13,123	1.0	4,207	0.3	167,354	R
Kansas	979,795	566,812	57.9	326,150	33.3	68,231	7.0	14,470	1.5	4,132	0.4	240,662	R
Kentucky	1,294,627	635,274	49.1	616,417	47.6	31,127	2.4	5,531	0.4	6,278	0.5	18,857	R
Louisiana	1,548,591	792,853	51.2	708,453	45.7	26,345	1.7	8,240	0.5	12,700	0.8	84,400	R
Maine	523,011	238,522	45.6	220,974	42.3	53,327	10.2	5,119	1.0	5,069	1.0	17,548	R
Maryland	1,540,496	680,606	44.2	726,161	47.1	119,537	7.8	14,192	0.9	—		45,555	D
Massachusetts	2,524,298	1,057,631	41.9	1,053,802	41.7	382,539	15.2	22,038	0.9	8,288	0.3	3,829	R
Michigan	3,909,725	1,915,225	49.0	1,661,532	42.5	275,223	7.0	41,597	1.1	16,148	0.4	253,693	R
Minnesota	2,051,980	873,268	42.6	954,174	46.5	174,990	8.5	31,592	1.5	17,956	0.9	80,906	D
Mississippi	892,620	441,089	49.4	429,281	48.1	12,036	1.3	5,465	0.6	4,749	0.5	11,808	R
Missouri	2,099,824	1,074,181	51.2	931,182	44.3	77,920	3.7	14,422	0.7	2,119	0.1	142,999	R
Montana	363,952	206,814	56.8	118,032	32.4	29,281	8.0	9,825	2.7	—		88,782	R
Nebraska	640,854	419,937	65.5	166,851	26.0	44,993	7.0	9,073	1.4	—		253,086	R
Nevada	247,885	155,017	62.5	66,666	26.9	17,651	7.1	4,358	1.8	4,193	1.7	88,351	R
New Hampshire	383,990	221,705	57.7	108,864	28.4	49,693	12.9	2,064	0.5	1,664	0.4	112,841	R
New Jersey	2,975,684	1,546,557	52.0	1,147,364	38.6	234,632	7.9	20,652	0.7	26,479	0.9	399,193	R
New Mexico	456,971	250,779	54.9	167,826	36.7	29,459	6.4	4,365	1.0	4,542	1.0	82,953	R
New York	6,201,959	2,893,831	46.7	2,728,372	44.0	467,801	7.5	52,648	0.8	59,307	1.0	165,459	R
North Carolina	1,855,833	915,018	49.3	875,635	47.2	52,800	2.8	9,677	0.5	2,703	0.1	39,383	R
North Dakota	301,545	193,695	64.2	79,189	26.3	23,640	7.8	3,743	1.2	1,278	0.4	114,506	R
Ohio	4,283,603	2,206,545	51.5	1,752,414	40.9	254,472	5.9	49,033	1.1	21,139	0.5	454,131	R
Oklahoma	1,149,708	695,570	60.5	402,026	35.0	38,284	3.3	13,828	1.2	—		293,544	R
Oregon	1,181,516	571,044	48.3	456,890	38.7	112,389	9.5	25,838	2.2	15,355	1.3	114,154	R
Pennsylvania	4,561,501	2,261,872	49.6	1,937,540	42.5	292,921	6.4	33,263	0.7	35,905	0.8	324,332	R
Rhode Island	416,072	154,793	37.2	198,342	47.7	59,819	14.4	2,458	0.6	660	0.2	43,549	D
South Carolina	894,071	441,841	49.4	430,385	48.1	14,153	1.6	5,139	0.6	2,553	0.3	11,456	R
South Dakota	327,703	198,343	60.5	103,855	31.7	21,431	6.5	3,824	1.2	250	0.1	94,488	R
Tennessee	1,617,616	787,761	48.7	783,051	48.4	35,991	2.2	7,116	0.4	3,697	0.2	4,710	R
Texas	4,541,636	2,510,705	55.3	1,881,147	41.4	111,613	2.5	37,643	0.8	528		629,558	R
Utah	604,222	439,687	72.8	124,266	20.6	30,284	5.0	7,226	1.2	2,759	0.5	315,421	R
Vermont	213,299	94,628	44.4	81,952	38.4	31,761	14.9	1,900	0.9	3,058	1.4	12,676	R
Virginia	1,866,032	989,609	53.0	752,174	40.3	95,418	5.1	12,821	0.7	16,010	0.9	237,435	R
Washington	1,742,394	865,244	49.7	650,193	37.3	185,073	10.6	29,213	1.7	12,671	0.7	215,051	R
West Virginia	737,715	334,206	45.3	367,462	49.8	31,691	4.3	4,356	0.6	—		33,256	D
Wisconsin	2,273,221	1,088,845	47.9	981,584	43.2	160,657	7.1	29,135	1.3	13,000	0.6	107,261	R
Wyoming	176,713	110,700	62.6	49,427	28.0	12,072	6.8	4,514	2.6	—		61,273	R
Dist. of Col.	175,237	23,545	13.4	131,113	74.8	16,337	9.3	1,114	0.6	3,128	1.8	107,568	D
Totals	**86,515,221**	**43,904,153**	*50.7*	**35,483,883**	*41.0*	**5,720,060**	*6.6*	**921,299**	*1.1*	**485,826**	*0.6*	**8,420,270**	**R**

PRESIDENTIAL ELECTION OF
1984

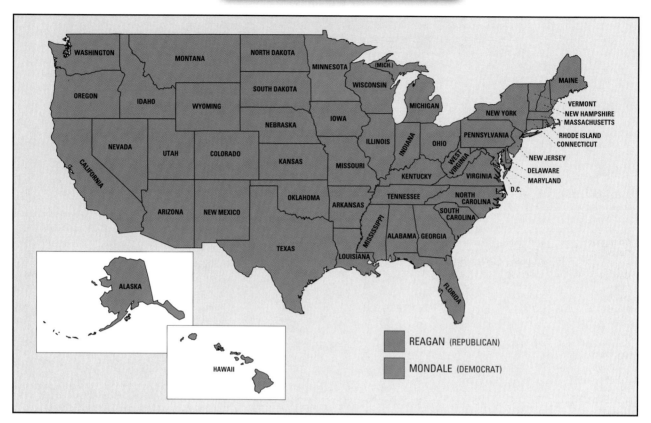

States	Electoral Votes	Reagan	Mondale	States	Electoral Votes	Reagan	Mondale
Alabama	(9)	9	-	Montana	(4)	4	-
Alaska	(3)	3	-	Nebraska	(5)	5	-
Arizona	(7)	7	-	Nevada	(4)	4	-
Arkansas	(6)	6	-	New Hampshire	(4)	4	-
California	(47)	47	-	New Jersey	(16)	16	-
Colorado	(8)	8	-	New Mexico	(5)	5	-
Connecticut	(8)	8	-	New York	(36)	36	-
Delaware	(3)	3	-	North Carolina	(13)	13	-
District of Columbia	(3)	-	3	North Dakota	(3)	3	-
Florida	(21)	21	-	Ohio	(23)	23	-
Georgia	(12)	12	-	Oklahoma	(8)	8	-
Hawaii	(4)	4	-	Oregon	(7)	7	-
Idaho	(4)	4	-	Pennsylvania	(25)	25	-
Illinois	(24)	24	-	Rhode Island	(4)	4	-
Indiana	(12)	12	-	South Carolina	(8)	8	-
Iowa	(8)	8	-	South Dakota	(3)	3	-
Kansas	(7)	7	-	Tennessee	(11)	11	-
Kentucky	(9)	9	-	Texas	(29)	29	-
Louisiana	(10)	10	-	Utah	(5)	5	-
Maine	(4)	4	-	Vermont	(3)	3	-
Maryland	(10)	10	-	Virginia	(12)	12	-
Massachusetts	(13)	13	-	Washington	(10)	10	-
Michigan	(20)	20	-	West Virginia	(6)	6	-
Minnesota	(10)	-	10	Wisconsin	(11)	11	-
Mississippi	(7)	7	-	Wyoming	(3)	3	-
Missouri	(11)	11	-	**Totals**	**(538)**	**525**	**13**

1984

PRESIDENTIAL ELECTION RETURNS

STATE	TOTAL VOTE	RONALD REAGAN (Republican)		WALTER F. MONDALE (Democrat)		DAVID BERGLAND (Libertarian)		LYNDON H. LaROUCHE JR. (Independent)		OTHER		PLURALITY	
		Votes	%	Votes	%	Votes	%	Votes	%	Votes	%		
Alabama	1,441,713	872,849	60.5	551,899	38.3	9,504	0.7	—		7,461	0.5	320,950	R
Alaska	207,605	138,377	66.7	62,007	29.9	6,378	3.1	—		843	0.4	76,370	R
Arizona	1,025,897	681,416	66.4	333,854	32.5	10,585	1.0	—		42		347,562	R
Arkansas	884,406	534,774	60.5	338,646	38.3	2,221	0.3	1,890	0.2	6,875	0.8	196,128	R
California	9,505,423	5,467,009	57.5	3,922,519	41.3	49,951	0.5	—		65,944	0.7	1,544,490	R
Colorado	1,295,380	821,817	63.4	454,975	35.1	11,257	0.9	4,662	0.4	2,669	0.2	366,842	R
Connecticut	1,466,900	890,877	60.7	569,597	38.8	204		—		6,222	0.4	321,280	R
Delaware	254,572	152,190	59.8	101,656	39.9	268	0.1	—		458	0.2	50,534	R
Florida	4,180,051	2,730,350	65.3	1,448,816	34.7	754		—		131		1,281,534	R
Georgia	1,776,120	1,068,722	60.2	706,628	39.8	152		34		584		362,094	R
Hawaii	335,846	185,050	55.1	147,154	43.8	2,167	0.6	654	0.2	821	0.2	37,896	R
Idaho	411,144	297,523	72.4	108,510	26.4	2,823	0.7	—		2,288	0.6	189,013	R
Illinois	4,819,088	2,707,103	56.2	2,086,499	43.3	10,086	0.2	—		15,400	0.3	620,604	R
Indiana	2,233,069	1,377,230	61.7	841,481	37.7	6,741	0.3	—		7,617	0.3	535,749	R
Iowa	1,319,805	703,088	53.3	605,620	45.9	1,844	0.1	6,248	0.5	3,005	0.2	97,468	R
Kansas	1,021,991	677,296	66.3	333,149	32.6	3,329	0.3	—		8,217	0.8	344,147	R
Kentucky	1,369,345	821,702	60.0	539,539	39.4	—		1,776	0.1	6,328	0.5	282,163	R
Louisiana	1,706,822	1,037,299	60.8	651,586	38.2	1,876	0.1	3,552	0.2	12,509	0.7	385,713	R
Maine	553,144	336,500	60.8	214,515	38.8	—		—		2,129	0.4	121,985	R
Maryland	1,675,873	879,918	52.5	787,935	47.0	5,721	0.3	—		2,299	0.1	91,983	R
Massachusetts	2,559,453	1,310,936	51.2	1,239,606	48.4	—		—		8,911	0.3	71,330	R
Michigan	3,801,658	2,251,571	59.2	1,529,638	40.2	10,055	0.3	3,862	0.1	6,532	0.2	721,933	R
Minnesota	2,084,449	1,032,603	49.5	1,036,364	49.7	2,996	0.1	3,865	0.2	8,621	0.4	3,761	D
Mississippi	941,104	582,377	61.9	352,192	37.4	2,336	0.2	1,001	0.1	3,198	0.3	230,185	R
Missouri	2,122,783	1,274,188	60.0	848,583	40.0	—		—		12		425,605	R
Montana	384,377	232,450	60.5	146,742	38.2	5,185	1.3	—		—		85,708	R
Nebraska	652,090	460,054	70.6	187,866	28.8	2,079	0.3	—		2,091	0.3	272,188	R
Nevada	286,667	188,770	65.8	91,655	32.0	2,292	0.8	—		3,950	1.4	97,115	R
New Hampshire	389,066	267,051	68.6	120,395	30.9	735	0.2	467	0.1	418	0.1	146,656	R
New Jersey	3,217,862	1,933,630	60.1	1,261,323	39.2	6,416	0.2	—		16,493	0.5	672,307	R
New Mexico	514,370	307,101	59.7	201,769	39.2	4,459	0.9	—		1,041	0.2	105,332	R
New York	6,806,810	3,664,763	53.8	3,119,609	45.8	11,949	0.2	—		10,489	0.2	545,154	R
North Carolina	2,175,361	1,346,481	61.9	824,287	37.9	3,794	0.2	—		799		522,194	R
North Dakota	308,971	200,336	64.8	104,429	33.8	703	0.2	1,278	0.4	2,225	0.7	95,907	R
Ohio	4,547,619	2,678,560	58.9	1,825,440	40.1	5,886	0.1	10,693	0.2	27,040	0.6	853,120	R
Oklahoma	1,255,676	861,530	68.6	385,080	30.7	9,066	0.7	—		—		476,450	R
Oregon	1,226,527	685,700	55.9	536,479	43.7	—		—		4,348	0.4	149,221	R
Pennsylvania	4,844,903	2,584,323	53.3	2,228,131	46.0	6,982	0.1	—		25,467	0.5	356,192	R
Rhode Island	410,492	212,080	51.7	197,106	48.0	277	0.1	—		1,029	0.3	14,974	R
South Carolina	968,529	615,539	63.6	344,459	35.6	4,359	0.5	—		4,172	0.4	271,080	R
South Dakota	317,867	200,267	63.0	116,113	36.5	—		—		1,487	0.5	84,154	R
Tennessee	1,711,994	990,212	57.8	711,714	41.6	3,072	0.2	1,852	0.1	5,144	0.3	278,498	R
Texas	5,397,571	3,433,428	63.6	1,949,276	36.1	—		14,613	0.3	254		1,484,152	R
Utah	629,656	469,105	74.5	155,369	24.7	2,447	0.4	—		2,735	0.4	313,736	R
Vermont	234,561	135,865	57.9	95,730	40.8	1,002	0.4	423	0.2	1,541	0.7	40,135	R
Virginia	2,146,635	1,337,078	62.3	796,250	37.1	—		13,307	0.6	—		540,828	R
Washington	1,883,910	1,051,670	55.8	807,352	42.9	8,844	0.5	4,712	0.3	11,332	0.6	244,318	R
West Virginia	735,742	405,483	55.1	328,125	44.6	—		—		2,134	0.3	77,358	R
Wisconsin	2,211,689	1,198,584	54.2	995,740	45.0	4,883	0.2	3,791	0.2	8,691	0.4	202,844	R
Wyoming	188,968	133,241	70.5	53,370	28.2	2,357	1.2	—		—		79,871	R
Dist. of Col.	211,288	29,009	13.7	180,408	85.4	279	0.1	127	0.1	1,465	0.7	151,399	D
Totals	92,652,842	54,455,075	58.8	37,577,185	40.6	228,314	0.2	78,807	0.1	313,461	0.3	16,877,890	R

PRESIDENTIAL ELECTION OF
1988

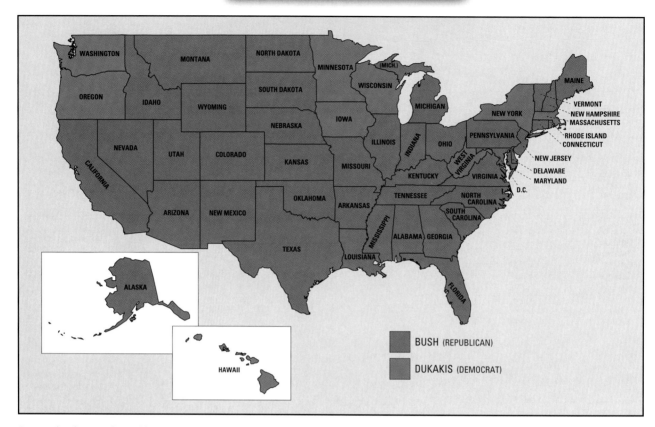

BUSH (REPUBLICAN)

DUKAKIS (DEMOCRAT)

Congressional Quarterly's Guide to U.S. Elections, 3rd. edition, copyright ©1994. Used with permission. All rights reserved.

States	Electoral Votes	Bush	Dukakis	Bentsen	States	Electoral Votes	Bush	Dukakis	Bentsen
Alabama	(9)	9	-	-	Montana	(4)	4	-	-
Alaska	(3)	3	-	-	Nebraska	(5)	5	-	-
Arizona	(7)	7	-	-	Nevada	(4)	4	-	-
Arkansas	(6)	6	-	-	New Hampshire	(4)	4	-	-
California	(47)	47	-	-	New Jersey	(16)	16	-	-
Colorado	(8)	8	-	-	New Mexico	(5)	5	-	-
Connecticut	(8)	8	-	-	New York	(36)	-	36	-
Delaware	(3)	3	-	-	North Carolina	(13)	13	-	-
District of Columbia	(3)	-	3	-	North Dakota	(3)	3	-	-
Florida	(21)	21	-	-	Ohio	(23)	23	-	-
Georgia	(12)	12	-	-	Oklahoma	(8)	8	-	-
Hawaii	(4)	-	4	-	Oregon	(7)	-	7	-
Idaho	(4)	4	-	-	Pennsylvania	(25)	25	-	-
Illinois	(24)	24	-	-	Rhode Island	(4)	-	4	-
Indiana	(12)	12	-	-	South Carolina	(8)	8	-	-
Iowa	(8)	-	8	-	South Dakota	(3)	3	-	-
Kansas	(7)	7	-	-	Tennessee	(11)	11	-	-
Kentucky	(9)	9	-	-	Texas	(29)	29	-	-
Louisiana	(10)	10	-	-	Utah	(5)	5	-	-
Maine	(4)	4	-	-	Vermont	(3)	3	-	-
Maryland	(10)	10	-	-	Virginia	(12)	12	-	-
Massachusetts	(13)	-	13	-	Washington	(10)	-	10	-
Michigan	(20)	20	-	-	West Virginia	(6)	-	5	1
Minnesota	(10)	-	10	-	Wisconsin	(11)	-	11	-
Mississippi	(7)	7	-	-	Wyoming	(3)	3	-	-
Missouri	(11)	11	-	-	**Totals**	**(538)**	**426**	**111**	**1**

1988

PRESIDENTIAL ELECTION RETURNS

STATE	TOTAL VOTE	GEORGE BUSH (Republican)		MICHAEL S. DUKAKIS (Democrat)		RON PAUL (Libertarian)		LENORA B. FULANI (New Alliance)		OTHER		PLURALITY	
		Votes	%	Votes	%	Votes	%	Votes	%	Votes	%		
Alabama	1,378,476	815,576	59.2	549,506	39.9	8,460	0.6	3,311	0.2	1,623	0.1	266,070	R
Alaska	200,116	119,251	59.6	72,584	36.3	5,484	2.7	1,024	0.5	1,773	0.9	46,667	R
Arizona	1,171,873	702,541	60.0	454,029	38.7	13,351	1.1	1,662	0.1	290		248,512	R
Arkansas	827,738	466,578	56.4	349,237	42.2	3,297	0.4	2,161	0.3	6,465	0.8	117,341	R
California	9,887,065	5,054,917	51.1	4,702,233	47.6	70,105	0.7	31,181	0.3	28,629	0.3	352,684	R
Colorado	1,372,394	728,177	53.1	621,453	45.3	15,482	1.1	2,539	0.2	4,743	0.3	106,724	R
Connecticut	1,443,394	750,241	52.0	676,584	46.9	14,071	1.0	2,491	0.2	7		73,657	R
Delaware	249,891	139,639	55.9	108,647	43.5	1,162	0.5	443	0.2	—		30,992	R
Florida	4,302,313	2,618,885	60.9	1,656,701	38.5	19,796	0.5	6,655	0.2	276		962,184	R
Georgia	1,809,672	1,081,331	59.8	714,792	39.5	8,435	0.5	5,099	0.3	15		366,539	R
Hawaii	354,461	158,625	44.8	192,364	54.3	1,999	0.6	1,003	0.3	470	0.1	33,739	D
Idaho	408,968	253,881	62.1	147,272	36.0	5,313	1.3	2,502	0.6	—		106,609	R
Illinois	4,559,120	2,310,939	50.7	2,215,940	48.6	14,944	0.3	10,276	0.2	7,021	0.2	94,999	R
Indiana	2,168,621	1,297,763	59.8	860,643	39.7	—		10,215	0.5	—		437,120	R
Iowa	1,225,614	545,355	44.5	670,557	54.7	2,494	0.2	540		6,668	0.5	125,202	D
Kansas	993,044	554,049	55.8	422,636	42.6	12,553	1.3	3,806	0.4	—		131,413	R
Kentucky	1,322,517	734,281	55.5	580,368	43.9	2,118	0.2	1,256	0.1	4,494	0.3	153,913	R
Louisiana	1,628,202	883,702	54.3	717,460	44.1	4,115	0.3	2,355	0.1	20,570	1.3	166,242	R
Maine	555,035	307,131	55.3	243,569	43.9	2,700	0.5	1,405	0.3	230		63,562	R
Maryland	1,714,358	876,167	51.1	826,304	48.2	6,748	0.4	5,115	0.3	24		49,863	R
Massachusetts	2,632,805	1,194,635	45.4	1,401,415	53.2	24,251	0.9	9,561	0.4	2,943	0.1	206,780	D
Michigan	3,669,163	1,965,486	53.6	1,675,783	45.7	18,336	0.5	2,513	0.1	7,045	0.2	289,703	R
Minnesota	2,096,790	962,337	45.9	1,109,471	52.9	5,109	0.2	1,734	0.1	18,139	0.9	147,134	D
Mississippi	931,527	557,890	59.9	363,921	39.1	3,329	0.4	2,155	0.2	4,232	0.5	193,969	R
Missouri	2,093,713	1,084,953	51.8	1,001,619	47.8	434		6,656	0.3	51		83,334	R
Montana	365,674	190,412	52.1	168,936	46.2	5,047	1.4	1,279	0.3	—		21,476	R
Nebraska	661,465	397,956	60.2	259,235	39.2	2,534	0.4	1,740	0.3	—		138,721	R
Nevada	350,067	206,040	58.9	132,738	37.9	3,520	1.0	835	0.2	6,934	2.0	73,302	R
New Hampshire	451,074	281,537	62.4	163,696	36.3	4,502	1.0	790	0.2	549	0.1	117,841	R
New Jersey	3,099,553	1,743,192	56.2	1,320,352	42.6	8,421	0.3	5,139	0.2	22,449	0.7	422,840	R
New Mexico	521,287	270,341	51.9	244,497	46.9	3,268	0.6	2,237	0.4	944	0.2	25,844	R
New York	6,485,683	3,081,871	47.5	3,347,882	51.6	12,109	0.2	15,845	0.2	27,976	0.4	266,011	D
North Carolina	2,134,370	1,237,258	58.0	890,167	41.7	1,263	0.1	5,682	0.3	—		347,091	R
North Dakota	297,261	166,559	56.0	127,739	43.0	1,315	0.4	396	0.1	1,252	0.4	38,820	R
Ohio	4,393,699	2,416,549	55.0	1,939,629	44.1	11,989	0.3	12,017	0.3	13,515	0.3	476,920	R
Oklahoma	1,171,036	678,367	57.9	483,423	41.3	6,261	0.5	2,985	0.3	—		194,944	R
Oregon	1,201,694	560,126	46.6	616,206	51.3	14,811	1.2	6,487	0.5	4,064	0.3	56,080	D
Pennsylvania	4,536,251	2,300,087	50.7	2,194,944	48.4	12,051	0.3	4,379	0.1	24,790	0.5	105,143	R
Rhode Island	404,620	177,761	43.9	225,123	55.6	825	0.2	280	0.1	631	0.2	47,362	D
South Carolina	986,009	606,443	61.5	370,554	37.6	4,935	0.5	4,077	0.4	—		235,889	R
South Dakota	312,991	165,415	52.8	145,560	46.5	1,060	0.3	730	0.2	226	0.1	19,855	R
Tennessee	1,636,250	947,233	57.9	679,794	41.5	2,041	0.1	1,334	0.1	5,848	0.4	267,439	R
Texas	5,427,410	3,036,829	56.0	2,352,748	43.3	30,355	0.6	7,208	0.1	270		684,081	R
Utah	647,008	428,442	66.2	207,343	32.0	7,473	1.2	455	0.1	3,295	0.5	221,099	R
Vermont	243,328	124,331	51.1	115,775	47.6	1,000	0.4	205	0.1	2,017	0.8	8,556	R
Virginia	2,191,609	1,309,162	59.7	859,799	39.2	8,336	0.4	14,312	0.7	—		449,363	R
Washington	1,865,253	903,835	48.5	933,516	50.0	17,240	0.9	3,520	0.2	7,142	0.4	29,681	D
West Virginia	653,311	310,065	47.5	341,016	52.2	—		2,230	0.3	—		30,951	D
Wisconsin	2,191,608	1,047,499	47.8	1,126,794	51.4	5,157	0.2	1,953	0.1	10,205	0.5	79,295	D
Wyoming	176,551	106,867	60.5	67,113	38.0	2,026	1.1	545	0.3	—		39,754	R
Dist. of Col.	192,877	27,590	14.3	159,407	82.6	554	0.3	2,901	1.5	2,425	1.3	131,817	D
Totals	91,594,809	48,886,097	53.4	41,809,074	45.6	432,179	0.5	217,219	0.2	250,240	0.3	7,077,023	R

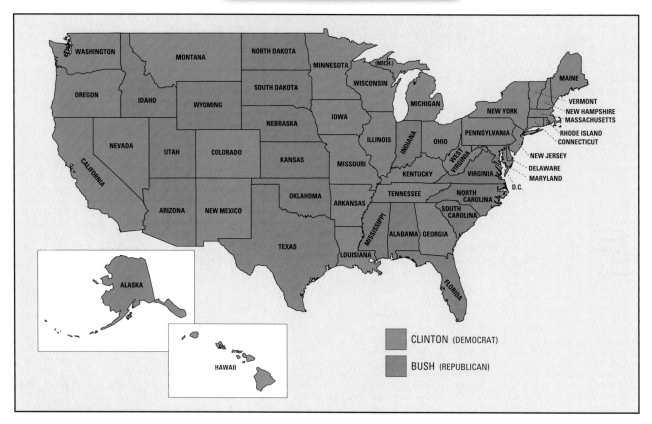

PRESIDENTIAL ELECTION OF
1992

Congressional Quarterly's Guide to U.S. Elections, 3rd. edition, copyright ©1994. Used with permission. All rights reserved.

States	Electoral Votes	Clinton	Bush	States	Electoral Votes	Clinton	Bush
Alabama	(9)	-	9	Montana	(3)	3	-
Alaska	(3)	-	3	Nebraska	(5)	-	5
Arizona	(8)	-	8	Nevada	(4)	4	-
Arkansas	(6)	6	-	New Hampshire	(4)	4	-
California	(54)	54	-	New Jersey	(15)	15	-
Colorado	(8)	8	-	New Mexico	(5)	5	-
Connecticut	(8)	8	-	New York	(33)	33	-
Delaware	(3)	3	-	North Carolina	(14)	-	14
District of Columbia	(3)	3	-	North Dakota	(3)	-	3
Florida	(25)	-	25	Ohio	(21)	21	-
Georgia	(13)	13	-	Oklahoma	(8)	-	8
Hawaii	(4)	4	-	Oregon	(7)	7	-
Idaho	(4)	-	4	Pennsylvania	(23)	23	-
Illinois	(22)	22	-	Rhode Island	(4)	4	-
Indiana	(12)	-	12	South Carolina	(8)	-	8
Iowa	(7)	7	-	South Dakota	(3)	-	3
Kansas	(6)	-	6	Tennessee	(11)	11	-
Kentucky	(8)	8	-	Texas	(32)	-	32
Louisiana	(9)	9	-	Utah	(5)	-	5
Maine	(4)	4	-	Vermont	(3)	3	-
Maryland	(10)	10	-	Virginia	(13)	-	13
Massachusetts	(12)	12	-	Washington	(11)	11	-
Michigan	(18)	18	-	West Virginia	(5)	5	-
Minnesota	(10)	10	-	Wisconsin	(11)	11	-
Mississippi	(7)	-	7	Wyoming	(3)	-	3
Missouri	(11)	11	-	**Totals**	**(538)**	**370**	**168**

1992

PRESIDENTIAL ELECTION RETURNS

STATE	TOTAL VOTE	BILL CLINTON (Democrat)		GEORGE BUSH (Republican)		ROSS PEROT (Independent)		ANDRE V. MARROU (Libertarian)		OTHER [1]		PLURALITY	
		Votes	%	Votes	%	Votes	%	Votes	%	Votes	%		
Alabama	1,688,060	690,080	40.9	804,283	47.6	183,109	10.8	5,737	0.3	4,851	0.3	114,203	R
Alaska	258,506	78,294	30.3	102,000	39.5	73,481	28.4	1,378	0.5	3,353	1.3	23,706	R
Arizona	1,486,975	543,050	36.5	572,086	38.5	353,741	23.8	6,759	0.5	11,339	0.8	29,036	R
Arkansas	950,653	505,823	53.2	337,324	35.5	99,132	10.4	1,261	0.1	7,113	0.7	168,499	D
California	11,131,721	5,121,325	46.0	3,630,574	32.6	2,296,006	20.6	48,139	0.4	35,677	0.3	1,490,751	D
Colorado	1,569,180	629,681	40.1	562,850	35.9	366,010	23.3	8,669	0.6	1,970	0.1	66,831	D
Connecticut	1,616,332	682,318	42.2	578,313	35.8	348,771	21.6	5,391	0.3	1,539	0.1	104,005	D
Delaware	289,735	126,054	43.5	102,313	35.3	59,213	20.4	935	0.3	1,220	0.4	23,741	D
Florida	5,314,392	2,072,698	39.0	2,173,310	40.9	1,053,067	19.8	15,079	0.3	238		100,612	R
Georgia	2,321,125	1,008,966	43.5	995,252	42.9	309,657	13.3	7,110	0.3	140		13,714	D
Hawaii	372,842	179,310	48.1	136,822	36.7	53,003	14.2	1,119	0.3	2,588	0.7	42,488	D
Idaho	482,142	137,013	28.4	202,645	42.0	130,395	27.0	1,167	0.2	10,922	2.3	65,632	R
Illinois	5,050,157	2,453,350	48.6	1,734,096	34.3	840,515	16.6	9,218	0.2	12,978	0.3	719,254	D
Indiana	2,305,871	848,420	36.8	989,375	42.9	455,934	19.8	7,936	0.3	4,206	0.2	140,955	R
Iowa	1,354,607	586,353	43.3	504,891	37.3	253,468	18.7	1,076	0.1	8,819	0.7	81,462	D
Kansas	1,157,335	390,434	33.7	449,951	38.9	312,358	27.0	4,314	0.4	278		59,517	R
Kentucky	1,492,900	665,104	44.6	617,178	41.3	203,944	13.7	4,513	0.3	2,161	0.1	47,926	D
Louisiana	1,790,017	815,971	45.6	733,386	41.0	211,478	11.8	3,155	0.2	26,027	1.5	82,585	D
Maine	679,499	263,420	38.8	206,504	30.4	206,820	30.4	1,681	0.2	1,074	0.2	56,600	D
Maryland	1,985,046	988,571	49.8	707,094	35.6	281,414	14.2	4,715	0.2	3,252	0.2	281,477	D
Massachusetts	2,773,700	1,318,662	47.5	805,049	29.0	630,731	22.7	9,024	0.3	10,234	0.4	513,613	D
Michigan	4,274,673	1,871,182	43.8	1,554,940	36.4	824,813	19.3	10,175	0.2	13,563	0.3	316,242	D
Minnesota	2,347,948	1,020,997	43.5	747,841	31.9	562,506	24.0	3,374	0.1	13,230	0.6	273,156	D
Mississippi	981,793	400,258	40.8	487,793	49.7	85,626	8.7	2,154	0.2	5,962	0.6	87,535	R
Missouri	2,391,565	1,053,873	44.1	811,159	33.9	518,741	21.7	7,497	0.3	295		242,714	D
Montana	410,611	154,507	37.6	144,207	35.1	107,225	26.1	986	0.2	3,686	0.9	10,300	D
Nebraska	737,546	216,864	29.4	343,678	46.6	174,104	23.6	1,340	0.2	1,560	0.2	126,814	R
Nevada	506,318	189,148	37.4	175,828	34.7	132,580	26.2	1,835	0.4	6,927	1.4	13,320	D
New Hampshire	537,943	209,040	38.9	202,484	37.6	121,337	22.6	3,548	0.7	1,534	0.3	6,556	D
New Jersey	3,343,594	1,436,206	43.0	1,356,865	40.6	521,829	15.6	6,822	0.2	21,872	0.7	79,341	D
New Mexico	569,986	261,617	45.9	212,824	37.3	91,895	16.1	1,615	0.3	2,035	0.4	48,793	D
New York	6,926,925	3,444,450	49.7	2,346,649	33.9	1,090,721	15.7	13,451	0.2	31,654	0.5	1,097,801	D
North Carolina	2,611,850	1,114,042	42.7	1,134,661	43.4	357,864	13.7	5,171	0.2	112		20,619	R
North Dakota	308,133	99,168	32.2	136,244	44.2	71,084	23.1	416	0.1	1,221	0.4	37,076	R
Ohio	4,939,967	1,984,942	40.2	1,894,310	38.3	1,036,426	21.0	7,252	0.1	17,037	0.3	90,632	D
Oklahoma	1,390,359	473,066	34.0	592,929	42.6	319,878	23.0	4,486	0.3	—		119,863	R
Oregon	1,462,643	621,314	42.5	475,757	32.5	354,091	24.2	4,277	0.3	7,204	0.5	145,557	D
Pennsylvania	4,959,810	2,239,164	45.1	1,791,841	36.1	902,667	18.2	21,477	0.4	4,661	0.1	447,323	D
Rhode Island	453,477	213,299	47.0	131,601	29.0	105,045	23.2	571	0.1	2,961	0.7	81,698	D
South Carolina	1,202,527	479,514	39.9	577,507	48.0	138,872	11.5	2,719	0.2	3,915	0.3	97,993	R
South Dakota	336,254	124,888	37.1	136,718	40.7	73,295	21.8	814	0.2	539	0.2	11,830	R
Tennessee	1,982,638	933,521	47.1	841,300	42.4	199,968	10.1	1,847	0.1	6,002	0.3	92,221	D
Texas	6,154,018	2,281,815	37.1	2,496,071	40.6	1,354,781	22.0	19,699	0.3	1,652		214,256	R
Utah	743,999	183,429	24.7	322,632	43.4	203,400	27.3	1,900	0.3	32,638	4.4	119,232	R
Vermont	289,701	133,592	46.1	88,122	30.4	65,991	22.8	501	0.2	1,495	0.5	45,470	D
Virginia	2,558,665	1,038,650	40.6	1,150,517	45.0	348,639	13.6	5,730	0.2	15,129	0.6	111,867	R
Washington	2,288,230	993,037	43.4	731,234	32.0	541,780	23.7	7,533	0.3	14,646	0.6	261,803	D
West Virginia	683,762	331,001	48.4	241,974	35.4	108,829	15.9	1,873	0.3	85		89,027	D
Wisconsin	2,531,114	1,041,066	41.1	930,855	36.8	544,479	21.5	2,877	0.1	11,837	0.5	110,211	D
Wyoming	200,598	68,160	34.0	79,347	39.6	51,263	25.6	844	0.4	984	0.5	11,187	R
Dist. of Col.	227,572	192,619	84.6	20,698	9.1	9,681	4.3	467	0.2	4,107	1.8	171,921	D
Totals	104,425,014	44,909,326	43.0	39,103,882	37.4	19,741,657	18.9	291,627	0.3	378,522	0.4	5,805,444	D

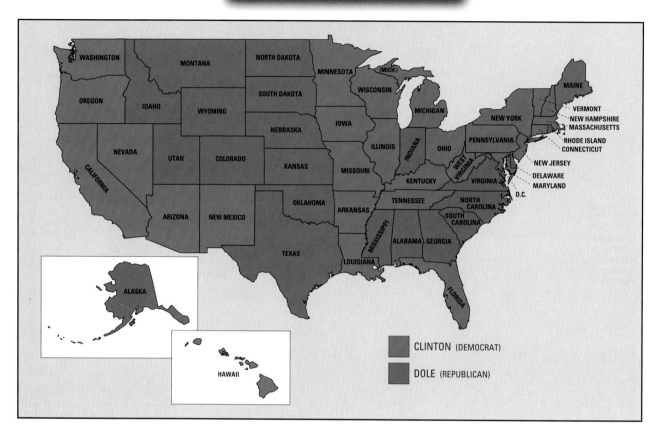

PRESIDENTIAL ELECTION OF
1996

CLINTON (DEMOCRAT)

DOLE (REPUBLICAN)

States	Electoral Votes	Clinton	Dole	States	Electoral Votes	Clinton	Dole
Alabama	(9)	-	9	Montana	(3)	-	3
Alaska	(3)	-	3	Nebraska	(5)	-	5
Arizona	(8)	8	-	Nevada	(4)	4	-
Arkansas	(6)	6	-	New Hampshire	(4)	4	-
California	(54)	54	-	New Jersey	(15)	15	-
Colorado	(8)	-	8	New Mexico	(5)	5	-
Connecticut	(8)	8	-	New York	(33)	33	-
Delaware	(3)	3	-	North Carolina	(14)	-	14
District of Columbia	(3)	3	-	North Dakota	(3)	-	3
Florida	(25)	25	-	Ohio	(21)	21	-
Georgia	(13)	-	13	Oklahoma	(8)	-	8
Hawaii	(4)	4	-	Oregon	(7)	7	-
Idaho	(4)	-	4	Pennsylvania	(23)	23	-
Illinois	(22)	22	-	Rhode Island	(4)	4	-
Indiana	(12)	-	12	South Carolina	(8)	-	8
Iowa	(7)	7	-	South Dakota	(3)	-	3
Kansas	(6)	-	6	Tennessee	(11)	11	-
Kentucky	(8)	8	-	Texas	(32)	-	32
Louisiana	(9)	9	-	Utah	(5)	-	5
Maine	(4)	4	-	Vermont	(3)	3	-
Maryland	(10)	10	-	Virginia	(13)	-	13
Massachusetts	(12)	12	-	Washington	(11)	11	-
Michigan	(18)	18	-	West Virginia	(5)	5	-
Minnesota	(10)	10	-	Wisconsin	(11)	11	-
Mississippi	(7)	-	7	Wyoming	(3)	-	3
Missouri	(11)	11	-	**Totals**	**(538)**	**379**	**159**

1996

PRESIDENTIAL ELECTION RETURNS

STATE	BILL CLINTON (Democrat)		ROBERT DOLE (Republican)		ROSS PEROT (Reform)		OTHER		PLURALITY	
	Votes	%	Votes	%	Votes	%	Votes	%		
Alabama	658,431	43	771,651	50	92,163	6	9,629	1	113,220	R
Alaska	66,508	33	101,234	51	21,536	11	8,673	5	34,726	R
Arizona	609,761	47	572,847	44	104,287	8	13,294	1	36,914	D
Arkansas	448,057	54	307,419	37	67,300	8	12,576	2	140,638	D
California	4,639,935	51	3,412,563	38	667,702	7	330,752	4	1,227,372	D
Colorado	670,656	44	691,095	46	99,440	7	47,115	3	20,439	R
Connecticut	709,149	52	484,638	36	136,723	10	32,960	2	224,511	D
Delaware	140,209	52	98,906	37	28,693	11	2,670	1	41,303	D
Florida	2,533,553	48	2,226,099	42	481,225	9	25,343	0	307,454	D
Georgia	1,045,466	46	1,077,161	47	144,368	6	18,534	1	31,695	R
Hawaii	205,012	57	113,943	32	27,358	8	10,532	4	91,069	D
Idaho	163,866	34	253,769	52	61,861	13	7,037	1	89,903	R
Illinois	2,302,054	54	1,576,534	37	343,942	8	34,159	1	725,520	D
Indiana	871,033	41	1,010,170	48	218,068	10	15,270	1	139,137	R
Iowa	615,523	50	489,729	40	102,922	8	14,051	1	125,794	D
Kansas	383,795	36	577,426	54	91,911	9	9,699	1	193,631	R
Kentucky	635,804	46	622,339	45	118,768	9	7,769	1	13,465	D
Louisiana	928,564	52	709,136	40	122,892	7	20,447	1	219,428	D
Maine	299,894	52	178,683	31	82,773	14	17,381	3	121,211	D
Maryland	924,284	54	651,682	38	113,684	7	14,584	1	272,602	D
Massachusetts	1,567,223	62	717,622	28	225,394	9	28,817	1	849,601	D
Michigan	1,786,702	52	1,332,706	39	302,751	9	29,207	1	453,996	D
Minnesota	1,087,263	51	746,890	35	250,512	12	41,219	2	340,373	D
Mississippi	382,621	44	433,439	50	51,258	6	7,538	1	50,818	R
Missouri	1,023,505	48	889,123	41	216,734	10	24,253	1	134,382	D
Montana	163,208	41	175,162	44	54,191	14	4,199	1	11,954	R
Nebraska	231,840	35	355,482	53	76,056	11	5,729	1	123,642	R
Nevada	196,050	44	187,421	42	41,820	9	16,046	4	8,629	D
New Hamphire	245,260	50	196,740	40	48,140	10	4,807	1	48,520	D
New Jersey	1,592,267	53	1,086,374	36	262,265	9	59,531	2	505,893	D
New Mexico	252,215	49	210,791	41	30,978	6	16,293	3	41,424	D
New York	3,493,548	59	1,852,097	31	479,953	8	112,430	2	1,641,451	D
North Carolina	1,094,025	44	1,211,844	49	164,593	7	11,877	0	117,819	R
North Dakota	106,136	40	124,215	47	32,481	12	1,934	1	18,079	R
Ohio	2,098,870	47	1,821,580	41	470,188	11	38,696	1	277,290	D
Oklahoma	488,102	40	582,310	48	130,788	11	5,505	0	94,208	R
Oregon	318,222	47	249,052	37	71,015	11	36,720	5	69,170	D
Pennsylvania	2,202,372	49	1,792,493	40	429,248	10	56,015	1	409,879	D
Rhode Island	217,495	60	96,498	27	39,137	11	8,051	2	120,997	D
South Carolina	496,146	44	564,979	50	62,733	6	7,371	1	68,833	R
South Dakota	139,296	43	150,508	46	31,218	10	2,698	1	11,212	R
Tennessee	905,538	48	860,809	46	105,577	6	15,047	1	44,729	D
Texas	2,455,735	44	2,731,998	49	377,530	7	33,938	1	276,263	R
Utah	220,197	33	359,394	54	66,100	10	15,442	2	139,197	R
Vermont	138,400	54	80,043	31	30,912	12	8,277	3	58,357	D
Virginia	1,065,737	45	1,117,690	47	158,253	7	26,937	1	51,953	R
Washington	899,645	51	639,743	36	161,642	9	70,153	4	259,902	D
West Virginia	320,913	51	230,997	37	70,158	11	2,968	0	89,916	D
Wisconsin	1,071,385	49	844,540	39	227,223	10	49,074	2	226,845	D
Wyoming	77,897	37	105,347	50	25,854	12	2,317	1	27,450	R
Dist. of Col.	152,031	85	16,637	9	3,479	2	5,676	3	135,394	D
Totals	**45,341,398**	**49.1**	**37,691,548**	**40.9**	**7,825,797**	**8.5**	**1,401,240**	**1.5**	**7,649,850**	**D**

*Incomplete results; not all precincts reporting. Partial source: Associated Press.

The Constitution of the United States

We the People of the United States, in Order to form a more perfect Union, establish Justice, insure domestic Tranquility, provide for the common defence, promote the general Welfare, and secure the Blessings of Liberty to ourselves and our Posterity, do ordain and establish this Constitution of the United States of America.

ARTICLE I.

Section. 1. All legislative Powers herein granted shall be vested in a Congress of the United States, which shall consist of a Senate and House of Representatives.

Section. 2. The House of Representatives shall be composed of Members chosen every second Year by the People of the several States, and the Electors in each State shall have the Qualifications requisite for Electors of the most numerous Branch of the State Legislature.

No Person shall be a Representative who shall not have attained to the Age of twenty five Years, and been seven Years a Citizen of the United States, and who shall not, when elected, be an Inhabitant of that State in which he shall be chosen.

Representatives and direct Taxes shall be apportioned among the several States which may be included within this Union, according to their respective Numbers, which shall be determined by adding to the whole Number of free Persons, including those bound to Service for a Term of Years, and excluding Indians not taxed, three fifths of all other Persons. The actual Enumeration shall be made within three Years after the first Meeting of the Congress of the United States, and within every subsequent Term of ten Years, in such Manner as they shall by Law direct. The Number of Representatives shall not exceed one for every thirty Thousand, but each State shall have at Least one Representative; and until such enumeration shall be made, the State of New Hampshire shall be entitled to chuse three, Massachusetts eight, Rhode-Island and Providence Plantations one, Connecticut five, New-York six, New Jersey four, Pennsylvania eight, Delaware one, Maryland six, Virginia ten, North Carolina five, South Carolina five, and Georgia three.

When vacancies happen in the Representation from any State, the Executive Authority thereof shall issue Writs of Election to fill such Vacancies.

The House of Representatives shall chuse their Speaker and other Officers; and shall have the sole Power of Impeachment.

Section. 3. The Senate of the United States shall be composed of two Senators from each State, chosen by the Legislature thereof, for six Years; and each Senator shall have one Vote.

Immediately after they shall be assembled in Consequence of the first Election, they shall be divided as equally as may be into three Classes. The Seats of the Senators of the first Class shall be vacated at the Expiration of the second Year, of the second Class at the Expiration of the fourth Year, and of the third Class at the Expiration of the sixth Year, so that one third may be chosen every second Year; and if Vacancies happen by Resignation, or otherwise, during the Recess of the Legislature of any State, the Executive thereof may make temporary Appointments until the next Meeting of the Legislature, which shall then fill such Vacancies.

No Person shall be a Senator who shall not have attained to the Age of thirty Years, and been nine Years a Citizen of the United States, and who shall not, when elected, be an Inhabitant of that State for which he shall be chosen.

The Vice President of the United States shall be President of the Senate, but shall have no Vote, unless they be equally divided.

The Senate shall chuse their other Officers, and also a President pro tempore, in the Absence of the Vice President, or when he shall exercise the Office of President of the United States.

The Senate shall have the sole Power to try all Impeachments. When sitting for that Purpose, they shall be on Oath or Affirmation. When the President of the United States is tried, the Chief Justice shall preside: And no Person shall be convicted without the Concurrence of two thirds of the Members present.

Judgment in Cases of Impeachment shall not extend further than to removal from Office, and disqualification to hold and enjoy any Office of honor, Trust or Profit under the United States: but the Party convicted shall nevertheless be liable and subject to Indictment, Trial, Judgment and Punishment, according to Law.

Section. 4. The Times, Places and Manner of holding Elections for Senators and Representatives, shall be prescribed in each State by the Legislature thereof; but the Congress may at any time by Law make or alter such Regulations, except as to the Places of chusing Senators.

The Congress shall assemble at least once in every Year, and such Meeting shall be on the first Monday in December, unless they shall by Law appoint a different Day.

Section. 5. Each House shall be the Judge of the Elections, Returns and Qualifications of its own Members, and a Majority of each shall constitute a Quorum to do Business; but a smaller Number may adjourn from day to day, and may be authorized to compel the Attendance of absent Members, in such Manner, and under such Penalties as each House may provide.

Each House may determine the Rules of its Proceedings, punish its Members for disorderly Behaviour, and, with the Concurrence of two thirds, expel a Member.

Each House shall keep a Journal of its Proceedings, and from time to time publish the same, excepting such Parts as may in their Judgment require Secrecy; and the Yeas and Nays of the Members of either House on any question shall, at the Desire of one fifth of those Present, be entered on the Journal.

Neither House, during the Session of Congress, shall, without the Consent of the other, adjourn for more than three days, nor to any other Place than that in which the two Houses shall be sitting.

Section. 6. The Senators and Representatives shall receive a Compensation for their Services, to be ascertained by Law, and paid out of the Treasury of the United States. They shall in all Cases, except Treason, Felony and Breach of the Peace, be privileged from Arrest during their Attendance at the Session of their respective Houses, and in going to and returning from the same; and for any Speech or Debate in either House, they shall not be questioned in any other Place.

No Senator or Representative shall, during the Time for which he was elected, be appointed to any civil Office under the Authority of the United States, which shall have been created, or the Emoluments whereof shall have been encreased during such time; and no Person holding any Office under the United States, shall be a Member of either House during his Continuance in Office.

Section. 7. All Bills for raising Revenue shall originate in the House of Representatives; but the Senate may propose or concur with Amendments as on other Bills.

Every Bill which shall have passed the House of Representatives and the Senate, shall, before it become a Law, be presented to the President of the United States; If he approve he shall sign it, but if not he shall return it, with his Objections to that House in which it shall have originated, who shall enter the Objections at large on their Journal, and proceed to reconsider it. If after such Reconsideration two thirds of that House shall agree to pass the Bill, it shall be sent, together with the Objections, to the other House, by which it shall likewise be reconsidered, and if approved by two thirds of that House, it shall become a Law. But in all such Cases the Votes of both Houses shall be determined by yeas and Nays, and the Names of the Persons voting for and against the Bill shall be entered on the Journal of each House respectively. If any Bill shall not be returned by the President within ten Days (Sundays excepted) after it shall have been presented to him, the Same shall be a Law, in like "Manner as if he had signed it, unless the Congress by their Adjournment prevent its Return, in which Case it shall not be a Law.

Every Order, Resolution, or Vote to which the Concurrence of the Senate and House of Representatives may be necessary (except on a question of Adjournment) shall be presented to the President of the United States; and before the Same shall take Effect, shall be approved by him, or being disapproved by him, shall be repassed by two thirds of the Senate and House of Representatives, according to the Rules and Limitations prescribed in the Case of a Bill.

Section. 8. The Congress shall have Power To lay and collect Taxes, Duties, Imposts and Excises, to pay the Debts and provide for the common Defence and general Welfare of the United States; but all Duties, Imposts and Excises shall be uniform throughout the United States;

To borrow Money on the credit of the United States;

To regulate Commerce with foreign Nations, and among the several States, and with the Indian tribes;

To establish an uniform Rule of Naturalization, and uniform Laws on the subject of Bankruptcies throughout the United States;

To coin Money, regulate the Value thereof, and of foreign Coin, and fix the Standard of Weights and Measures;

To provide for the Punishment of counterfeiting the Securities and current Coin of the United States;

To establish Post Offices and post Roads;

To promote the Progress of Science and useful Arts, by securing for limited Times to Authors and Inventors the exclusive Right to their respective Writings and Discoveries;

To constitute Tribunals inferior to the supreme Court;

To define and punish Piracies and Felonies committed on the high Seas, and Offences against the Law of Nations;

To declare War, grant Letters of Marque and Reprisal, and make Rules concerning Captures on Land and Water;

To raise and support Armies, but no Appropriation of Money to that Use shall be for a longer Term than two Years;

To provide and maintain a Navy;

To make Rules for the Government and Regulation of the land and naval Forces;

To provide for calling forth the Militia to execute the Laws of the Union, suppress Insurrections and repel Invasions;

To provide for organizing, arming, and disciplining, the Militia, and for governing such Part of them as may be employed in the Service of the United States, reserving to the States respectively, the Appointment of the Officers, and the Authority of training the Militia according to the discipline prescribed by Congress;

To exercise exclusive Legislation in all Cases whatsoever, over such District (not exceeding ten Miles square) as may, by Cession of particular States, and the Acceptance of Congress, become the Seat of the Government of the United States, and to exercise like Authority over all Places purchased by the Consent of the Legislature of the State in which the Same shall be, for the Erection of Forts, Magazines, Arsenals, dock- Yards, and other needful Buildings;—And

To make all Laws which shall be necessary and proper for carrying into Execution the foregoing Powers, and all other Powers vested by this Constitution in the Government of the United States, or in any Department or Officer thereof.

Section. 9. The Migration or Importation of such Persons as any of the States now existing shall think proper to admit, shall not be prohibited by the Congress prior to the Year one thousand eight hundred and eight, but a Tax or duty may be imposed on such Importation, not exceeding ten dollars for each Person.

The Privilege of the Writ of Habeas Corpus shall not be suspended, unless when in Cases of Rebellion or Invasion the public Safety may require it.

No Bill of Attainder or ex post facto Law shall be passed.

No Capitation, or other direct, Tax shall be laid, unless in Proportion to the Census or Enumeration herein before directed to be taken.

No Tax or Duty shall be laid on Articles exported from any State.

No Preference shall be given by any Regulation of Commerce or Revenue to the Ports of one State over those of another: nor shall Vessels bound to, or from, one State, be obliged to enter, clear, or pay Duties in another.

No Money shall be drawn from the Treasury, but in Consequence of Appropriations made by Law; and a regular Statement and Account of the Receipts and Expenditures of all public Money shall be published from time to time.

No Title of Nobility shall be granted by the United States: And no Person holding any Office of Profit or Trust under them, shall, without the Consent of the Congress, accept of any present, Emolument, Office, or Title, of any kind whatever, from any King, Prince, or foreign State.

Section. 10. No State shall enter into any Treaty, Alliance, or Confederation; grant Letters of Marque and Reprisal; coin Money; emit Bills of Credit; make any Thing but gold and silver Coin a Tender in Payment of Debts; pass any Bill of Attainder, ex post facto Law, or Law impairing the Obligation of Contracts, or grant any Title of Nobility.

No State shall, without the Consent of the Congress, lay any Imposts or Duties on Imports or Exports, except what may be absolutely necessary for executing it's inspection Laws: and the net Produce of all Duties and Imposts, laid by any State on Imports or Exports, shall be for the Use of the Treasury of the United States; and all such Laws shall be subject to the Revision and Controul of the Congress.

No State shall, without the consent of Congress, lay any Duty of Tonnage, keep Troops, or Ships of War in time of Peace, enter into any Agreement or Compact with another State, or with a foreign Power, or engage in War, unless actually invaded, or in such imminent Danger as will not admit of delay.

ARTICLE II.

SECTION. 1. The executive Power shall be vested in a President of the United States of America. He shall hold his Office during the Term of four Years, and, together with the Vice President, chosen for the same Term, be elected, as follows

Each State shall appoint, in such Manner as the Legislature thereof may direct, a Number of Electors, equal to the whole Number of Senators and Representatives to which the State may be entitled in the Congress; but no Senator or Representative, or Person holding an Office of Trust or Profit under the United States, shall be appointed an Elector.

The Electors shall meet in their respective States, and vote by Ballot for two Persons, of whom one at least shall not be an inhabitant of the same State with themselves. And they shall make a List of all the Persons voted for, and of the Number of Votes for each; which List they shall sign and certify, and transmit sealed to the Seat of the Government of the United States, directed to the President of the Senate. The President of the Senate shall, in the Presence of the Senate and House of Representatives, open all the Certificates, and the Votes shall then be counted. The Person having the greatest Number of Votes shall be the President, if such Number be a Majority of the whole Number of Electors appointed; and if there be more than one who have such Majority, and have an equal Number of Votes, then the House of Representatives shall immediately chuse by Ballot one of them for President; and if no Person have a Majority, then from the five highest on the List the said House shall in like Manner chuse the President. But in chusing the President, the Votes shall be taken by States, the Representation from each State having one Vote; A quorum for this purpose shall consist of a Member or Members from two thirds of the States, and a Majority of all the States shall be necessary to a Choice. In every Case, after the Choice of the President, the Person having the greatest Number of Votes of the Electors shall be the Vice President. But if there should remain two or more who have equal Votes, the Senate shall chuse from them by Ballot the Vice President.

The Congress may determine the Time of chusing the Electors, and the Day on which they shall give their Votes; which Day shall be the same throughout the United States.

No Person except a natural born Citizen, or a Citizen of the United States, at the time of the Adoption of this Constitution, shall be eligible to the Office of President; neither shall any Person be eligible to that Office who shall not have attained to the Age of thirty five Years, and been fourteen Years a Resident within the United States.

In Case of the Removal of the President from Office, or of his Death, Resignation, or

Inability to discharge the Powers and Duties of the said Office, the Same shall devolve on the Vice President, and the Congress may by Law provide for the Case of Removal, Death, Resignation or Inability, both of the President and the Vice President, declaring what Officer shall then act as President, and such Officer shall act accordingly, until the Disability be removed, or a President shall be elected.

The President shall, at stated Times, receive for his Services, a Compensation, which shall neither be encreased nor diminished during the Period for which he shall have been elected, and he shall not receive within that Period any other Emolument from the United States, or any of them.

Before he enter on the Execution of his Office, he shall take the following Oath of Affirmation:—"I do solemnly swear (or affirm) that I will faithfully execute the Office of President of the United States, and will to the best of my Ability, preserve, protect and defend the Constitution of the United States."

SECTION. 2. The President shall be Commander in Chief of the Army and Navy of the United States, and of the

Militia of the several States, when called into the actual Service of the United States; he may require the Opinion, in writing, of the principal Officer in each of the executive Departments, upon any Subject relating to the Duties of their respective Offices, and he shall have Power to grant Reprieves and Pardons for Offences against the United States, except in Cases of Impeachment.

He shall have Power, by and with the Advice and Consent of the Senate, to make Treaties, provided two thirds of the Senators present concur; and he shall nominate, and by and with the Advice and Consent of the Senate, shall appoint Ambassadors, other public Ministers and Consuls, Judges of the supreme Court, and all other Officers of the United States, whose Appointments are not herein otherwise provided for, and which shall be established by Law: but the Congress may by Law vest the Appointment of such inferior Officers, as they think proper, in the President alone, in the Courts of Law, or in the Heads of Departments.

The President shall have Power to fill up all Vacancies that may happen during the Recess of the Senate, by granting Commissions which shall expire at the End of their next Session.

Section. 3. He shall from time to time give to the Congress Information of the State of the Union, and recommend to their Consideration such Measures as he shall judge necessary and expedient; he may, on extraordinary Occasions, convene both Houses, or either of them, and in Case of Disagreement between them, with Respect to the Time of Adjournment, he may adjourn them to such Time as he shall think proper; he shall receive Ambassadors and other public Ministers; he shall take Care that the Laws be faithfully executed, and shall Commission all the Officers of the United States.

Section. 4. The President, Vice President and all civil Officers of the United States, shall be removed from Office on Impeachment for, and Conviction of, Treason, Bribery, or other high Crimes and Misdemeanors.

ARTICLE III.

Section. 1. The judicial Power of the United States, shall be vested in one supreme Court, and in such inferior Courts as the Congress may from time to time ordain and establish. The Judges, both of the supreme and inferior Courts, shall hold their Offices during good Behaviour, and shall, at stated Times, receive for their Services, a Compensation, which shall not be diminished during their Continuance in Office.

Section. 2. The judicial Power shall extend to all Cases, in Law and Equity, arising under this Constitution, the Laws of the United States, and Treaties made, or which shall be made, under their Authority;—to all cases affecting Ambassadors, other public Ministers and Consuls;—to all Cases of admiralty and maritime Jurisdiction;—to Controversies to which the United States shall be a Party;—to Controversies between two or more States;—between a State and Citizens of another State;—between Citizens of different States;—between Citizens of the same State claiming Lands under Grants of different States, and between a State, or the Citizens thereof, and foreign States, Citizens or Subjects.

In all Cases affecting Ambassadors, other public Ministers and Consuls, and those in which a State shall be Party, the supreme Court shall have original Jurisdiction. In all the other Cases before mentioned, the supreme Court shall have appellate Jurisdiction, both as to Law and Fact, with such Exceptions, and under such Regulations as the Congress shall make.

The Trial of all Crimes, except in Cases of Impeachment, shall be by Jury; and such Trial shall be held in the State where the said Crimes shall have been committed; but when not committed within any State, the Trial shall be at such Place or Places as the Congress may by Law have directed.

Section. 3. Treason against the United States, shall consist only in levying War against them, or in adhering to their Enemies, giving them Aid and Comfort. No Person shall be convicted of Treason unless on the Testimony of two Witnesses to the same overt Act, or on Confession in open Court.

The Congress shall have Power to declare the Punishment of Treason, but no Attainder of Treason shall work Corruption of Blood, or Forfeiture except during the Life of the Person attainted.

ARTICLE IV.

SECTION. 1. Full Faith and Credit shall be given in each State to the public Acts, Records, and judicial Proceedings of every other State. And the Congress may by general Laws prescribe the Manner in which such Acts, Records and Proceedings shall be proved, and the Effect thereof.

SECTION. 2. The Citizens of each State shall be entitled to all Privileges and Immunities of Citizens in the several States.

A Person charged in any State with Treason, Felony, or other Crime, who shall flee from Justice, and be found in another State, shall on Demand of the executive Authority of the State from which he fled, be delivered up, to be removed to the State having Jurisdiction of the Crime.

No Person held to Service or Labour in one State, under the Laws thereof, escaping into another, shall, in Consequence of any Law or Regulation therein, be discharged from such Service or Labour, but shall be delivered up on Claim of the Party to whom such Service or Labour may be due.

SECTION. 3. New States may be admitted by the Congress into this Union; but no new State shall be formed or erected within the Jurisdiction of any other State; nor any State be formed by the Junction of two or more States, or Parts of States, without the Consent of the Legislatures of the States concerned as well as of the Congress.

The Congress shall have Power to dispose of and make all needful Rules and Regulations respecting the Territory or other Property belonging to the United States; and nothing in this Constitution shall be so construed as to Prejudice any Claims of the United States, or of any particular State.

Section. 4. The United States shall guarantee to every State in this Union a Republican Form of Government, and shall protect each of them against Invasion; and on Application of the Legislature, or of the Executive (when the Legislature cannot be convened) against domestic Violence.

ARTICLE V.

The Congress, whenever two thirds of both Houses shall deem it necessary, shall propose Amendments to this Constitution, or, on the Application of the Legislatures of two thirds of the several States, shall call a Convention for proposing Amendments, which, in either Case, shall be valid to all Intents and Purposes, as Part of this Constitution, when ratified by the legislatures of three fourths of the several States, or by Conventions in three fourths thereof, as the one or the other Mode of Ratification may be proposed by the Congress; Provided that no Amendment which may be made prior to the Year One thousand eight hundred and eight shall in any Manner affect the first and fourth Clauses in the Ninth Section of the first Article; and that no State, without its Consent, shall be deprived of it's equal Suffrage in the Senate.

ARTICLE VI.

All Debts contracted and Engagements entered into, before the Adoption of this Constitution, shall be as valid against the United States under this Constitution, as under the Confederation.

This Constitution, and the Laws of the United States which shall be made in Pursuance thereof; and all Treaties made, or which shall be made, under the Authority of the United States, shall be the supreme Law of the Land; and the Judges in every State shall be bound thereby, any Thing in the Constitution or Laws of any State to the Contrary notwithstanding.

The Senators and Representatives before mentioned, and the Members of the several State Legislatures, and all executive and judicial Officers, both of the United States and of the several States, shall be bound by Oath or Affirmation, to support this Constitution; but no religious Test shall ever be required as a Qualification to any Office or public Trust under the United States.

ARTICLE VII.

The Ratification of the Conventions of nine States, shall be sufficient for the Establishment of this Constitution between the States so ratifying the Same.

The Word "the", being interlined between the seventh and eighth Lines of the first Page, the Word "Thirty" being partly written on an Erazure in the fiftieth Line of the first Page, The Words "is tried" being interlined between the thirty second and thirty third Lines of the first Page and the Word "the" being interlined between the forty third and forty fourth Lines of the second Page.
Attest William Jackson
Secretary

Done in Convention by the Unanimous Consent of the States present the Seventeenth Day of September in the Year of our Lord one thousand seven hundred and Eighty seven and of the Independance of the United States of America the Twelfth. In Witness whereof We have hereunto subscribed our Names.
G° WASHINGTON
Presidᵗ and deputy from Virginia

DELAWARE	Geo: Read Gunning Bedford jun John Dickinson Richard Bassett Jaco: Broom
MARYLAND	James McHenry Dan of St. Thos. Jenifer Danl. Carroll
VIRGINIA	John Blair— James Madison Jr.
NORTH CAROLINA	Wm. Blount Richd. Dobbs Spaight Hu Williamson
SOUTH CAROLINA	J. Rutledge Charles Cotesworth Pinckney Charles Pinckney Pierce Butler
GEORGIA	William Few Abr Baldwin

NEW HAMPSHIRE	John Langdon Nicholas Gilman
MASSACHUSETTS	Nathaniel Gorham Rufus King
CONNECTICUT	Wm. Saml. Johnson Roger Sherman
NEW YORK	Alexander Hamilton
NEW JERSEY	Wil: Livingston David Brearley Wm. Paterson Jona: Dayton
PENNSYLVANIA	B. Franklin Thomas Mifflin Robt. Morris Geo. Clymer Thos. FitzSimons Jared Ingersoll James Wilson Gouv Morris

AMENDMENT I [1791]

Congress shall make no law respecting an establishment of religion, or prohibiting the free exercise thereof; or abridging the freedom of speech, or of the press; or the right of the people peaceably to assemble, and to petition the Government for a redress of grievances.

AMENDMENT II [1791]

A well regulated Militia, being necessary to the security of a free State, the right of the people to keep and bear Arms, shall not be infringed.

AMENDMENT III [1791]

No Soldier shall, in time of peace be quartered in any house, without the consent of the Owner, nor in time of war, but in a manner to be prescribed by law.

AMENDMENT IV [1791]

The right of the people to be secure in their persons, houses, papers, and effects, against unreasonable searches and seizures, shall not be violated, and no Warrants shall issue, but upon probable cause, supported by Oath or affirmation, and particularly describing the place to be searched, and the persons or things to be seized.

AMENDMENT V [1791]

No person shall be held to answer for a capital, or otherwise infamous crime, unless on a presentment or indictment of a Grand Jury, except in cases arising in the land or naval forces, or in the Militia, when in actual service in time of War or public danger; nor shall any person be subject for the same offence to be twice put in jeopardy of life or limb; nor shall be compelled in any criminal case to be a witness against himself, nor be deprived of life, liberty or property, without due process of law; nor shall private property be taken for public use, without just compensation.

AMENDMENT VI [1791]

In all criminal prosecutions, the accused shall enjoy the right to a speedy and public trial, by an impartial jury of the State and district wherein the crime shall have been committed, which district shall have been previously ascertained by law, and to be informed of the nature and cause of the accusation; to be confronted with the witnesses against him; to have compulsory process for obtaining Witnesses in his favor, and to have the assistance of counsel for his defence.

AMENDMENT VII [1791]

In Suits at Common law, where the value in controversy shall exceed twenty dollars, the right of trial by jury shall be preserved, and no fact tried by a jury, shall be otherwise re-examined in any Court of the United States, than according to the rules of the common law.

AMENDMENT VIII [1791]

Excessive bail shall not be required, nor excessive fines imposed, nor cruel and unusual punishments inflicted.

AMENDMENT IX [1791]

The enumeration in the Constitution, of certain rights, shall not be construed to deny or disparage others retained by the people.

AMENDMENT X [1791]

The powers not delegated to the United States by the Constitution, nor prohibited by it to the States, are reserved to the States respectively, or to the people.

AMENDMENT XI [1798]

The Judicial power of the United States shall not be construed to extend to any suit in law or equity, commenced or prosecuted against one of the United States by Citizens of another State, or by Citizens or Subjects of any Foreign State.

AMENDMENT XII [1804]

The Electors shall meet in their respective states, and vote by ballot for President and Vice President, one of whom, at least, shall not be an inhabitant of the same state with themselves; they shall name in their ballots the person voted for as President, and in distinct ballots the person voted for as Vice President, and they shall make distinct lists of all persons voted for as President, and of all persons voted for as Vice President, and of the number of votes for each, which lists they shall sign and certify, and transmit sealed to the seat of the government of the United States, directed to the President of the Senate;—The President of the Senate shall, in the presence of the Senate and House of Representatives, open all the certificates and the votes shall then be counted;—The Person having the greatest number of votes for President, shall be the President, if such number be a majority of the whole number of Electors appointed; and if no person have such majority, then from the persons having the highest numbers not exceeding three on the list of those voted for as President, the House of Representatives shall choose immediately, by ballot, the President. But in choosing the President, the votes shall be taken by states, the representation from each state having one vote; a quorum for this purpose shall consist of a member or members from two-thirds of the states, and a majority of all the states shall be necessary to a choice. And if the House of Representatives shall not choose a President whenever the right of choice shall devolve upon them, before the fourth day of March next following, then the Vice President shall act as President, as in the case of the death or other constitutional disability of the President.—The person having the greatest number of votes as Vice President, shall be the Vice President, if such number be a majority of the whole number of Electors appointed, and if no person have a majority, then from the two highest numbers on the list, the Senate shall choose the Vice President; a quorum for the purpose shall consist of two-thirds of the whole number of Senators, and a majority of the whole number shall be necessary to a choice. But no person constitutionally ineligible to the office of President shall be eligible to that of Vice President of the United States.

AMENDMENT XIII [1865]

1. Neither slavery nor involuntary servitude, except as a punishment for crime whereof the party shall have been duly convicted, shall exist within the United States, or any place subject to their jurisdiction.

2. Congress shall have power to enforce this article by appropriate legislation.

AMENDMENT XIV [1868]

1. All persons born or naturalized in the United States, and subject to the jurisdiction thereof, are citizens of the United States and of the State wherein they reside. No State shall make or enforce any law which shall abridge the privileges or immunities of citizens of the United States; nor shall any State deprive any person of life, liberty, or property, without due process of law; nor deny to any person within its jurisdiction the equal protection of the laws.

2. Representatives shall be apportioned among the several States according to their respective numbers, counting the whole number of persons in each State, excluding Indians not taxed. But when the right to vote at any election for the choice of electors for President and Vice President of the United States, Representatives in Congress, the Executive and Judicial officers of a State, or the members of the Legislature thereof, is denied to any of the male inhabitants of such State, being twenty-one years of age, and citizens of the United States, or in any way abridged, except for participation in rebellion, or other crime, the basis of representation therein shall be reduced in the proportion which the number of such male citizens shall bear to the whole number of male citizens twenty-one years of age in such State.

3. No person shall be a Senator or Representative in Congress, or elector of President and Vice President, or hold any office, civil or military, under the United States, or under any State, who, having previously taken an oath, as a member of Congress, or as an officer of the United States, or as a member of any State legislature, or as an executive or judicial officer of any State, to support the Constitution of the United States, shall have engaged in insurrection or rebellion against the same, or given aid or comfort to the enemies thereof. But Congress may by a vote of two-thirds of each House, remove such disability.

4. The validity of the public debt of the United States, authorized by law, including debts incurred for payment of pensions and bounties for services in suppressing insurrection or rebellion, shall not be questioned. But neither the United States nor any State shall assume or pay any debt or obligation incurred in aid of insurrection or rebellion against the United States, or any claim for the loss or emancipation of any slave; but all such debts, obligations and claims shall be held illegal and void.

5. The Congress shall have power to enforce, by appropriate legislation, the provisions of this article.

AMENDMENT XV [1870]

1. The right of citizens of the United States to vote shall not be denied or abridged by the United States or by any State on account of race, color, or previous condition of servitude.

2. The Congress shall have power to enforce this article by appropriate legislation.

AMENDMENT XVI [1913]

The Congress shall have power to lay and collect taxes on incomes, from whatever source derived, without apportionment among the several States, and without regard to any census or enumeration.

AMENDMENT XVII [1913]

The Senate of the United States shall be composed of two Senators from each State, elected by the people thereof, for six years; and each Senator shall have one vote. The electors in each State shall have the qualifications requisite for electors of the most numerous branch of the State legislatures.

When vacancies happen in the representation of any State in the Senate, the executive authority of such State shall issue writs of election to fill such vacancies: Provided, That the legislature of any State may empower the executive thereof to make temporary appointments until the people fill the vacancies by election as the legislature may direct.

This amendment shall not be so construed as to affect the election or term of any Senator chosen before it becomes valid as part of the Constitution.

AMENDMENT XVIII [1919]

1. After one year from the ratification of this article the manufacture, sale, or transportation of intoxicating liquors within, the importation thereof into, or the exportation thereof from the United States and all territory subject to the jurisdiction thereof for beverage purposes is hereby prohibited.

2. The Congress and the several States shall have concurrent power to enforce this article by appropriate legislation.

3. This article shall be inoperative unless it shall have been ratified as an amendment to the Constitution by the legislatures of the several States, as provided in the Constitution, within seven years from the date of the submission hereof to the States by the Congress.

AMENDMENT XIX [1920]

The right of citizens of the United States to vote shall not be denied or abridged by the United States or by any State on account of sex.

Congress shall have power to enforce this article by appropriate legislation.

AMENDMENT XX [1933]

1. The terms of the President and Vice President shall end at noon on the 20th day of January, and the terms of Senators and Representatives at noon on the 3d day of January, of the years in which such terms would have ended if this article had not been ratified; and the terms of their successors shall then begin.

2. The Congress shall assemble at least once in every year, and such meeting shall begin at noon on the 3d day of January, unless they shall by law appoint a different day.

3. If, at the time fixed for the beginning of the term of the President, the President elect shall have died, the Vice President elect shall become President. If a President shall not have been chosen before the time fixed for the beginning of his term, or if the President elect shall have failed to qualify, then the Vice President elect shall act as President until a President shall have qualified; and the Congress may by law provide for the case wherein neither a President elect nor a Vice President elect shall have qualified, declaring who shall then act as President, or the manner in which one who is to act shall be selected, and such person shall act accordingly until a President or Vice President shall have qualified.

4. The Congress may by law provide for the case of the death of any of the persons from whom the House of Representatives may choose a President whenever the right of choice shall have devolved upon them, and for the case of the death of any of the persons from whom the Senate may choose a Vice President whenever the right of choice shall have devolved upon them.

5. Sections 1 and 2 shall take effect on the 15th day of October following the ratification of this article.

6. This article shall be inoperative unless it shall have been ratified as an amendment to the Constitution by the legislatures of three-fourths of the several States within seven years from the date of its submission.

AMENDMENT XXI [1933]

1. The eighteenth article of amendment to the Constitution of the United States is hereby repealed.

2. The transportation or importation into any State, Territory, or possession of the United States for delivery or use therein of intoxicating liquors, in violation of the laws thereof, is hereby prohibited.

3. This article shall be inoperative unless it shall have been ratified as an amendment to the Constitution by conventions in the several States, as provided in the Constitition, within seven years from the date of the submission hereof to the States by the Congress.

AMENDMENT XXII [1951]

1. No person shall be elected to the office of the President more than twice, and no person who has held the office of President, or acted as President, for more than two years of a term to which some other person was elected President shall be elected to the office of the president more than once. But this Article shall not apply to any person holding the office of President when this Article was proposed by the Congress, and shall not prevent any person who may be holding the office of President, or acting as President, during the term within which this Article becomes operative from holding the office of President or acting as president during the remainder of such term.

2. This article shall be inoperative unless it shall have been ratified as an amendment to the Constitution by the legislatures of three-fourths of the several States within seven years from the date of its submission to the States by the Congress.

AMENDMENT XXIII [1961]

1. The District constituting the seat of Government of the United States shall appoint in such manner as the Congress may direct:

A number of electors of President and Vice President equal to the whole number of Senators and Representatives in Congress to which the District would be entitled if it were a State, but in no event more than the least populous State; they shall be in addition to those appointed by the States, but they shall be considered, for the purposes of the election of President and Vice President, to be electors appointed by a State; and they shall meet in the District and perform such duties as provided by the twelfth article of amendment.

2. The Congress shall have power to enforce this article by appropriate legislation.

AMENDMENT XXIV [1964]

1. The right of citizens of the United States to vote in any primary or other election for President or Vice President, for electors for President or Vice President, or for Senator or Representatives in Congress, shall not be denied or abridged by the United States or any State by reason of failure to pay any poll tax or other tax.

2. The Congress shall have power to enforce this article by appropriate legislation.

AMENDMENT XXV [1967]

1. In case of the removal of the President from office or of his death or resignation, the Vice President shall become President.

2. Whenever there is a vacancy in the office of the Vice President, the President shall nominate a Vice President who shall take office upon confirmation by a majority vote of both Houses of Congress.

3. Whenever the President transmits to the President pro tempore of the Senate and the Speaker of the House of Representatives his written declaration that he is unable to discharge the powers and duties of his office, and until he transmits to them a written declaration to the contrary, such powers and duties shall be discharged by the Vice President as Acting President.

4. Whenever the Vice President and a majority of either the principal officers of the executive departments or of such other body as Congress may by law provide, transmit to the President pro tempore of the Senate and the Speaker of the House of Representatives their written declaration that the President is unable to discharge the powers and duties of his office, the Vice President shall immediately assume the powers and duties of the office as Acting President.

Thereafter, when the President transmits to the President pro tempore of the Senate and the Speaker of the House of Representatives his written declaration that no inability exists, he shall resume the powers and duties of his office unless the Vice President and a majority of either the principal officers of the executive department or of such other body as Congress may by law provide, transmit within four days to the President pro tempore of the Senate and the Speaker of the House of Representatives their written declaration that the President is unable to discharge the powers and duties of his office. Thereupon Congress shall decide the issue, assembling within forty-eight hours for that purpose if not in session. If the Congress, within twenty-one days after receipt of the latter written declaration, or, if Congress is not in session, within twenty-one days after Congress is required to assemble, determines by two-thirds vote of both Houses that the President is unable to discharge the powers and duties of his office, the Vice President shall continue to discharge the same as Acting President; otherwise, the President shall resume the powers and duties of his office.

AMENDMENT XXVI [1971]

1. The right of citizens of the United States, who are eighteen years of age or older, to vote shall not be denied or abridged by the United States or by any State on account of age.

2. The Congress shall have power to enforce this article by appropriate legislation.

AMENDMENT XXVII [1992]

No law, varying the compensation for the services of the Senators and Representatives, shall take effect, until an election of Representatives shall have intervened.

at a glance . . .

President	Volume	President	Volume	President	Volume
George Washington	1	James Buchanan	3	Calvin Coolidge	5
John Adams	1	Abraham Lincoln	3	Herbert Hoover	5
Thomas Jefferson	1	Andrew Johnson	3	Franklin D. Roosevelt	6
James Madison	1	Ulysses S. Grant	3	Harry S. Truman	6
James Monroe	1	Rutherford B. Hayes	4	Dwight D. Eisenhower	6
John Quincy Adams	2	James A. Garfield	4	John F. Kennedy	6
Andrew Jackson	2	Chester A. Arthur	4	Lyndon B. Johnson	6
Martin Van Buren	2	Grover Cleveland	4	Richard M. Nixon	7
William Henry Harrison	2	Benjamin Harrison	4	Gerald R. Ford	7
John Tyler	2	William McKinley	4	Jimmy Carter	7
James K. Polk	2	Theodore Roosevelt	5	Ronald Reagan	7
Zachary Taylor	3	William Howard Taft	5	George Bush	7
Millard Fillmore	3	Woodrow Wilson	5	Bill Clinton	7
Franklin Pierce	3	Warren G. Harding	5		

j

k

X

Y

Z